MW00334337

The Light of the Christ Within

Jesus Christ, from a painting by Heinrich Hoffmann

The Light of the Christ Within

INSPIRED TALKS BY
REVEREND JOHN LAURENCE

A DIRECT DISCIPLE
of PARAMHANSA YOGANANDA

Compiled and Edited by ELANA JOAN CARA

Crystal Clarity Publishers, Nevada City, CA 95959
Copyright © 2012 by Elana Joan Cara
All rights reserved. Published 2013

Printed in USA
ISBN 13: 978-1-56589-267-5
ePub: 978-1-56589-511-9

1 3 5 7 9 10 8 6 4 2

Cover and interior design by: Amala Cathleen Elliott

Library of Congress Cataloging-in-Publication Data

Laurence, John, 1908-2003.
  The light of the Christ within : inspired talks by Reverend John Laurence, a direct disciple of
Paramhansa Yogananda / compiled and edited by Elana Joan Cara.
    p. cm.
  ISBN 978-1-56589-267-5 (pbk. : alk. paper)
1. Yogananda, Paramahansa, 1893-1952. 2. Ananda Sangha (Organization) I. Cara, Elana Joan.
II. Title.

  BP605.S43Y638 2012
  294.5'44--dc23

                            2012024638

www.crystalclarity.com
800-424-1055
clarity@crystalclarity.com

THIS BOOK IS DEDICATED
TO TRUTH SEEKERS
OF BOTH EAST AND WEST,
THOSE WONDERFUL SOULS
OF ALL RELIGIONS
WHO ARE THIRSTY FOR DIRECT
EXPERIENCE OF GOD.

The illumined consciousness that speaks in these talks is a healing balm for the wounded spirit, a guiding light for one's daily journey within, and a gift of love designed to inspire, awaken, and expand our understanding and childlike trust in the infinitely compassionate and all-loving divine presence that lives within every heart.

CONTENTS

Oh Yoganandaji beloved
this day we mark
with love and gratitude
for tis thy natal day.

Thou who with infinite compassion
toucheth soul of devotee
awakening to birth in consciousness
that matchless path of love,
of dedication.

Could we fail to love thee
who has taught us how to love, to serve?
Who has led and guided,
even suffered in our stead?

Oh Yoganandaji beloved,
we hail thy natal day.*

—John Laurence

* A poem written by John for Paramhansa Yogananda. On January 5, 1952, the Master asked his disciple, Dr. M. W. Lewis, to read this poem at the banquet table of his last birthday on earth. (As mentioned in Yogananda's letter to John, published on page 13.)

FOREWORD

by Swami Kriyananda

If ever you feel tempted to lose faith in human nature, I suggest you read a few of the talks recorded in this volume by John Laurence. They exude goodness, kindness, humility, good humor, and wise insight. I strongly recommend reading what John said not only for what he said, but above all for who he was. Contact with such a soul is both purifying and uplifting.

I myself got to meet John while he was alive. My contact with him was not extensive, but I have always carried with me the sweet memory of a man with clear insight into reality, one who was not influenced by anyone's opinions regardless of that person's position or importance, and one, finally, whose focus always was on the spiritual heights.

I am grateful to Elana Joan Cara for the care with which she has edited these talks. It is seldom easy to edit talks by those who speak spontaneously, as John did. (And how few speakers are even able to speak spontaneously!) She has done an excellent job, combining clarity with intuitive understanding. In my opinion, she has done the world a signal service in producing this volume.

Swami Kriyananda and John Laurence

ACKNOWLEDGEMENTS

I gratefully acknowledge the many people who have contributed to the publishing of these wonderful talks by Reverend John Laurence.

First, I extend my never-ending gratitude to Kamala Silva, beloved disciple of Paramhansa Yogananda, for your masterful spiritual direction, and for encouraging me to write about John Laurence as part of my life's work.

I wish to express my deep appreciation to Swami Kriyananda, for the privilege of publishing The Light of the Christ Within through Ananda's publishing house, Crystal Clarity Publishers.

My heartfelt thanks go to all the people at Ananda who were involved in this project, especially Skip Barrett, President of Crystal Clarity Publishers—and Richard Salva, for your expertise, impeccable attention to detail, research and footnoting of the scriptural references in these talks, and for your valuable suggestions, fine tuning, and final editing of the texts.

Many thanks also to Rita Viscogliosi, for your tireless work in proofreading the first draft of these talks. Your brilliant and humorous comments made light work of an otherwise tedious task.

A special thanks to the Friends of John Laurence, for your generous support of this work. "JL" is smiling at you: Russ Anderson, Robert and AnaMaria Dean, Stephanie Costanza, Mike Ginoza, Herbert Grosser, Collen Laurence, Stuart McIntee, Sheila and Robert Nichols, Scott and Meridian Phillips, Linda Phon, Nancy Karpani Rakela, Grace Rinaldi, Lids Rinaldi, Mike Rinaldi, Vincenzo and Janes Rinaldi, Erik and AnaMaria Rose, Brad Roy, Scott Shnurman, Suma Vasudevan, and Robert and Maria Rita Viscogliosi.

And finally, a special thanks to you, my friends and students, for your enthusiasm, encouragement, and ongoing support. You are each reflections of the divine light, and I love you: Mary Colligan, Carol Calvert, Richard Gundry, Melinda Elwell, Patti Valdez, Virginia Gilstrap, Ashana Lobody, Ed Wiggins, Diane Benson, Lois DiMari, Dante Allegro, Lee Ann Davis, Jean Kraft, Scott Gilmore, Seva Khalsa, Nancy Broadhead, Bill O'Donnell, and Brother Brian Dybowski.

John Laurence serving in the US Navy

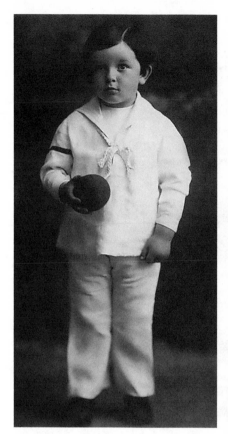

In clockwise order, John Laurence as a child, John Laurence's mother, John Laurence's father, and John with his sister and mother.

INTRODUCTION

THE LIFE of JOHN LAURENCE

John Laurence was born on January 6, 1908 on an Indian reservation in Wyoming, at an Army post named Fort Washakie. His father was in the Army Medical Corps, so the family, mother, father, and his older sister, Marian, lived in a small adobe house on the reservation.

John's mother was a short, slender, devout Roman Catholic, who was born and raised in Ireland in County Carey near the Lakes of Kilarney. She was a very sensible and positive woman who possessed courage and an abiding faith. Altogether, she had five children, three of whom died in infancy.

Because John's father was in the military, the family traveled a great deal. They left Wyoming when John was very young and moved to Fort Terry, an island off the coast of New London, Connecticut, where they stayed for four years. They moved again, this time to San Antonio, Texas, where John entered school for the first time. He was only in class for about three weeks before the family once again moved to another military base. It was two and a half years before John saw a classroom again.

He was not a very good student and not the brightest in the class. Besides that, he was always a little older than the other students. John attended public schools in Washington, D.C., but his mother decided to transfer him to a Catholic school—the Thomas Edward Shields Memorial School: a fine example of Catholic education, affiliated with the Catholic University of America. He remained there until he graduated.

John was deeply influenced by his mother's devout religious nature. He was also impressed by his family's natural love of music. Both religion and music played an important role throughout his life. John loved opera, concerts, and song recitals. Eventually he developed a deep love for orchestral works, particularly the piano concerti of Sergei Rachmaninoff and other great composers.

There were many happy hours in the home as the family gathered around the old wind-up record player, listening intently to the Red Seals 78 rpm recordings of the great opera singers and other artists of the day.

Enrico Caruso, Nellie Melba, John McCormack, Amelita Galli-Curci, Lucretia Bori, Ernestine Schumann-Heink, Tito Ruffo, and others became their joy. John loved to attend as many live performances as he could, and he would always go backstage after the concerts so that he could meet the artists and ask them to autograph their programs and photos. Over the span of seventy years, John grew an impressive collection of autographed programs and photographs.

In the midst of all his musical interests and activities, John intensified his spiritual practices and religious studies. He read the lives of mystics and saints wherever he could find them—Franciscan saints, Dominican saints, and various other saints of the Catholic Church. He savored that literary diet and couldn't get enough of these wonderful people who possessed such unusual powers.

While he was attending Thomas Edward Shields School, John began spending his after-school hours showing people through a famous Franciscan monastery that was only a few blocks from his home in Washington, D.C. He would take people through the Holy Land of America and Mount Saint Sepulcher shrines, which are to scale as they appear in the Holy Land and the catacombs of Rome. As a schoolboy, John enjoyed talking to people and explaining what the Latin inscriptions meant. This also gave him his first taste of public speaking, which turned out to be a lifelong pursuit.

The Holy Land of America was designed and built by Reverend Father Godfrey Shilling, O.F.M. It is a fascinating and picturesque place with a lovely summer rose garden. Father Shilling, a venerable and dear old gentleman with a white beard, was John's spiritual director and confessor from about 1918. He had been a priest for over fifty years. Even though his hands shook a good deal in the latter part of his life, Father Shilling was strong and very clear of mind. He was a kind and wonderful man with merry, twinkling blue eyes that reflected his great love for everyone. People from every religion and no religion loved this fine old gentleman. Even people who didn't particularly like Catholics automatically loved Father Shilling.

Now, he was something of a saint and seer, and he always kept a candle burning, a small vigil light, in his cell at night because so many souls from the spirit world would stop by to visit him. An endless stream of beautiful souls would walk by his bed, and he would give them a blessing. Then they would move on. Father Shilling was a visionary, and in a certain sense, a holy man, and John was very grateful to have known him well.

Another important influence from this part of John's life was a simple brother named Thomas Lee. Thomas had been a baseball player for the Boston Red Sox before joining the Order. As he moved closer to becoming fully vowed, Thomas took on more and more austerities. He almost never spoke; and certainly if he could get out of it, he wouldn't. He was always in a highly contemplative state.

At one time Thomas was assigned to be the doorkeeper. When people came and asked for someone, he would go and get them. But he was so honest that he could not tell even a little white fib. One day, a man came to the door and said, "I would like to speak to the Father Superior." Thomas replied, "All right, I'll call him." And he went in the back room and called the Superior on the phone. The Superior instructed him, "Tell him I'm not in." So Thomas went back in and artlessly said, "Father Superior tells me to tell you that he's not in."

If you happened to get up early in the morning, at two o'clock or so, and walked into the chapel of that monastery, Thomas would be there. He was in a state of continuous contemplation. As a little boy, when John was coming home from school, he would go up to the monastery and offer to help out in any way he could. He just loved the place and so earnestly wanted to be a good Franciscan. One afternoon, John was in the refectory where Brother Thomas, who was assigned at that time to work there, was cutting bread. The afternoon sun was shining through the window and the brother's face gave off an almost celestial beauty. As John looked at the old man, he sensed intuitively that Thomas was a visionary, and so John asked him, "Brother Thomas, have you ever seen any visions?" Thomas never looked up from the cutting board. He kept right on cutting the bread. He didn't answer the question directly. He simply said: "John, there is more merit before God in one little act of obedience than in all the visions you could see in ten years."

Brother Thomas Lee—this simple, radiant, and pious man— remained a powerful influence on John's spiritual life. Thomas was sent to Nazareth in the Holy Land, where he spent the last years of his life making bread—hundreds of loaves, not only for the monks, but for various uses by the convents and for the poor. When Brother Thomas passed away, the brothers wanted to put a little picture of him on a card to give to people, asking for prayers for his soul, but they had no picture of him. John had the only picture that existed, so one of the monks wrote to John and asked him if he would send it to them. John did, and they made a little holy card showing Thomas' face. And of course, in the photograph Thomas' eyes were downcast and he looked very contemplative.

When Archbishop Daeger consecrated the monastery church, in a vast and great ceremony, John was privileged to be one of the altar boys. John loved Saint Francis of Assisi and wanted to become a Franciscan. Even as a youngster, he gave away all his little possessions—his coins and other little treasures that youngsters have—in order to be, like Saint Francis, without worldly possessions. In 1924, when he was older, John received a scholarship to St. Joseph's Seminary in New York, which was conducted by the Franciscan Order.

Afterwards, John transferred to the Franciscan monastery in Washington. D.C. and became Friar Raymond. He was there for a year or so; and then in 1928 he went into his novitiate in Paterson, New Jersey. He was there a full year and took simple vows. (These are just as binding as solemn vows, but they automatically expire in three years, at which time one must decide whether or not to take the solemn vows.)

John's last year as a friar at the Franciscan monastery was in 1931. At that time, the Oxford Fellowship Ministerial Association at American University was sponsoring a series of lectures by speakers of various religious persuasions. Among them were Bishop Ryan, rector of the Catholic University of America, and many other religious notables. A good friend and former schoolmate invited John to be one of the speakers. And so John went, wearing his Franciscan habit, his brown robe and sandals, and gave a talk on Saint Francis of Assisi. His talk was well received. During the question and answer session, people from the psychology department joined in and it developed into a lively discussion. Later, the directors of the fellowship decided that John had given the best lecture of the year, and so they presented him with a beautiful gold cross. John treasured that cross, especially because the directors had chosen him from among so many notable speakers who were much more educated than he was.

At that time, in 1931, John was prepared to take lifelong vows. But there were pressing problems in his family on the occasion of his father's passing; and inasmuch as he was about to take a vow of poverty for life, it was advised that he should instead re-enter secular life, get a job, and help support his mother and sister. This was during the Great Depression, so John got a job as a desk attendant at the old Carnegie Library in Washington, D.C., where he earned the magnificent sum of $15 a week. (In those days, that was a pretty good wage.)

John was doing a good deal of reading and having some doubts about whether he should return to the monastery. He had received a letter from Father Theophilis Bellerini, O.F.M., who was Custos (a Franciscan official) of the Holy Land at that time. He told John that the papers for his vows had been forwarded from Jerusalem to Washington. Father Leonard Walsh, who at that time was Superior of the monastery, came to visit John. He asked John if he would like to come back and do his novitiate over again, repeating the entire program to become a full-fledged friar, and then taking his vows. John courteously told Father Leonard, whom he had known since he was first admitted to the monastery, that he didn't feel he would fit in very well. So many changes had taken place in his life that he didn't really feel he would be a good candidate.

You see, John had been attending lectures on Vedanta, reading about Eastern religions, and learning a bit about yoga. Once again, the lines of religion and music crossed. Madame Amelita Galli-Curci, a famous Italian coloratura soprano, had become a devotee of the great mystic known as Swami Yogananda. She wrote the preface to Yogananda's book, *Whispers from Eternity*, and because John had literally worshipped Galli-Curci as a great musical artist, he was very interested in this holy man from India.

Curiously enough, as fate would have it, John was walking down 16th Street in Washington, D.C. on the evening of November 2, 1933, just opposite the Mayflower Hotel (where, coincidentally, he had sung a number of times), when he saw a man in a dark suit coming down the walkway. John noticed the man's hat and cane, and also the dark hair tucked inside his coat collar, and said to himself, "Oh, that's Swami Yogananda." John thought it would be rude to accost him on the street, and he knew that the Swami had a small center in a downtown Washington hotel, so John ran ahead a short distance and went into the lobby and awaited the great teacher from the East. It wasn't long before Yogananda came in. John had a little autograph book with him, and he stepped up and asked for the swami's autograph. Yogananda smiled. He gazed at John intently. And, standing there, he wrote:

With unceasing blessings.
There is no East nor West, nor North nor South
But pervaded by my one Father
Whose children we all races are.

Swami Yogananda

November 2, 1933

They exchanged a few words; and of course, John asked about Galli-Curci. "Yes," Yogananda said modestly, "She is interested in my work." At that time, Yogananda was probably the only mystic from India who had ever been a guest at the White House. He had met President Calvin Coolidge, and was enormously popular in Washington—more than a thousand students attended one of the swami's many classes in that city.

Having been out of the monastery for only two years, John was not altogether ready to accept this incredible man and his teachings, but he was profoundly impressed by him. John was not quick to make changes, and it took him another ten years or so before he received initiation into Yogananda's exalted meditation technique of Kriya Yoga from the beautiful and saintly disciple of Yogananda, Kamala Silva.

Kamala was indeed a radiant example of what the philosophy and practice of Yogananda's teachings can bring about. Her wonderful book, *The Flawless Mirror*, tells of her experiences from the time she met Yogananda as a teenager, up to the time she wrote the book, shortly after Yogananda's passing from this earth plane.

Another meeting that John found particularly notable was with the Parsee mystic, Meher Baba. John had *darshan** with him, and it was a remarkable experience. In the last forty years or so of Meher Baba's life, he never spoke. He communicated with sign language to his brothers, who took care of him. He was on a tour throughout the United States, and it was during this time that John had the opportunity of meeting him. All one had to do, John said, was be in Meher Baba's presence, or just look at him, to receive a wonderful blessing. This experience was

* The spiritual blessing that comes from seeing a holy man or woman.

so intriguing that it spurred John to research the whole of Meher Baba's beautiful life story.

Influences from the East continued, and John met Swami Satchidananda, a disciple of Swami Sivananda. Some individuals had invited John to hear this teacher from India, saying that he was wonderful and that people were very excited about him. John said, "I'm really not interested. I've met a lot of holy men, and some less than that from the Far East, and I don't think I need to look further." However, in the end John was persuaded to go to the lecture at the local Unitarian Church. One of the young men who went along with them that evening was a very bright, intelligent chap, and John tried very hard to get him interested in Yogananda and his teachings, but somehow it never happened. But the young man went along, as John did, "for the ride."

The church was filled to capacity when Swami Satchidananda came in. He was tall and thin, with long hair and a gray beard, and there was certainly a most distinct spiritual personality that emerged as he approached the platform. After his talk, the swami said, "I would like to have the lights lowered, and we'll have a meditation." The lights were lowered and eighteen candles were lit against the stone wall behind him. (That's not much light in a big church.) As people started to meditate, John glanced up at the swami and saw the biggest, most vivid and wonderfully colorful human aura he had ever witnessed. It extended from the swami's person to the very edge of the vast hall, all the way to the windows on each side of the church. John was very glad after all that he had gone to that lecture, because he felt that he was indeed in the presence of a truly holy man. John attended a number of Swami Satchidananda's subsequent lectures, and he remained impressed by the yogi's extraordinary auric emanations.

Throughout much of his life, John had wanted to go to India and Tibet, but he never did. It is interesting, therefore, to note that the best of these distant places came to him, and John was always deeply grateful for those meetings. One of the more interesting holy men he met was the sixteenth Gupela Karmapa, presumed to be very close to the Dalai Lama. The Gupela Karmapa is the only one who can give the sacred Black Hat initiation. When John attended, about three thousand people came for darshan. When the Karmapa ascended the throne, he was wearing a miter and chanting "*Om Mani Padme Hum*" in a very light voice. He gave a talk in his own language, which was translated into English, and he said, "I am not the sixteenth incarnation of the Karmapa. I am the same Karmapa back for the sixteenth time." John found this most interesting. Later on in the service, the many monks who were with the Karmapa burned incense, blew on conch shells, and shook sacred rattles. At the end the attendees were allowed to go before the Karmapa, who sat on the edge of a throne several feet above the people. He reached over and touched each one as they went by. The administrative staff instructed everyone, "Don't look at the Karmapa." And, of course, John ignored them. When the Karmapa touched him, John glanced up at him. The holy man leaned over to John and said "hello" in a high-pitched voice. Then John left the stage and one of the monks draped a simple cord around his neck, which indicated that he had received the spiritual blessing of the Black Hat initiation. It was wonderful, and John had the joy of participating in the same ceremony again at another location. When he left the hall that night, he felt like he was walking six inches off the floor.

John had the blessing of spending time in the presence of several other holy men from the East, including the Dalai Lama. One of the most exciting meetings was with His Holiness Sri Swami Chidananda—the successor to Swami Sivananda, who founded the Divine Life Society in India (now a worldwide mission). John was very interested to meet this man, who was quite thin and frail and looked a bit like Mahatma Gandhi.

Now, John was not much for sitting on the floor, and he never could sit in the lotus posture, so Swami Chidananda's staff was kind enough to put out a chair for him. They let him sit on the left side of this great teacher for the whole afternoon. Chidananda asked John a question or two, and John answered as quickly as he could, because there were seventy-five other people there for the swami's darshan and John didn't want to take a minute away from that. John said the experience was electrifying. There was a subtle, soft, beautiful, and uplifting current pervading the atmosphere around this holy man.

After the event was over, Chidananda graciously gave John a little private time. As John sat with him, he asked for Chidananda's blessing. Chidananda put both his hands on the top of John's head and, speaking their names aloud, called on the blessings of all the gurus of Yogananda's lineage. John thought that was so thoughtful of Chidananda, and so typical of the people in the Divine Life Society. It demonstrated their broadness of mind and their ecumenical quality. At one point, Chidananda began to recite a beautiful poem that Yogananda had written, and, knowing the poem very well, John joined him. John certainly appreciated the blessing he received meeting this great swami.

In 1959, John was ordained a minister in the Universal Church of the Master, a Spiritualist Church in the Bay Area. He had become especially interested in metaphysics, and so he founded the Metaphysical Design for Living Church in San Francisco, and pastored a congregation there for twenty-five years. He was also a highly sought-after speaker, and on some Sundays he would speak in as many as three churches. He had his own church service at eleven AM, and in the afternoon at two o'clock he would give a short talk in one of the many churches in San Francisco, and in the evening he would speak again for another group. He was chaplain at the Presbyterian Heritage House for ten years, and also a regular guest speaker at the San Francisco Unity Temple, where some of the lectures contained in this book were given. His deep love for God fueled him with endless energy and a passion for the subjects he taught.

There is one more person who deeply influenced John Laurence. She was an American, but the mendicant life she lived and the way in which she taught can hardly be imagined in any other place but India. She was, like Yogananda, truly a bridge between East and West in terms of her spirituality and dedicated life. She was a college graduate with all the niceties of an abundant life, but one day she had a spiritual awakening. She was told that she must leave her home and just walk, forsaking all possessions. So she left her home and set out on pilgrimage, walking without any money or even a coat, in fulfillment of the gospel injunctions issued to the apostles. She sold all her things and even dropped her name, simply calling herself "Peace Pilgrim." She traversed the United Stated on foot so many times that at the time John met her, she had walked 25,000 miles without a nickel in her pocket. She met thousands of people, but she never told anybody her real name. Peace Pilgrim spoke on two occasions at John's church in San Francisco, and she ultimately became a radiant and wonderful saint. There is a book about her called *Peace Pilgrim: Her Life and Work in Her Own Words*. It is a magnificent and inspiring book about the life and work of a modern woman who followed without hesitation the injunctions of the Bible.

As Reverend John Laurence has identified with his spiritual teachers, so has he become like them. His blazing devotion to Yogananda, his adoration of Saint Francis, his enormous respect for Mahatma Gandhi (on whose life and work John lectured all over the United States), were woven into the fabric of John's consciousness. His childlike sweetness and acceptance of God's life and laws made him one with those who walked before him, calling him to follow. John *lived* his teachings and indeed reflected the truth of them in his own life. Even when he was in his eighties and nineties, Reverend Laurence bounced through his days with the joyous energy that comes from being in love, and he could never do enough for his divine Beloved. He always taught that every one of us has the same spark of the Infinite within us, and that the only difference between Jesus and us, between Yogananda and us, is that they *know* who they are. Reverend Laurence had a deep devotion and connection to Padre Pio, and as the years moved forward, he began demonstrating many of the profound spirit gifts of that saint. John was often seen in more than one place at the same time, exhibiting what is known as "bilocation." His clairvoyance was a vehicle of healing for countless people, and his prayers were a powerful intercession for those who were in great need. In his last years, people reported that after praying to Reverend Laurence, their prayers were answered. His words and prayers transformed lives and gave people hope and new beginnings.

Through these inspired talks, Reverend Laurence leads us from doubt and uncertainty to a true *knowing* that if we turn our gaze toward the Light, we too can eventually become spiritual giants like the saints and sages who are our older brothers and sisters.

Of all the things I treasure about my twenty-five-year friendship with Reverend John Laurence, what touched me most was his great and simple joy and his commitment to awakening and elevating every person he met. By his words, his joyful spirit, his daily prayers, and most especially with his deep love and compassion, Reverend Laurence lifted us into an atmosphere of divine light-heartedness. Many people came to him with sorrows and heavy burdens, and in an instant, with a twinkle of his shining eyes and an oceanic smile that drowned all sorrows, those troubles simply evaporated. In the presence of John's total love and unconditional acceptance, countless people were brought to God, and to an understanding of the divine nature of their true being.

These wonderful, simple talks speak in the language of all religions. The truths expressed in them cross all boundaries of time and religious expression. From the depths of his soul realization, he reiterates what the great world teacher Paramhansa Yogananda wrote to him in 1933, *"There is no East nor West, nor North nor South but pervaded by my one Father whose children we all races are."* Every page of this wonderful book contains universal wisdom and transforming messages of hope, courage, joy, and love that literally awaken and lift the reader into a higher, freer, and more beautiful awareness of the omnipresence of Good.

At the time these talks were delivered, in 1981 and 1982, Reverend John Laurence was teaching on the Psalms. It is for this reason that many of the texts chosen in these talks are based on the Psalms. In a broad and all-inclusive ecumenical spirit of oneness, Reverend Laurence brings to life the deeper meaning of the Psalms and other biblical passages he often quoted at the opening of his talks.

Within these pages you will find a true friend and knower of God, whose sole desire is to serve. With humor and an occasional bit of irreverence, "JL" places before us a picture of ourselves, and holds a divine mirror in which we may see ourselves as God sees us. His encouragement and positive belief in us stirs our own imagination of what great spiritual strides are possible for us in this very life.

Indeed, every moment of his life was dedicated to service and to *living* the prayer of his beloved Paramhansa Yogananda, "May Thy love shine forever on the sanctuary of my devotion, and may I be able to awaken Thy love in all hearts."

Elana Joan Cara, Santa Fe, New Mexico

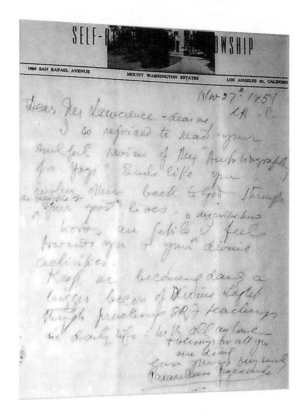

Nov. 27th, 1951
LA, C.

Dear Mr. Lawrence – dear one,

I so rejoiced to read your soulful review of my "Autobiography of a Yogi." Souls like you usher others back to God through the examples of your good lives.

Words are futile to describe how I feel towards you and your divine activities.

Keep on becoming daily a bigger beacon of Divine Light through practicing SRF teachings in daily life.

With all my love + blessings for all you are doing.

Ever yours, very sincerely,

Paramhansa Yogananda

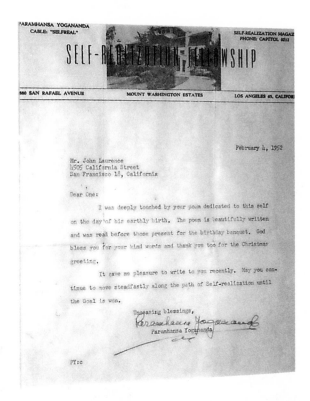

February 4, 1952

Mr. John Laurence
4505 California Street
San Francisco 18, California

Dear One:

I was deeply touched by your poem dedicated to this self on the day of his earthly birth. The poem is beautifully written and was read before those present for the birthday banquet. God bless you for your kind words and thank you too for the Christmas greeting.

It gave me pleasure to write to you recently. May you continue to move steadfastly along the path of Self-realization until the Goal is won.

Unceasing blessings,
Paramhansa Yogananda

· PART ONE ·

SPIRITUAL TALKS OF 1981

Reverend Laurence at the altar of the Trinity Episcopal Church in San Francisco, where he held weekly healing services

Serve the Lord with Gladness

Heritage House Presbyterian Chapel, San Francisco, CA
January 25, 1981

"Serve the LORD with gladness; . . Make a joyful noise unto the LORD, all ye lands." With great emphasis and enthusiasm the Psalmist tells us of the importance of being joyful, and living a healthy and pleasing life. In Psalm 100 he gets completely carried away with the lyric beauty of his religious fervor. As he strums his harp and sings to the Lord, he gives full voice to his feelings with these words, *"Serve the LORD with gladness; . . Make a joyful noise unto the LORD, all ye lands."* (Ps. 100:1-2.)

This Psalm deals entirely with joyfulness, praise, gladness, and thanksgiving. All of these qualities are constructive and health-enhancing if we cultivate them, and all of them make us more pleasant people to be around. So I hope that during the coming week you will take a little time to read Psalm 100 and meditate on its deeper meaning.

Everybody loves to see a smiling face. That's why we love to be around children. We love their joyous nature and merry responses to everything. Nobody looks nice with a frown on his face; and no one wants to be with somebody who goes around moping and sulking all the time, scowling at the world. Even a saint looks unpleasant with a frown on his face. As Saint Francis de Sales put it, "A sad saint is a very sad saint indeed." So if you walk around with a puckered brow, all sad and grumbling at the world, not only do *you* feel miserable, but you make the people around you pretty unhappy too.

If a person has really found some attunement with the all-pervading reality of goodness and love, then in truth and in deed his heart should be gladdened. To be truly in touch with the consciousness of love and mercy, and the restorative power of God, one cannot but beget a happy and joyous heart. Being glad of heart also brings joy to the cells and tissues of your body. If you have a glad and joyous heart, even those microscopic wild animals called viruses are much less likely to attack you. The scriptures mention more than once that those who have a glad heart spend their days in health and in doing good works, not in sickness and sorrow.

So today we want to think about the spiritual riches that are contained in this beautiful Psalm. It says, *"Know ye that the LORD he is God: it is he that hath made us."* (Ps. 100:3.) All right, are you going to take the scripture at its word? Did God make you or didn't He? If He did, then He made you perfect. That doesn't mean you are never going to have any difficulties, or occasional illnesses. These things do happen in our lives; but the scriptures tell us that what the Lord has made, He declared good, He declared whole, and He declared perfect. So in spite of the imperfections that may have come into your mind and experience through errors in the way you've been going about life's journey, always remember this essential truth: God made you, and He made you perfect. God doesn't make mistakes, and He didn't make a mistake when he made *you*; no matter how many mistakes you think you have made. As far as you can, try to see yourself as God sees you. Visualize your most perfect and noble self, and then try to live up to God's vision for you by attuning to His love, His goodness, His forgiveness, and His joy. He will help you uncover the real you, the person He knows you really are.

When you are experiencing an illness or when something is going wrong in your life, it is a little hard to see God's perfection. If you have a swelling in your knee, trouble with your business, or a problem in your family, you can't just say, "I'm perfect, and there is no problem here," because you can see and feel it. But you can begin to meditate on your knee (and so on) with a hopeful and happy heart, and lean with confidence upon God's healing power. Even if your senses testify to the contrary, begin to think of your situation as if it *were* perfect, because it truly *is* perfect in the sight of the Lord. Turn your mind away from thinking about your body and the affairs of your material world, and place your attention on the divine idea that you are well and whole. Yield to the mind of God and let His perception of you become your perception: as good and as perfect. In that way, you will be imprinting upon the mechanism that is your subconscious mind—that marvelous instrument of manifestation—a positive statement of health, well-being, and success. The result will be the wondrous perpetual phenomenon of regeneration: the very foundation of healing and health within the structure of your body economy. Pretty soon you will see the swelling, the pain, or other difficulty subside a little (if not completely), and a simple solution to your problem will come into your mind.

Now, fortunately, many of the processes of your physical organism—such as your heartbeat, circulation, respiration, and metabolism—are totally under the control of your subconscious mind. If it were not so, you would die when you fell asleep if you forgot to tell these systems what to do. Imagine having to say to your body, *"Now, don't forget to pump my heart and keep me breathing, and don't forget to circulate my blood. Remember to rinse my lymph system, and please digest that big pizza I ate for dinner."* Fortunately, you don't have to worry about those things because they are under complete and automatic control. This gives you the freedom to explore the spiritual side of your nature, and to plant positive ideas in the fertile ground of your mind. It liberates you from worry and gives you time to offer quiet and simple thanks for good health and for the beauty of your life. Instead of fretting about whether your brain is picking up the proper signal from your little toe so that you can stand up and walk across the room, you are free to focus on thoughts of God, to generate gratitude for a healthy and efficient body, and to gives thanks for a glad and happy heart. This is the way to stay young.

Your concentrated thought, combined with your mental picture of wellness, is a dynamo of regeneration that affects the entire structure and function of all your body cells. Just as a hypnotist can raise a blister on your arm with a feather by telling you it is a hot iron, so can your thoughts bring about healing of your body and mind, as well as your outer conditions. Your entire body is responsive to your emotions in the same way that your face blushes with embarrassment, or pales when you receive bad news. So realize that no matter what your situation seems to be, if you respond to it with conviction and spiritual vision, you will soon see positive changes in your health, your business, your creative endeavors, and in your family and relationships. In no time at all, in a very simple and natural way, the answer to every question comes forward to give you exactly what you need.

The faculty of creative consciousness within the human mind, as I have said many times before, is an endless wellspring from which we may imbibe and distill the knowledge of the universe. Geniuses in music and art, science, literature, business, and statesmanship have all been people who have consciously or unconsciously touched on this incredible creative factor of mind. Without logical dissertation or intellectual argument, the intuitive mind gives back to you exactly what you put into it. Since we employ this part of our consciousness all the time, we must make good and careful use of it. I often like to point this out to spiritual seekers and devotees because even though they are sincere and love the Lord with all their hearts, they sometimes pour negative and unhappy thoughts into their coffee pot of consciousness; and instead of getting a cup of the richest, mountain-grown coffee, they end up drinking a muddy and bitter-tasting brew.

You know, we all watch TV once in a while, and it seems like there are more commercials than programs. When I talk about this marvelous instrument of consciousness—the "servomechanism" of the subconscious mind—I like to use the analogy of an old Folgers Coffee commercial. Remember Mrs. Olsen? She would measure a scoop of Folgers coffee and put it into the percolator, and in her lilting Scandinavian accent she would smilingly say, "It's the richest kind. It's mountain grown." See, if you put in the richest and best coffee, you'll pour *out* the richest and best-tasting cup of coffee. If Mrs. Olsen had put lousy coffee in the pot, she would have gotten a lousy cup of coffee. But no, she puts in the best, the richest, mountain-grown coffee, and everybody says, "Ummm, this is the best-tasting coffee I've ever had!"

Of course, they had to say that because they were paid to do so, and we don't know if Mrs. Olsen's is really the best brand—but we do know this: what we put into the coffee pot of our consciousness is what comes out. Likewise, the thoughts we pour into the subconscious mind (which never sleeps) are the thoughts that come out and change our lives. Saint Paul said so. Jesus said so. The great healers and teachers have said so; and now, even our medical doctors are saying so. Therefore, we should believe what they said and work with our thoughts every day.

We have to practice these things. We can't change all our habitual thoughts in an instant; we have to practice. We must look in on our thoughts from time to time and check for habitual worriments and doubts that wither and shrink the spirit. It is a nice little exercise to look in on your thoughts every once in a while. You might be surprised to find quite a bit of negative chattering going on in your mind, along with some less-than-lovely thoughts about your fellow humans.

There was a wonderful comedy show many years ago called the Duncan Sisters (Topsy and Eva). I wonder how many of you remember *that* far back! It was a marvelous show full of comic lines that left you in stitches. Topsy would get all mad at everybody, and she would say, *"I hate everybody in the world. And I wish there were **more** people in the world, so I could hate them too!"* Of course, it was meant to be funny, and we all laughed at the simplicity of the character. But, you know, there really are people like that.

The thing is, we must be very careful never to hate or hold negative feelings about anyone, because those thoughts seep into the obedient ground of your mind like germinating seeds and inevitably shoot negative experiences right back into your life. Like the coffee pot, what you put in comes right back out into your cup of life's experiences. If you sink into the habit of unhappiness or allow yourself to harden with sarcasm, cynicism, and judgment, then you are likely to reap stiffness in your joints and resistance in your relationships. If you fall victim to discouragement, unworthiness, and self-condemnation, dishonoring your true selfhood, you will most certainly bring forth only more to be discouraged about. If you concede to criticism and condemnation, convicting yourself and those around you, then like morning follows the night, you will draw to yourself disapproval and judgment. You see, the same law of creation which made you operates in and through you, expressing itself and working its way out in your body and affairs.

All of us have had to battle some illness, deal with a troubled relationship, or weather the failure of a business or financial venture at one time or another. But when we understand the deeper meaning of Psalm 100 and learn to habitually *"make a joyful noise,"* we always rise more quickly from these trials. I like this beautiful Psalm because it urges us to have a happy and grateful heart. Why? Because, in the consciousness of joy and gratitude, there isn't any room for disease or disharmony. The consciousness of gladness and thankfulness is a consciousness of light, so we must remember to pour ever more light into our thoughts. You know, your thoughts have an awful lot to do with how you look, how you feel, and how you go through life. Now, I don't mean that you should skip down the street, dancing and whistling like Fred Astaire all the time. Naturally, some days will be a little less than perfect, but you have already learned how to handle those vexations and problems. When things occur that you wish would not, simply stand still, get quiet, and remind yourself that you *can* change it all. How? By following Saint Paul, who said, *"I am changed by the renewing of my mind."* (Rom. 12:2: "be ye transformed by the renewing of your mind.") That's the kind of determination we need.

Whatever your challenge or limitation, always remember that the key to your liberation lies deeply within your consciousness of Christ, within your divine Self, right here and right now. We can all use this heavenly power of thought anytime, anywhere; and it doesn't matter how long you've had your problem or how old you are. When you change your mind, you can revivify your body and bring new zest to your life. To drink of the fountain of youth is to drink of joyousness. It is setting aside old and weary habits of thought and putting on the newness and resilience of a little child.

You know, children are naturally optimistic and trusting. When they are hurt, or when they suffer some sort of illness like the measles, they generally recover very quickly. Children bounce back swiftly from life's disappointments and losses, and in no time at all they return to their natural state, which is joyous and light. We must practice being like them. See, old and tired thoughts make old and tired bodies, but fresh and cheerful thoughts make healthy bodies and happy lives. Did you know that every time you fill your spirit with good cheer you literally postpone old age and death? So remember to *"make a joyful noise unto the LORD"* every day, and thereby bring to your life new zest, and the healing power of renewed enthusiasm and joy.

I have been taking singing lessons with a wonderful gentleman down in San Jose who is ninety-one years young. He plays the piano magnificently and sings like a brilliant Italian tenor. He is a superb conversationalist, and if you spoke to him on the phone you'd think he was thirty-five years old. He is very alert, sweetly dignified, and has an entirely positive and passionate approach to music and to his life. He walks faster than I do, and I walk fairly fast. He has a mop of white hair and thick bushy eyebrows; and if you don't pay attention and do what he says during your singing lesson, he peers out from under those big bushy white eyebrows, and his look lets you know you're out—you're just out! He doesn't waste his time or energy on anybody who isn't going to be intelligent and receptive to what he has to teach. I just think the world of him. He's sort of like a papa to me . . . and imagine, I'm in my seventies and he's in his nineties! He's just like a good father who teaches with love and discipline.

He teaches you how to sing a note by first telling you what to do, and letting you hear what it's supposed to sound like. Then he shows you how to do it the *wrong* way. He says, "Now, you don't want to make *that* kind of a sound, do you? You want to make a resonant sound that has brilliance, one that carries beautifully. And this can be accomplished very easily, once you learn how."

One day he said, "Now, listen to this . . ." and he went right up to a high C and sustained it. It was a brilliant and glorious tone that sent shivers up and down my arms. He once took his voice, in falsetto, all the way up to D above high C, and held it. That's pretty high, even for a tenor. Imagine, this wonderful man is ninety-one, and he's playfully saying to me, "I can sing better than you because I know what I'm doing!" His positivity and joyfulness, plus his enthusiasm for music and all of life, continue to keep him vibrantly alive and available to share his experience and knowledge with others.

When you study with this man you get not only lessons in singing, but also a treasure trove of marvelous and lasting spiritual lessons that he has gleaned over his many years as a musician and knower of the Great Artist within. From music, as from any endeavor, we can learn spiritual lessons. Even in the most mundane activities of our lives we have the prospect of perceiving Spirit at work. In all of these things, the innate capacities of the mind play such an important part. And we must never forget to work wisely and persistently with our innate faculties of creative consciousness, for they are the designers and builders of both our bodies and our experiences. Realize that you are the architect of your days; and never let a day go by without first plugging the extension cord of your consciousness into the Infinite, and bringing forth your divine ability to effectively arrange and manage your life and affairs. When you wake up in the morning, before you have even gotten out of bed, begin to impress your mind with positive spiritual statements, such as, *"This is a beautiful day—one of the best days of my life. I see only beauty and good today, and I am filled with gladness."*

Saint Paul told us to *"think on those things that are lovely."* (Phil. 4:8.) Why did he say that? Because he was something of a psychologist and metaphysician, and even in his day he knew that the tone and mood of people's thinking at the beginning of the week had a great deal to do with how they went through the rest of their week, and the whole of their lives. And it doesn't matter how old you are. Never think, "Oh well. I'm too old. It's too late for me. I'm too tired and weak. I can't change now." *It's never too late.* Don't permit yourself to shrink from the promise of a new and better life. Remember that you are a bubble of God, floating in a boundless ocean of ongoing, ever-continuing newness of life. You cannot be lost at sea or marooned anywhere, except in the marshes of your own murky thinking. So, instead of sinking into the swamplands of discouragement, let the rescue boat of optimism and good cheer tow you to the safety of hopefulness and the promise of new beginnings.

Every day, right in front of us, are wonderful examples of so-called elderly people who are mentally very sharp and physically full of vitality. These people thrive and prosper with purpose. They are continuously creative and actively concerned for the welfare of others. They thrive in the consciousness of joy and friendship. Such people are around us all the time, but we often don't notice them because they are "busy about their Father's business." They are the ones who have truly achieved a state of inner gladness wherein the light of a happy heart is reflected in their bodies as radiant health, and mirrored in their daily lives as uncountable blessings.

When you are in the presence of elders who have ripened into the luminous consciousness of joy, you are touched and lifted by the atmosphere of grace that surrounds them. It is like walking through a garden fully grown: rich with well-rooted plants and overflowing with fragrant flowers. There are no more thorns of anger or contempt to pluck out, no more weeds of sorrow and regret to pull; there are only clear and easy walkways within the conservatories of their consciousness, wherein they cultivate seeds of kindness and yield blossoms of beautiful soul qualities.

"Enter into his gates with thanksgiving, and into his courts with praise." (Ps. 100:4.) Now, what does it mean to "enter into his gates with thanksgiving" and "into his courts with praise?" These are wonderful symbols. They mean that you should leave your worldly concerns and all your material ideas outside the gate, and enter into the deepest chambers and courts of your consciousness. Close the door and leave all distracting thoughts behind you. Enter that quiet place and do what Jesus did: meditate on the meaning of a happy heart, and give thanks to the Lord that you *have* a glad heart. By reiterating and rehearsing the spirit of praise and thanksgiving, you steadily build a consciousness of joy within the tabernacle of the self. The residual therapeutic benefits are numerous and most wonderful. So if you want to stay young, efficient, and active as you go about the business of your life, remember to serve the Lord with gladness. Believe me, it will add years to your life, and life to your years.

"Be thankful unto him, and bless his name. For the LORD is good; his mercy is everlasting, and his truth endureth [forever]." (Ps. 100:4-5.) Now, it's nice to know that God is infinitely merciful, and that He is very compassionate of us little ones. Because once in a while we all make

minor errors here and there, and we need all the help we can get. God is not peering down on us from some distant cloud, shaking a stick at us and growling, "I'm gonna get you!" No. God is right here, loving us with the infinite love and compassion that are His nature. He is not a punishing God (though many people still can't quite get that notion out of their heads). He doesn't measure His love, and it is not dependent on whatever points you think you may or may not have scored along the way. He has compassion for the mistakes His children have made, and He offers understanding forgiveness for the foolish things that we, His little wandering sheep, have done.

So let us make up our minds that, beginning today, we are going to be glad of heart and filled with thanksgiving. *"Make a joyful noise unto the LORD, all ye lands."* That means everybody, everywhere: all people. Make a praiseful noise. Say a little prayer, reminding the subconscious mind, and the Lord within, that you are aware of His constant compassion and love. Then, you see, your days cannot but be better and brighter.

"Serve the LORD with gladness." The Lord doesn't want His children going around with long, dreary faces. He wants them to enjoy the playground of the earth experience, and He wants them to be glad in their work of serving His divine presence in all things. If people see you going around frowning all the time, they begin to wonder what kind of a Lord you are serving—because you don't seem to be very happy about it. Now, of course, that doesn't mean you should ignore or suppress your true feelings. Sometimes things happen that naturally provoke a negative emotion. And it is very important to release those negative emotions in a safe and sound way, and get them off your chest, so to speak, so that you can be free of any emotional toxicity. Parading around with a silly grin on your face, and baring your teeth from ear to ear when you don't mean it would be false and insincere; that's not what I'm talking about. *"Serve the Lord with gladness"* means remembering that He is your Lord, the One Great Self. It means that when you enter the gates and go into the inner courts, do so with praise and thanksgiving, and bless His holy name.

Now, in order to serve the Lord and *"pray without ceasing,"* (1 Thess. 5:17.) you don't have to kneel on a stone floor for seventeen hours every day. To *"pray without ceasing"* means to keep constant remembrance of the all-embracing, all-loving God within, without, and all about you. To be mindful means that as you walk through your building, the mall, a park, or the streets of your community—you just whisper a little prayer of thanksgiving for the beautiful surroundings in which, through the goodness of the Lord, you find yourself. As you go through your day, let your loving and joyful inner thoughts be like a fragrance: a silent prayer that blesses the people you work with, the people you live with, and the stranger you pass on the street.

I know that most of you seniors in this congregation have been here on planet earth for quite a while. Give thanks for your longevity, and what you have learned in the classroom of this wonderful earth experience. If you are an elder, give thanks for a sharp and positive mind, and for a vibrant and well-functioning body. That way your health will be sustained and immeasurably improved. If you are a young person and just setting out on your voyage through life, give thanks that you are being given an incredible array of opportunities and experiences that will help you learn, grow, and become. Each of them is a stepping-stone that leads you in the direction of your dreams, and helps to awaken in you a sense of your true identity.

Who are you? You are a child of God and heir to the Kingdom. You are a spark of the Infinite: the boundless and all-pervading consciousness, and beingness of Love without condition or end. *That's* who you are, and that is why you are here in the classroom of the earth experience. Such good news should cause anyone to *"Make a joyful noise unto the LORD."* Amen. Thank you.

O Rest in the Lord

Heritage House Presbyterian Chapel, San Francisco, CA
March 29, 1981

Good morning, dear friends. Today we read: *"O rest in the LORD. Wait patiently for him, and he shall give thee thy heart's desires. Commit thyself unto him and trust in him. And fret not thyself because of evildoers. O rest in the LORD, and wait patiently for him."* (This reading is a loose compilation of phrases taken from Ps. 37:1,4,5,7.)

You know, we do an awful lot of fretting, we really do. We read the newspaper and get all churned up, our blood pressure starts to rise, and pretty soon we're pounding the table, shaking our fists, and shouting at the television. Now, if you can do something about the situation, then most definitely do. But if there is nothing you can do, you would be very wise to follow the instruction of the inspired psalmist David when he says, *"Fret not thyself because of evildoers."* David got a great deal of solace from these beautiful words of wisdom because they came to him inspirationally. Those words carry as much import and inspiration for us today as they did in the time of David, so we should read them again and again.

Often we inadvertently admit into our body temple a tension and stress we don't need at all. It's natural for us to become outraged by what we read sometimes in the paper. I tell you, sometimes I almost feel like not reading the news for a while; but I always do. We need to be informed about what is going on in the world. And especially, when it comes to some of the shenanigans of the people in governments around the world, it isn't wise for us to put our heads in the sand. However, I think it a good idea to skip the bummers: those sensational and disturbing stories that merely cause anxiety and raise our blood pressure. Getting upset over something we cannot control doesn't do us any good, and it certainly doesn't help anybody else. If we get all worked up over the stories we read in the news, we may lose our balance and even get sick. Of course, we want to be aware of the current temper of things politically, socially, medically, financially, philosophically, and artistically. But we must learn to discriminate and take in only those things which are in harmony with our interests. This will add to our peaceful and positive approach to life. Otherwise, we fill ourselves with fretfulness and stress.

Now, the word "fret" means to worry, bother, or stress about something. If you fret about something, you are stressing both your mind and body. David counsels us in Psalm 37: *"Trust in the Lord and thou shalt dwell in the land, and verily thou shalt be fed."* In other words, when we stop fretting and begin to trust in God, all things come to us. We are fed in the spirit by divine wisdom. We are also fed in the physical sense with a steady supply of good food, opportunities, loving relationships, and all the other things we need on the earth plane.

You know, some people get so aggravated about things that they become quite cynical and end up with a total lack of trust in God. But we must remember that it is the Lord eternal who keeps this globe of mud in its orbit around the sun, just as He keeps the rest of the galaxies in their place in the universes of infinite space. We are told in scripture that the Lord is mindful of even the fallen sparrow. Certainly, then, the Lord is mindful of us, His children, because He made us in His own image and likeness.

The question people often ask is, "In what way am I made in His image and likeness? Exactly what does God look like, and how are we little ones like Him?" Well, we are made in the *spiritual* image and likeness of God, because God is spirit. It is important for us to realize that this "image and likeness" refers to the spirit within us that pauses and says, "I AM." Your "likeness" is your divine essence, that eternal spark of the Infinite living within you. That is the *real* you. When Moses heard the voice speaking from the burning bush, he asked, *"Who is it that speaks?"* The answer was quite simply, "I AM." (Exod. 3:13-14.) Moses understood the deep metaphysical meaning of the words "I AM." He intuitively perceived that "I AM" is another name for God, for he knew it was the voice of the divine that spoke to him from that burning bush.

Understanding who the "I AM" really is should cause us to be rather careful about how we use those two little words. Every time we say, "I AM" we are making a powerful declaration in the name of the eternal One, the spiritual presence within our own divine being. You may say, "I am sick. I am poor. I am sad. I am lonely." You are giving power to all these negatives when you speak or think such words, because you are declaring them in the name and through the power of "I AM"—that is, in the name of God. Whenever you say something about yourself and you precede it with "I AM," you must be careful to declare only that which is like unto God. Why? Because God said, *"I have made all things, and I have declared them good."* (Gen. 1:31.) So if you didn't know it before, you know it today: *you are good.* Accept that as truth, no matter what your conditioning has told you, and live up to it.

You know, for centuries it was the custom of preachers to pound the pulpit and send everybody off to perdition to roast on the perpetual rotisserie over the scorching fires of hell. This did not make people better. It sometimes made them very much afraid, but it didn't make them better. Later on, people began to take a second look at the words of God, and they discovered the subtle metaphysical meaning contained in them. They changed their minds and began to recognize that the immutable, imperishable, and eternal truths that Christ spoke of dwell, in fact, within themselves. Christ taught them that within the body temple resides a spark of the infinite One. That is the eternal nature of your being. That is the real and imperishable you. That is the "I AM" that goes on after this exercise in the classroom of the earth experience is all over.

When we graduate from *terra firma*, this solid earth plane, we move into another expression of life that is exquisitely more beautiful. When we leave this carnal figure behind and enter the eternal worlds, we do so clad in a garment made of more delicate material, a body made of light. These are more than beautiful ideas. They are absolute and unchangeable truths. So let us take hold of them, and work with them, incorporating them into our consciousness through daily contemplation and meditation.

I often speak about the marvelous research going on today into what is called the "near-death experience." More and more, because of our sophisticated medical technology, people pronounced clinically dead, due to accidents or illness, are being resuscitated through mechanical and medical means. In every one of the cases reported to Dr. Raymond Moody and others, the patient describes passing through some kind of tunnel or tube into a beautiful place of light where they saw family members and friends who had left the body and were called "dead."

There is one story I think is especially interesting about a man we'll call Joe, who "died" of cardiac arrest in the hospital. He had the experience of going up through a tunnel and coming out onto the shores of the heaven world, where he was greeted with great love by his mother and father. He turned to his right and saw his friend, Mr. Stevens, standing nearby. He thought, "What is Mr. Stevens doing here? He's not dead." Joe shook Mr. Stevens' hand; and suddenly a powerful urge rose up from within him and he knew that he must return to his earthly body. In a flash, as if pulled by a vacuum, Joe found himself back in the hospital operating room, floating over the table, listening to every word the doctors were saying about him.

They were trying to get his heart going again, and he heard one of the doctors say, "Look, we've done everything we can for Joe; that's all we can do." One of the other doctors said, "Oh, come on, let's give him one more blast with the defibrillator and see if we can get his heart started." Well, it worked, but it was quite painful for Joe as he came back into his dense body.

One day, after he got out of intensive care, he was talking with his wife and he said, "Tell me, dear, how is Mr. Stevens?" His wife said,

"Oh, we didn't want to tell you while you were so ill, but Mr. Stevens was killed in an automobile accident."

Now, this is a fascinating story, because here we have a man who remembers meeting someone on the other side of the veil, whom he didn't even know had passed on. Mr. Stevens was over there on the spiritual plane, the other side of earthly life, because he had "graduated" from the earth plane. There are hundreds of cases like this one, and more all the time, because as our technology improves, we are able to bring people back before they complete the dying process. These stories offer a lot of hope; and they strengthen our faith in the eternal and ongoing nature of the deepest aspect of the self, which is the eternal, ever-living Soul. And so, truly, we must take heed of these things and be joyful in the knowledge that indeed there are "many mansions" in our Father's infinite house.

Now, let us return to our reading, *"Delight thyself also in the Lord and He shall give thee thy heart's desire."* Okay, are you going to believe that God wants to give you your heart's desire, or do you think this is just a nice little poem that somebody wrote on a whim? This Psalm means exactly what it says, and it is as simple as that. The master teacher said that if we give our attention to first things first (meaning to the Lord Himself), and to bringing this wonderful eternal soul into alignment with God through devotion, meditation, and prayer, then those things we have need of, and those things which are our hearts' desire, *will* be given to us. We must put the eternal One first in our thinking, then all other things shall be added unto us. What a wonderful and consoling teaching this is.

Now, some people say, "I prayed, but I didn't get my heart's desire." Well, sometimes your heart's desire wasn't really good for you in the broader view of your life. Maybe it was the wrong thing to ask for. You know, Saint Teresa of Avila, the great Carmelite mystic of Catholicism, said that there are more tears shed over answered prayers because we know so little about what is best for us. That is quite a statement of wisdom. However, when you do know what you want and that it *is* good for you, then you must ask aright. You cannot murmur weakly. You have to fire up your prayers with the power of enthusiasm and the force of faith. You cannot be timid. Sometimes you have to storm the gates of heaven. When you know what you really want—what is right and good for you—then you mustn't be afraid to ask abundantly, with total commission of your mind and heart, for every worthy and noble desire of yours. Sometimes people say, "But I really don't know what I should ask for." When it is all boiled down, what people want most is an untroubled mind, a means of providing for their physical needs, the feeling of love in their hearts, and a sense of quiet in their souls. Isn't that what you want, too? All the material riches of the world cannot give you that.

I recently read an article about a man who was thoroughly laden with gold. He had everything that anybody could ever want or beget from this planet. He had every new gadget and technological toy invented by man. He owned planes and yachts, penthouses and villas. He was surrounded by the most beautiful women in the world, and his tables were overflowing with gastronomical delicacies and the finest of rare wines. And yet, he was utterly miserable.

Of course, gold by itself doesn't make you miserable. Gold *can* make you miserable, but it doesn't have to. It depends on your attitude toward it. You may have anything you wish: even the most beautiful homes in the world, filled with paintings and other works of art. You may have jewelry and clothes, cars, yachts and planes, or any number of other material objects that may please your heart—and it's perfectly all right to own all of them, provided you don't let them own *you*. The minute we lose touch and think, "This is so precious that if I lost it I would not want to live anymore," then we're in trouble. That's the wrong attitude. We may be custodians of all beauty, all art, and all wealth, but we must never let those material things own us. When we ascribe qualities to perishable things that we should really reserve for God the imperishable, we make a mistake.

Now, let's continue with our reading: *"Commit thy way unto Him. Trust also in Him and He shall bring it to pass."* It is very important to make a spiritual commitment at some time in your life. It's never too early, and never too late. Many of the saints started out early, while others began rather late in life. But ultimately, all of them made a profound commitment that no matter what came about in the affairs of their lives, devotion to God was always the most important. I hope that you practice a little meditation every day. There are many ways to meditate, and you must find your own. Take a passage from a nice inspirational book, or one of the Psalms or another passage you like from the Bible, and read a little bit. Then become very still. See, it is only during that very still time, after you have tuned out the noises of daily living and have even lost consciousness of your body, that you can perceive the inner voice of inspiration whispering the eternal and immutable truths of God. When you perceive the nature of your true Self, you begin to live as a spiritual giant.

See, we are not supposed to be lowly servants, crawling around on the parched pavement of the world, begging for crumbs. We're supposed to stand tall and walk straight in the light, as sons and daughters of God and heirs of heaven, because that is exactly what we have been told by Christ and all the other spiritual masters who have walked the earth. But, you know, humanity is slow to learn. If something is too hard and we can't understand it right away, or if we don't want to practice the teaching, we simply close the door on it or stash it in a box and tuck it away somewhere. On Sunday mornings we open the box and take a little peek and say, "Well, I can't accept *that* yet!" and close the box up tightly again. Sometimes it takes meeting a saint or a mystic in order to reopen that door and accept what we have been so reluctant to see.

There was a teacher who came to this country many years ago. He was not a Christian, but he was more Christian than anyone I ever met. This remarkable man had such love for God and such incredible devotion to Christ that every person he met felt the power of that divine love in him. He traveled across America giving lectures to packed houses; and as he did, he awakened and transformed thousands of lives. He always urged everyone to put first things first, and never begin the day without reserving some time for devotion to God. He knew that devotion was the quickest way to bring into consciousness the most marvelous factor of being, namely your relatedness to your Divine Mother/Father God. This man was able to do that with such beauty and power that his whole life was a miracle.

He wrote a book which was a synthesis of the teachings of East and West. Now, because he had long hair and sometimes wore a turban, some people called him a pagan and didn't want to read his book. But I like to read his book, and I've read it many times over the years, because he talks about God with such clarity and blazing devotion. He could not have written about the divine in that way unless he had experienced it intimately. This man worshipped God in truth and in deed, and in temples everywhere. He filled himself with the consciousness of the joy, love, compassion, and power that was ever available to him through his contact with the living Christ and with the all-pervading reality we call God.

I think many of you might enjoy reading his book. It is called *Autobiography of a Yogi*, and the name of the man who wrote it is *Paramhansa Yogananda*. I met Yogananda in 1933, and I was tremendously impressed by the overwhelming love he expressed for everyone. People everywhere, no matter what religion they followed, all loved him on sight because he expressed God. He was filled with a consciousness of the omnipresence of God, especially within the temple of his own being.

So when you commit your way unto Him and trust in Him, as today's text says, you are doing one of the greatest things you can do in your life. Sometimes we don't show real trust in God, and we try to do things by ourselves. We can do an enormous amount *with* God, and very little without God. We have to trust in Him and lean upon Him, the sustaining Infinite, *knowing* in mind, body, and emotions that whatever we need for the peace of our soul will come about in a wonderful way, through silent interior communion. Then we will know what the psalmist David was talking about when he said, *"O rest in the LORD. Wait patiently for him, and he shall give thee thy heart's desires. Commit thyself unto him and trust in him. And fret not thyself because of evildoers. O rest in the LORD, wait patiently for Him."* When we do that, we really have something to go on, because then we are working in a truly Christian, truly spiritual, dimension. The end is never. The sinner becomes a saint, and nobody really knows what comes after that. Consciousness is ever unfolding, and life is ever continuing. As we grow, little by little, and as we accept more and more, we are building within the consciousness of our being an incredibly beautiful gift for God, and for the world. Thank you. *Amen.*

The Secret Place of the Most High

Heritage House, San Francisco, CA
May 1981

Good morning, dear friends. Today I am going to read from Psalm 91. I am partial to the Psalms because they are filled with wonderful lessons of hope and joy. The beautiful songs of David give us great confidence in the love and continuing protection of the Heavenly Father. So let us read from Psalm 91: *"He that dwelleth in the secret place of the most High shall abide under the shadow of the Almighty. . . . Surely he shall deliver thee from the snare of the fowler, and from the noisome pestilence. He shall cover thee with his feathers, and under his wings shalt thou trust. . . . Thou shalt not be afraid for the terror by night; nor for the arrow that flieth by day; nor for the pestilence that walketh in darkness; nor for the destruction that wasteth at noonday."* (Ps. 91:1,3-6.)

Heavenly Father, fill us with a sense of confidence in the divine providence that this beautiful scriptural reading brings to our innermost being. For as we sensitize ourselves and begin to be filled with the truth of these beautiful utterances, so then shall we stay our souls in Thee, and thus be comforted and at rest. And, dear Father, fill us with a sense of Your almighty, eternal, infinite, and ongoing protection and love. Thank You. *Amen.*

People sometimes refer to Psalm 91 as a scriptural hymn, and that's really what it is. The very first line is sufficient to give us a whole morning of positive and profitable thinking. *"He that dwelleth in the secret place of the most High shall abide under the shadow of the Almighty."* Now, sometimes when we read these lovely words, we are immediately impressed by their lyrical beauty, and yet there is more here than just lovely poetry. We need to investigate a little more and discover the deeper meaning in these lines. What *is* the secret place of the most high? *Where* is the secret place of the most high? Well, Jesus told us. And because he knew that we are simple children who often get mixed up and wander off into other pastures in our understanding, he explained it in very simple, direct terms. He said that heaven (or expanded awareness) is *within* us; it is a state of consciousness.

Occasionally we meet people in life who have enormous serenity. They have a kind of inner glow that affects everybody who comes in contact with them. They shine, as it were. Now, just what is it about them that touches us so deeply? Very simply, it is the fact that they have felt the presence of God within the temple of the self as a state of consciousness. They live in full awareness that the eternal, immutable, ongoing and changeless spirit of God is in them. That same spirit is the deepest part of you. Jesus came in fulfillment of the law. He came to alert us by making statements that would force us to think in terms of the divine, all-pervading reality: which is God within, without, and all about.

Anyone can find "the secret place of the most High," and anyone can dwell in that secret place, because you don't have to go anywhere to find it. I remember during the 1960s when the big hippie movement was going on. Everybody had to go to India, or they had to live in a mountain cave in some strange place far, far away in order to find God. But they didn't really have to go anywhere, because the answer was already right there within them. Jesus said quite simply and directly, "Don't look here, nor there, for behold"—I like the way he put it— "*behold*"—take *hold* of this—"*The kingdom of heaven is within you.*" (Luke 17:21.) That which has been the goal of your deepest spiritual seeking is already there. It has always been, and will forever be, a part of the innermost facets of your being. This is truly wonderful! So when things get a little stormy, or when we are beset by noises and pestilence and all sorts of tumults as described in Psalm 91, where do we go to take refuge? We go within.

Many years ago, I met a wonderful mystic. This man had a beautiful spiritual understanding, and he was one of the greatest healers I ever met in my life. Having just come back from World War II, I was having some problems and struggling to find the answers to my difficulties. One day when we were talking, I said, "You know, I really don't feel very happy. There is so much confusion, and so much going on in the world. I am rather disturbed about it." Immediately this man said, "Well, John, that's because you haven't been very close to God. That's why you're disturbed." Then he vehemently declared, "I don't care if this whole ball of mud we call planet earth should burst into trillions of pieces in the next three minutes. I know where I am!"

Now, that's quite a statement. This was a Christian who took Christ at his word. He knew where he was. Why? Because he constantly entered into that "secret place of the most High": into the temple of being, where silence dwells. In the midst of that marvelous silence, the whispered words of eternal truth came into his consciousness.

This inspired teacher changed the lives of countless people all over the United States. He was a marvelous man who had all kinds of hobbies. He was an inventor, and a brilliant chess player who played chess by mail with people in all parts of the world. He had a vast library with over five thousand volumes on every kind of religious thought and human experience you could ever imagine. He read all these things because he wanted to stay abreast of what the greatest minds in science, art, politics, and religion had to say. But he knew that if he never read another book in his life, he would still have access to all the knowledge necessary at any time. Daily he entered "the secret place of the most High," and daily he meditated. With this daily practice he became part of the consciousness wherein dwells peace and truth: wherein dwells God.

I've always had a particular love for Psalm 91. It points out the marvelous truth of our being, centuries before Jesus came to spell it out for us. We're so apt to say, "Oh, if I had only been born in the time of Jesus, I would have recognized him. I would have walked with the master. I would have been one of his great disciples." Well, you don't know if you would have been a great disciple or not. You might not have recognized Jesus at all because, you see, most of the time when he was walking about the countryside, he was walking among the poor, the diseased, the hungry, and the dying. He was not clad in the raiment of those who dwelled in the houses of kings, but in the simplest robes of the poor people of his time. How could we have recognized him? If we were very lucky we might, through spiritual grace and the touch of his love, have recognized Jesus as a true Son of God, as divinity in the person Jesus.

Through the miraculous activities of his ministry, Jesus revealed the divine nature of his being. In healing, serving, and feeding the multitudes, and later on through his death and resurrection, Jesus demonstrated the presence and power of that indwelling divinity. Jesus constantly reminded us not to look for God in the razzle-dazzle of big things; for Christ consciousness, or God's love and power, dwells in the temple of silence. Those who have truly felt the presence of God within are very sure of that, and they walk through life with a kind of gentle, easy grace because they know that life is eternal. The end is never. You may lose your body (we're all going to lose our bodies someday), and it doesn't matter that much, because life is ongoing. The person you say is 'me,' John or Mary, goes on and on in the eternal home, in the "many mansions" which God has prepared for those who love Him.

Resounding through the corridors of time, religion has said, "Yes, yes, and *yes*" to eternal life, and still it is something of a mystery. It is a matter of moving from coarser to finer vibrations: from the density of physical form to the lightness of spiritual form. These subtle vibrations have always been with us, but we aren't always able to pick them up. It is only through regular meditation, in silence in "the secret place of the most High," that we begin to discern the nature of Spirit. With practice you will get used to these subtle energies, and you will find that noises round about you will bother you less.

Tumult and troubles naturally come up in human affairs. Problems and disharmonies are part of the classroom of the earth experience, as I often say, and sometimes they can be a little overwhelming. We all seem to have a threshold of resistance, and when that breaks down, what do we do? We let go and let God. How do we do that? We quietly enter that still place wherein dwells silence—wherein dwells the presence of the Christ Spirit—wherein dwells the presence of God. When we do that, we are absolutely renewed.

In the busy-ness of our activities, let us constantly cry out to God and Christ with reverence and love; and let us remember that the Christ Spirit dwells deep within us, for that *is* "the secret place of the most High." Jesus brought this eternal, immutable truth to our level in simple language so that we might understand—and still we insist on looking for God in other places. We're almost afraid that we're going to find it, and then we'll have to be too good! Well, don't worry about that, because it takes a little time, as we all know! You won't get so holy that you'll go flying off into the ether. We're still grounded here on *terra firma* for the time that we're supposed to be. So we enter that still place, we meditate, and we become more acquainted with spiritual reality every day, until at last it reveals its vast and undreamed-of riches in the totally conscious experience of the divine.

I'm pretty active and busy even at my age. I speak in a lot of churches, and at colleges and universities. I give weekly classes and I see a lot of people privately. I wouldn't dream of going out into my daily world without first entering "the secret place of the most High": the interior realm wherein dwells the light of God. Yesterday afternoon I gave a two-hour lecture at Foothill College, and it was a success. I hope that I awakened at least a dozen people to the reality that we are spiritual beings, temporarily residing in this earth plane, clad in the garment of the body and yet immortal in our spirit. You don't have to die to be spirit, you know; you're *already* spirit. You'll never be spirit more than you are right now. Later on, you'll graduate and enter another of the infinite realms of spirit. By entering into meditation every day, you will be prepared for that ongoing journey because you will have already acquainted yourself with the spiritual realities.

As I say, I wouldn't dream of beginning my day without at least an hour of meditation and prayer. I used to pray only for others, but I've learned to include myself. You know, in the holy scriptures it says that it is a good and wholesome thing to pray for the dead so that they may be loosed from their mistakes. Man is spirit, and with our prayers, our love, and good will, we can touch even those who have entered the larger expression of life.

So if you want to know a little bit about the essence of your being, which is spirit, then communicate at least once a day by becoming very still. There are many side benefits of meditation; it is very therapeutic. So sit in the best, most comfortable chair you can find, and put a pillow in back of you so that your spine is straight. Deeply quiet yourself, and declare total relaxation to every part of your body. Start with your feet, and move right up to your head. Some people do it the other way round, beginning with the head and moving downward to the feet; but I like to keep my head till last, so I begin at the feet and move upward. With this total relaxation, you see, you will gradually lose all body consciousness. Then you're on the launching pad, so to speak—ready to send the rockets of your consciousness into inner space; and inner space is what it's all about. That's "the secret place of the most High."

So dear friends, let us remember, *"He that dwelleth in the secret place of the most High shall abide under the shadow of the Almighty."* We all want to dwell in the shadow of the Almighty. We don't want to go where God is not. We can't anyway. No matter what you think, you can't get away from God; He is everywhere. He is, in a certain deep sense, in every one of us. Occasionally, you might meet someone who isn't behaving too well, or at least you don't think they are. (Maybe they don't think you are either.) Forgive them anyway, and remind yourself that the spirit of God is in them just as it is in you. The light of that spirit may be dimmed and covered over by a deep sense of sadness, failure, guilt, regret, or some other form of heartache or negativity, but always remember that knowing who we really are is a matter of degree. The saint *knows* who he or she is. We ordinary people don't always apprehend spiritual truth with such clarity, but we're on our way. We believe, but Christ *knew*. So enter into the knowing Christ spirit and take him at his word. Realize that the kingdom of expanded awareness is within you, and that all conditions—

those of the here and now as well as those of the hereafter—are areas of eternal and infinite consciousness.

We really have neglected to realize how powerful our prayers can be. When we unite our simple, humble selves with the power of Christ, then "God and one become a majority." That's when marvelous healings take place; that's when wonders occur which the uninitiated call "miracles."

And so, dear friends, don't neglect to daily enter "the secret place of the most High," and seek with diligence. Nobody can really take you there but you. The preacher, the practitioner, the minister, the rabbi, the rimpoche, the swami, or the priest can say, "Go that-a-way; it's over there," but you have to do it yourself. The great democracy of the spiritual trip, as I often say, is that YOU do it. In America we have total freedom of religion—and that is a marvelous thing, which we must never lose. Each person is responsible for his or her own spiritual destiny. If it were not so, the millionaire could buy Heaven, couldn't he? He could buy spiritual gifts. But it is not so.

Remember the story of the simple widow who put only a mite into the collection basket in the temple? Others were very lavish in their giving to the temple, offering gold coins and other treasures. Jesus turned to this simple old widow who put in just a mite, and pointed out that before God, her small offering was to be counted as far greater, because she gave it with so much love. So you see, it is not always whether you give gold and glitter, but whether you give of yourself in deep earnestness, as the simple widow did in the gospel story. Obviously, this simple Hebrew lady had discovered something about "the secret place of the most High." She had no doubt heard the rabbi speak about the Ninety-first Psalm, and she understood. You see, she had potential in the presence of God. Dwelling in "the secret place of the most High," she knew that that was her salvation and her treasure. And she understood that nothing could be found to be greater.

So I urge you to re-read Psalm 91 and give a little time to meditation every day this week. You don't have to give an hour; start with ten minutes. Oh, I can hear some of you saying, "But when I sit for meditation, I think of all sorts of other things. I start to meditate, and then I find myself thinking about how terrible it is that they laid off another seven thousand people this week." Well, that *is* a terrible thing, and that kind of thing can disturb you. Other thoughts will be disturbing, too. Sometimes in meditation, bothersome thoughts do creep in; but don't let that bother you. Don't get annoyed. And don't say, "I just can't meditate." Simply brush aside those thoughts and ask the Christ spirit for a deep understanding of "the secret place." Give thanks for a quiet mind and a peaceful heart, and for the ability to rest in the silence within. That which you ask for will be given to you.

Little by little, you will find that you *are* dwelling in "the secret place of the most High," and you *are* "abiding under the shadow of the Almighty." In that secret place you will know that He delivers you from the noisome pestilence and covers you with His feathers. You will realize that under His wings, you can trust and not be afraid of the terror of the night, nor the arrow that flies by day. Thus you will be filled with a sense of confidence in the eternal and infinitely ongoing protection and love of God within the temple of your very own being. *Amen.*

The Democracy of the Spiritual Trip

Unity Temple, San Francisco, CA
June 26, 1981

Good morning, dear friends. It's nice to be with you again. Today I want to talk a little bit about spiritual freedom.

Each one of us is an individualized concept of the Heavenly Father, who made all things and declared them good. In the gospel of St. John we are told, *"In the beginning was the Word, and the Word was with God, and the Word was God . . . and without him was not anything made that was made."* (John 1:1,3.)

Now, occasionally we are confronted by things which can only be described as *not* good. But God makes no mistakes, even though we, His children, often do. Sometimes we walk in darkness, as if we were blind. The Scripture continues, *"[The light of God is] the light of men. And the light [which is God] shineth in the darkness; and the darkness comprehended it not."* (John 1:4-5.)

This refers to spiritual illusion, or spiritual ignorance, and often it means living in total worship of the material. When we are asleep to the light of God (which is the light of man), we are certainly in darkness.

We don't want any part of that, do we? No. We want to take God at His word when He declared our divinity.

It is very difficult for us to come to grips with the essential nature of our true being. As we grow in understanding, we realize that God is not outside and separate from us—but inside, as part of our true self. As we move toward spiritual maturity, we are better able to embrace spiritual sovereignty.

Now, we have all read history, and we know that sometimes, in his ignorance, man has curbed the religious freedoms of other people. If you didn't believe "this creed" or "that doctrine," you were damned. One of the beautiful things about our ancestors leaving the religious oppression of the Old World and coming to America in search of religious freedom, is that we were granted the freedom to discover the essential truth and divine nature of our being. With this new freedom we were able to move into the byways of metaphysical understanding, and this gave us great latitude for development, understanding, and expression. Wrapped in this body garment, we journey through the classroom of the earth expression in order that we may grow, unfold, and infinitely expand.

There is a great leap between believing and knowing. The saints, sages, prophets, and holy ones *know* who they are with a kind of inner divine assurance. This certainty and knowledge gives them an inner sense of the infallibility of the pathway they are walking—and for them it *is* the only way. The only difference between us and Teresa of Avila, John the Evangelist, Francis of Assisi, and other great saints of the Christian path, is that we *believe* and they *knew*.

We must realize that God expresses Himself in a myriad of marvelous ways. Each one of us is highly individualized; no two people have the same fingerprints. And in the consciousness of the all-pervading Father, no two of us are identical. There is only *one* you. (Of course, I can hear some of our neighbors whispering, "*Thank God!*")

Now, we all need teachers, ministers, rabbis, priests, and other kinds of leadership. But never take the attitude that the practitioner, pastor, or priest can make the spiritual journey *for* you. You see, the great democracy of the spiritual trip, as I always say, is that *YOU do it*. Nobody is hammering you on the head, saying, "You have to believe *this* way," or "You have to do it *that* way." Not at all.

I am grateful that today the ecumenical spirit in religion is gaining acceptance throughout the world. Pope John XXIII was one of the leaders in the western Christian movement, and in true ecumenical spirit he spoke of the acceptance of good everywhere. This beloved religious leader was a Catholic—which, in its truest sense, means *universal*. With this sense of universality, you are at liberty to move in a spiritual way according to the dictates of your conscience, and in so doing express your free will and independence, as long as it does not interfere with the rights of anyone else.

Some people who enter churches and temples of every description, and visit metaphysicians and other kinds of healers, have somehow gotten a wrong notion that the practitioner is going to shoulder their burdens and do all the work for them. They have to get over that idea. Certainly a healer, minister, priest, guru, or practitioner can give you some direction. They may say, "Look, here's your problem. And this is the way you might go about unraveling the entanglement to solve your problem. But do not imagine for a moment that I can, or should, carry it for you—because the minute I did, I would have destroyed the essential nature of your spiritual independence."

The divine democracy of religion and of seeking after truth is indeed that *you* do it, and it is incumbent upon you to do it. Now, I would not be up here talking if I didn't believe that we all need speakers and teachers to guide and encourage us. We need those who are a little ahead of us on the path to remind us, again and again. This is the way we grow into an increasing understanding of truth, until, little by little, we are truly transformed and liberated. We are transmuted in a kind of divine alchemy within our consciousness, as we lean totally and with absolute faith upon the sustaining Infinite—upon God within, without, and all about.

Now, we all want spiritual freedom, and the best way any teacher, minister, priest, or rabbi can give you that is to make you independent of everything, including him or her. They may guide and help you; they may lift you and exhort you, but YOU do the work. You must make the effort. You must seek, and knock, and ask for what you need. Quite simply, the great democracy of the spirit is that *you*, and you alone, must traverse the road to an increasing elevation and awareness of the truth, so that ultimately you are raised to conscious identification with the divine. And the way to do that is through daily meditation upon the infinite and all-pervading Reality.

There are a lot of people who never meditate. I don't know how you can expect to get anywhere if you don't meditate just a little. You see, it is in the stillness that the voice of truth can be heard whispering silently into the deep regions of consciousness, urging you onward to change this and that—in order to liberate you from all materiality, all inordinate love of the mortal things of this world.

Now, some people misquote Scripture. They say, "Money is the root of all evil." This is not so. It is greed and the *inordinate love of money* that is "the root of all evil."(1 Tim. 6:10.) An excessive love of money imprisons you, and in the grip of such a passion you become an absolutely confirmed materialist. That is not spiritual freedom. In fact, such an obsession might indeed inhibit not only *your* freedom, but the freedom of others too.

And so, dear friends, let us concern ourselves deeply with the task of attaining the spiritual and material freedom we need through the practice of daily introspection, self-examination, and meditation. Meditation is a definite and positive assistance in the ever-increasing elevation of our consciousness as we move toward God. We approach the divine realization of the truth we all seek by making a commitment to become utterly and completely still within—so that wisdom insights may come like a beautiful, harmonious cloud of knowing. As we work and move with that truth, we are truly able to declare our independence from the tyranny of materiality and over-possessiveness.

You know, water can serve as a symbol for Spirit. If you look into a very still lake you will see a perfect reflection of yourself; but if you drop a stone into the water, many ripples arise and your reflection becomes distorted. We don't want to throw any stones of turbulence into the still pool of meditation and conscious realization. We don't want to distort the recognition of ourselves as individualized sons and daughters of God, and heirs of heaven with Christ. The sooner you begin to realize the essential divine nature of your being, the quicker will be your elevation on the pathway of spiritual liberation.

Spiritual independence is an absolute essential to spiritual growth. In America there are hundreds of different denominations of Christianity, and I regret to say that sometimes the only thing they have in common is that each one is "the only true church"! What is really essential in religion is that truth *is*, and truth is triumphant.

When I was a little boy I was a very good Catholic. My mother was a wonderful, devout Irish lady with a lot of wisdom and wit. She warned me of spiritual pride; she also urged me to be mindful, and to realize that we make our own pathway. She taught me that we create our own tomorrows by the dynamic power of our thinking today. When I first went to seminary, she said, *"Now be careful, John. Sometimes the nearer the altar, the farther from God."* Don't let yourself become proud, spiritually. Walk in humility, and in divine acceptance of the all-pervading Light. Then you will become one with that Light.

One of the greatest and most marvelous aspects of spiritual freedom is our divine imagination. This marvelous factor of consciousness is the greatest gift because it helps us become co-creators with God. Whatever we can envision with great power upon the inner screen of the mind can become a profound reality in our lives and in our affairs.

In the past, few of us were told that we had any power to create or become the architects of our own lives. We were told only that if we didn't go to church, terrible things would happen to us. Thankfully, we are much more liberated now. We know we are responsible for ourselves, and nobody out there with a magic hat and wand is going to save us. We know that within the temple of our very being there is a divine intelligence and power that will truly save us, materially, financially, and spiritually. We are saved by leaning upon the sustaining Infinite and by declaring our independence. We do that by becoming totally dependent upon God, and by asking for the help that comes from the divine Self, from the kingdom of heaven within.

You know, Jesus said so many marvelous things, and he said them with such simplicity. In almost every talk I give I repeat what he told us, because we need to hear it again and again. He said, "Don't look here nor there, for *behold* (take *hold* of this), the kingdom of heaven (of freedom, or expanded awareness) is *within you.*" (Luke 17:21.)

It takes a long time for people to accept that. They either feel they are not good enough, or they think that somebody else who *is* good enough will pray for them or do it all for them. Of course, it is a beautiful thing to pray for each other and help each other along the way, and I urge you to do that. But nobody is going to save you. Great teachers help and guide us; they tell us how we can best move into our own fulfillment. If we follow their wisdom, do the work, and devote ourselves to a life of meditation and prayer, then surely we will grow and become more attuned to Spirit. In that sense, we will be saved. But if we don't do the work, all the spiritual advice in the world will fall flat upon the untilled ground.

Recently, on the Fourth of July, we celebrated our national birthday and our Declaration of Independence. It is important that you make your own *spiritual* "declaration of independence"—one that entails freedom from all the troubles that befall us in our human condition. Freedom from trauma. Freedom from anxiety. Freedom from fear, superstitions, and a lot of other nonsense we were fed growing up.

The way to God is extremely simple. If it were not so, then all the great scientists of the world would be God-realized. A PhD, by itself, doesn't do it for you. A person with a PhD *might* become God-realized (and I'm sure we have some here today!), but Jesus had no trace of a Harvard accent, and neither did any of his followers. They were simple fishermen living the very uncomplicated ways of their times, and they uttered liberating wisdom insights, which were made available to "those who could hear."

During the time of Jesus, people couldn't read; there were no newspapers, and there was certainly no nightly news on television or radio. So how did Jesus reach the people? Well, first and foremost, he taught by example; and again, by the miracle-working power of his absolute faith; and by simple, direct instruction. When people accepted what Jesus taught, they were liberated from a thousand ills and misconceptions; they were freed, and they were able to declare their spiritual independence. By their own free will, they came to the Christ and to the truth he brought: the truth that set them free. No one coerced them, and no one need ever coerce *us*. Our conscience will coerce us sufficiently, if we are going wrong. If we put aside a little time every day to tune in to the Infinite, we will surely know when we are wrong.

If you had the best television set in the world, costing ten thousand dollars, but you never bothered to plug it in, nothing would come onto your screen. You would go around whining, "I never get anything on my television set!" First, you have to plug in the TV. Similarly, if you want spiritual freedom, you have to tune in first and quiet the self.

There is a marvelous capacity and a great healing power in stillness. Today, many scientists in the field of medicine are recognizing the wonderful benefits of meditation. Patients who learn to become very still are quickly relieved of pain, both physical and emotional, and they are able to find answers to problems which perhaps have been vexing them for a very long time. When you quiet the mind, you'll quiet the body, and in so doing you'll accrue many benefits. You'll bring your blood pressure down, and your circulation will improve. You'll quiet the heart, and your emotions will simmer down a bit too. All these wonderful benefits will be added to your physical and emotional health, simply by taking the time to plug into the Infinite and listen quietly. In that deep silence, health benefits are immeasurable. Insights emerge, and answers to long-standing problems will become very clear. In simply being still, you *can* hear His voice, and you can truly become one with Him, who abideth in stillness.

And so, dear friends, let us remember to keep our daily appointment with God, for it is by being in the presence of God within that you can rightly declare your freedom and total spiritual independence. Thank you. *Amen.*

Judge Not

Heritage House, San Francisco, CA
June 28, 1981

Good morning. Today we read in scripture: *"Judge not, that ye be not judged. For with what judgment ye judge, ye shall be judged: and with what measure ye mete, it shall be measured to you again. And why beholdest thou the mote that is in thy brother's eye, but considerest not the beam that is in thy own eye? Or how wilt thou say to thy brother, Let me pull out the mote out of thine eye; and behold, a beam is in thine own eye?"* (Matt. 7:1-4.)

Heavenly Father, emblazon upon our hearts this important Christian attitude of being non-judgmental. Teach us to tend the garden of our own souls so that each one of us, in so caring for the spiritual self, will have no time for bearing judgment against another. Though this is the fundamental wisdom of Your Christian teaching, Lord, it is sometimes sorely neglected. Bless us as we consider this scripture in our talk today, and fill us with a sense of ongoing love and compassion. Amen.

Dear friends, today I am going to talk about a subject that we frequently hear in sermons, but just as frequently forget. It is one of those texts that seems to have a little oil or something on it; because even though we hear about it often, it slips through the fingers of our soul very quickly and easily. Life can be much more beautiful when we relegate to the Divine the judgment and correction of people, instead of taking that job upon ourselves. You do a great disservice to yourself when you criticize someone, because in so judging, you see, you lose your own peace of mind. Being inordinately conscious of the failings of other people can make you depressed. Of course, we don't like to hear this, but modern psychologists tell us very often that the thing we criticize in other people is the thing that goes unrecognized in us. If you see the mote in the eye of another person, do not criticize it, because in your own eye there might also be a beam. Instead, follow the pure and direct Christian attitude of mercy and loving compassion. How does anybody watching us know if we are Christians? Because we love one another.

It's not easy to refrain from criticizing. Sometimes I get very critical about what I read in the newspaper. Dreadful things *are* going on in our world, and that's bad enough. But if we start being critical of our fellow men and women, then we have lost our essential Christian spirituality. I am certainly not a model yet of complete tranquility, but I have found that I am a little more mellow than I was ten or twenty years ago. Generally, I don't waste my time criticizing others, because I realize that before the eye of the omniscient, all-pervading One, I too have innumerable faults. Were it not for the loving and redemptive activities of the Christ Spirit on our behalf, we could not be, shall we say, spared from this natural tendency to criticize and judge.

Most of the things we read in scripture have a remarkably practical application, and this one certainly does. Saint Matthew gives us a beautiful teaching here, and he brings it down to the bottom line with infinite simplicity. He doesn't make a big Shakespearean speech out of it. He notes that Jesus said, quite simply, *"Judge not, that ye be not judged."* We find this to be applicable not only in our ordinary physical world, but also in the metaphysical, spiritual aspect of man. The thoughts that you habitually send out into the ether are real things, and they come back into your consciousness and your being like doves coming home to roost. Be careful, therefore, what you think because, *"As a man thinketh in his heart, so is he."* (Prov. 23:7.)

If you are tempted, as we all are from time to time, to say, "Oh, I like everybody *except* Mrs. So-and-So; she really gets on my nerves," turn your thoughts in a different direction, and wisely begin to concentrate instead on healthy, happy, and outgoing thoughts. It's very normal and natural to criticize someone who is behaving inappropriately. When you see someone stumbling into the furniture and faltering in his speech, it is quite natural to say, "Oh, he's drunk." That's an observation. But if you say, "Isn't that terrible? Just look at that bum, what a despicable man he is," that's a judgment. Leave the judgments to God. We have a lot to do in this world in order to develop our own consciousness and elevate it toward the mountaintop of truth. If we waste time judging others and dare to assume prerogatives that belong to the Lord Himself, then we are disobeying the simple injunction of the gospel: namely that we should "judge not."

Now, I'm sure that none of us wants to be unkind, but sometimes we catch ourselves being a little impatient and harsh anyway. It is at those times that we need to take hold of our criticizing thoughts and change them to positive and loving thoughts. You know, it doesn't make people feel very good if you send them unlovely thoughts, and it certainly doesn't make you feel very good either. So instead of wasting energy you could be using in so many constructive ways, why not let God be in His heavens and leave all judgment in His hands. We get into trouble when we try to take over the work of the Father. We can't do it; we shouldn't do it; and in chapter seven, verse one, Matthew tells us *not* to do it.

The Bible tells us to love one another, but that doesn't mean it has to be a big *emotional* love. It is simply a call to kindness and charity, an offering to uplift the soul of every living being. You can't have an emotional attachment and involvement with all living beings, but you can have a spiritual love for all. You are really offering Christian love to your fellow humans when you treat them as you would like to be treated. Then you are fulfilling the law, which is love, charity, and compassion. It is very important, you see, for us to love everyone because, according to the Lord Jesus, each and every one of us has within a spark of the Infinite. In the temple of the self there dwells the divine essence that is your true nature. We must live up to that by being very compassionate with others and with ourselves.

Over the years, I've counseled many people who were carrying around a huge and heavy sack of injuries, regrets, sorrows, and a host of other things that were quite painful and burdensome. If you are carrying a sack of such weighty troubles, realize that they do nothing but obstruct and retard your easy march toward the supreme truth and light of God. Now, I think that hatred is probably the darkest of all sins, and I know that nobody here would ever give way to it. Though it may arise in you in response to something that has hurt you very deeply, you must let it go and forgive, even as you would want to be forgiven, for that is the law. It is the truth as expounded by Jesus the Christ as he walked the countryside in what today is called the Holy Land.

Sometimes people feel that if they give up their negative feelings and "forgive," it means they must condone what happened to them—that it was okay. It was *not* okay, and forgiving doesn't mean you condone what someone did. It simply means you stop carrying around the negative feelings about what happened. You release your anger and resentment. You are not necessarily doing this to set the other person free. You are doing it to liberate yourself.

You know, psychologists tell us that the mind is never still, and that in the tape recordings of the mind there are continuous conversations going on. Stop sometime and take notice of what kind of thoughts you are having and what kind of mental conversations are going on within you. You may be quite shocked to find that they are often rather negative. What you must do is reverse the whole picture and throw out the negatives—the "baddies"—and bring in the good and prospering thoughts. You see, thoughts which are beautiful and uplifting, health-giving and joyful, are the ones that sustain you.

On the ordinary social level of interacting with people, as well as on the spiritual level, you must realize that there is an *inner* man or woman. That inner man or woman is mind, consciousness, or spirit, and it is always at work. What things do you say to yourself? How do you treat yourself? Are you kind and compassionate? Do you encourage yourself, or are you always criticizing, demanding, and putting yourself down? How do you mentally talk to others? Are you always arguing with them and casting mental barbs at them?

I'm sure you've heard people say, "Well, I wouldn't do that if I were him." Well, you *would* do it if you were him—because he just did it! We don't always know what motivates people, or what is behind an unhappy mood. Let things go and forgive. If you see somebody trudging down the hall, looking desperate and unhappy, and she passes you by without even saying hello, don't let that bother you. Give her a silent blessing. Maybe she is in physical pain or dealing with something very difficult in her life. Perhaps she is so concentrated that she doesn't even see you go by. Now, you can see how easy it would be to make a mountain out of a molehill in such a situation, but instead of that, simply say, "God bless

Mrs. So-and-So. Lord, let the sunlight of a positive attitude toward life blossom in her heart and liberate her from all the ills that beset her, and make her a true child of the Christ light."

See, the people around you are part of your Christian interaction with the world. Your workplace, as well as your home, should be filled with fraternity, love, compassion, and charity of heart. So if you are inclined one day, because somebody stepped on your pet corn, to say something sharp, save it. Instead, change your mind and silently say, "I send you the Christ light and blessing." That will not only brighten your day, it will brighten the day of the person toward whom you perhaps didn't feel too charitable.

Now, everywhere we go we find people who neglect charity and love. But when we become conscious of the fact that we are all one in the Christ Spirit, we bow to our fellow man, because we realize that we are in fact saluting the divinity in him or her. Understand that within each and every person, no matter how deeply buried it may seem, there is a spark of the Infinite. Remembering that should help us overlook our tendency to be uncharitable or unkind. Being critical and impatient with someone seems like such a little thing in the moment, but it can snowball into something rather significant, so that by Christmastime there are seventeen people you don't want to talk to anymore. When you live with people, it's natural to become impatient or frustrated with them once in a while. We're all human, and sometimes people annoy us. Christ promised us a rich and satisfying life if we would simply follow his most important and direct message: namely that we become one with his spirit of compassion and charity for others.

You know, once in a while we have to review these portions of the scripture, because they are very easily passed by. We are apt to say, "Well, the Bible is a wonderful book, and Mrs. So-and-So should read this part; it would really help her." Well, we have to realize that these scriptures help us and take care of *our* needs. Whenever you have a need of any kind, pick up the Bible, or any other spiritual book you like, and begin to read the positive statements contained in it, and right away you will feel a kind of uplift. Happiness is contagious, and when you are lifted up by reading some inspiring passage, you automatically lift those around you. It is a transfer of energy, and it is very tangible. Of course, it wouldn't be natural to go around grinning ear to ear twenty-four hours a day, but you can decide to become a person who is habitually happy, someone who has a kind of serenity and a pleasant, outgoing attitude. Then, you see, in a silent way, you begin to spread the true message of love and charity, which is the spirit of the Christ.

So I urge upon you to take a second look at Matthew, chapter seven, verse one this week. There is a little more to it than what we talked about today. Read it over, and reaffirm the basic, fundamental aspects of your Christian heritage. In this way, not only will you be healthier and freer in your own spirit, but you will find that you get along with everybody, and you'll see that everybody likes you better too. When you develop a loving and charitable attitude, you can even handle people who are desperately unhappy, dreadfully ill, or even rather evil.

There are people walking the streets who are so miserable and wicked that you'd be afraid to meet them in a dark place. When you meet such people, what do you do? You bless them silently as you pass by, and pray that they will see the light and know that they, too, can be one with Christ. One of the great saints used to say, "When you take one step toward God, He has already taken two steps toward you." Fortunately, we don't have to be very often around people who are filled with ugly and toxic emotions, because we don't walk down to the skid row district every day. But if you should meet someone who is terribly out of balance and forlorn, always send out from your inner self a sense of light, an ongoing aura of divine light and love, and leave it to the Christ Spirit to touch those whom He will. In that way, you become a silent missionary of God. I urge this upon you, not only because it is the right thing to do, but also because it will bring you a great and abiding joy, a deep serenity, and an ongoing sense of well being. I'm sure we all want that. Thank you. *Amen.*

Have You Tuned In?

Unity Temple, San Francisco, CA
June 28, 1981

The title of my talk today is, "Have You Tuned In?" Well, have you? Tuned in to what? When you are at home and you turn on the radio or the television, you want to tune in a program you like, one that makes you feel good. If you tuned in a program and really didn't like what you heard coming from it, you'd just turn the dial to a different station, wouldn't you? We are all responsible for what we allow ourselves to hear, not only through the media, but also in the conversational aspects of our minds. Scientists tell us that there are conversations going on within our minds all the time, even if we are not quite aware of them. So it is very wise for us occasionally to pause and listen to what is going on within the self. You might be quite shocked at the negativity going on within the tape-recorded conversations of your mind.

Just what do we do when we find a negative program going on in our mind? Well, we do the same thing that we do with any television or radio program we don't like. We absolutely switch it off channel "negative," and put it on channel "positive." That's the only way to fly! Now, tuning in to the conversations of the mind is only one way to tune in, but there is another level. Have you tuned in to the Infinite?

You may remember a book written many years ago by a man named Ralph Waldo Trine called *In Tune with the Infinite*. It is a beautiful book which gives us some very fine hints as to how we may tune in to the Infinite.

Now, of course, this is something you must do for yourself. Nobody's going to tune in to the Infinite for you. If you get up in the morning and go through all the ramifications of gaining your daily bread in the marketplace without first tuning in to the consciousness that can bring you poise, power, peace, and dominion, then you've certainly missed the bus, at least for that day. So the very first thing you have to accomplish (and this is absolutely obligatory) is to give a little time to quietness before you begin your day.

Now, I can almost hear some of you say, "But I'm in a big hurry in the morning. I'm getting the coffee ready. I have to turn the egg over. I've got to run to catch the bus. I have to take the kids to school," and a thousand and one other things. But you can always make time to tune in to the Infinite. That is one of the things within your power. You can make time simply by determining that you will get up ten minutes earlier. What's ten minutes? You organize these little ten minutes so that after you've gotten everything out of the way except breakfast, you can sit down and quiet your mind, quiet your body, and breathe deeply.

The therapeutic benefits that accrue from merely quieting the body-mind-spirit relatedness are enormous. First of all, meditation relieves stress and tension, which is literally killing people. We run off to work in a big tension, we work in a big tension, and we eat in a big tension. Then we fight our way home in a big tension. With such constant stress, what kind of a life do you expect to have? And don't tell me you can't do anything about it, because you can. I do. I tune in every day. I wouldn't dream of beginning my day out in the world without having first tuned in to the Infinite. See, I'm not preaching something I'm not practicing. I believe so implicitly that, as the beginning of the day and your attunement to the divine and all-pervading goes, so goes the rest of your day. And so goes your protection, your inner intelligent guidance, and the perception and insight that might emerge in your vast consciousness as direction. But of course, if we're never quiet, we are never going to hear "that still small voice": the whispering voice within. And so, dear friends, tune in, because if you don't, it isn't going to tune in to you.

When we came down to this classroom of the earth experience we were given absolute dominion and free will. We can tune in to God: we can seek God, divine realization, and deep meditational and spiritual uplift and bliss. But we don't have to. No one is going to force us. We might push ourselves and accrue some pretty heavy karma now and then, but the bottom line is quite simply that God lets you do it. And isn't that marvelously democratic? We're allowed to seek for ourselves. Nobody's out there with a big stick, hitting you over the head shouting, "Meditate, grow, and be liberated!" It's your choice, your free will.

You know, the Zen Buddhists are wonderful people, and they are known to use a certain teaching technique that helps keep students awake. You enter their halls to meditate; and there you sit, becoming more and more quiet. After a while you think, "Wow, I've really made it! I've never been this quiet in my life." Then suddenly, POW, you get smacked right over your head with a bamboo stick, just because the teacher saw you move your little toe!

It's almost like the early American Quakers. In the Quaker meetings everyone would remain silent, and the only person who dared to get up and utter anything at all was the one who was at that moment inspired by the Holy Spirit. Unless he or she was inspired, nobody got up. There was a man who would walk around in the back of the room—I'm sure he was a very tall man with long arms—and he carried a big stick. If he saw anybody even nod, much less snore (no snoring allowed at all), he would rap you on the bean with the stick and wake you up. It was not exactly the highest moment of your life, having him land on you with that big stick! But at least they were teaching people to be aware and awake. You would be absolutely shocked at the number of people marching through life in a kind of comatose state because they have never tuned in.

Now, if you tune in, your life will change. Why? Because you have dominion. Remember, *"It is the Father's good pleasure to give you the kingdom."* (Luke 12:32.) If you reach out and take hold of it, glory be! If, on the other hand, you sit down and say, "I'm poor. I'm weak. I'm tired. I'm sick, and everybody hates me"—well, probably all those things will be true for you because you've declared them to be true. On the other hand, you can stand up and declare, "God has told me, in the bibles and holy books of all religions, that I have dominion." If you choose to be quiet and very still, even for a very short period of time (especially in the first hours of the morning), you will realize this marvelous interrelatedness of body, mind, and spirit. It is a connectedness that so involves itself with us that we are given total dominion over our lives by the very power of our thoughts.

I give weekly classes near San Jose, California, and part of my first night's teaching is to simply show people how to sit, how to still the body, and how to quiet the mind. Very often people become more deeply silent than they have ever been before. You would be surprised how many people have never really sat and become truly quiet. Once in a while someone will come up and say, "Oh, Mr. Laurence, I heard my heart; it was beating." It alarms some people when they hear their heart beating for the very first time, but I say, "That's great. Don't worry— unless it stops!" You see, when you get that quiet, you are able to hear sounds within the body temple you may have never heard before. When you are very quiet, you might also hear your blood circulating or feel your internal organs. You may sense your breath in various parts of your body, and you may even feel your digestion at work. Later on, after you have practiced for a while, you won't notice those things at all. In fact, after awhile you will lose all body consciousness.

It almost never fails that during the course of these classes, at least one person, and sometimes two or three, will have a healing. That is the beauty of teaching people to deeply quiet the mind and body. We had one dear lady in the class who was a nurse in the intensive care unit of one of the largest hospitals in the area. She was a wonderful lady, very intuitive and quite delightful. She suffered with debilitating headaches, and although she had worked in medicine all her adult life and knew all the various brands of headache medicine, none of them worked for her. This poor, dear lady had had a continuous headache for seventeen years—and there she was, right in the midst of a major hospital, but the boys in white couldn't help her. She couldn't find the right nostrum, and so she came to class. We had an eight-week class at that time; and before we finished the seventh class, she announced to us that for the first time in seventeen years she was free from pain and no longer concerned with the headache that had consumed her life. That's an example of a spontaneous healing. It took place because she became still enough in her mind to hear the voice of inspiration, the voice of healing, the voice that lifts us up and tells us over and over that we have dominion.

Too many of us have forgotten that. Many of us are spiritual somnambulists. We go trudging through life fast asleep. Of course, life isn't going to be very glorious for us when we are sleeping through it. But again, we have chosen our lives. Cicero said, "Oh man who suffers, know that you suffer from yourself." Some years later, Abraham Lincoln said, "Men [and women] suffer because they bring it upon themselves to suffer; they don't have to." Well now, you might say that statement is a little too broad, because sometimes things happen to us that we have very little control over, and sometimes we have to endure some kind of suffering through no fault of our own. That is true, but most of our suffering is created by our own thoughts and actions, or inactions. We do have the chance to move away from most of our suffering by participating in a few simple laws.

What we do first is learn to be still, because it is only when you are very still that you will hear the still small voice. You're not likely to hear the still small voice of God while doing "La Cucaracha" out on the dance floor, or while at a baseball game in the midst of a very big crowd and everybody's screaming and howling at the umpire. Why? Because, you see, God expects of us a certain degree of quietude of mind and heart. Being still is a simple exercise, so *do* it. Practice it every day, and you'll find the results to be beyond your wildest dreams. You'll experience better health, a more focused mind, and a joyful, love-filled spirit.

Now, as I mentioned a little while ago, we are all having little conversations within our minds all the time, and we should occasionally stop and listen to them. Maybe some of you don't know that you are talking to yourself all the time, even when you're outwardly quiet, but if you pause and look into the recesses of consciousness, you will discover what kinds of thoughts and words persist inside your mind. As I say, you may be shocked and amazed to find that a great deal of it is negative. Now, there isn't anybody in this room who wants to live in a negative state all the time. We're all looking for the positive. We're looking for health, freedom, and joy and love. And we're looking for healing of all sorts of conditions. These things can and do come about when we learn to be quiet, tune in, and listen.

Now, as I said, when you tune in to yourself, you may be quite surprised by what you find. You might become embarrassed to discover that you are engaging in persistent negative inner dialogue, and you're really rather glad that those conversations cannot be heard by everybody in the room! When you discover such negativity in yourself, what should you do? Do you stay and listen, or argue with it? No, you *change* it. How do you change it? By a conscious and continuous act of will. Pretty soon you begin to weed out the same negativities in your mind that have bedeviled human beings throughout the ages. You give yourself the chance to truly become master within your own kingdom, within your own body temple, rather than being a servant and slave to the negative conversations that persist and control you. You have a choice, and it's not a difficult one to carry out. It's really rather easy, and it can become sort of a game.

There is a wonderful little book many of you will remember called *The Game of Life and How to Play It* by Florence Scovel Shinn. I'm sure most of you have heard about that book. If you haven't, go get a copy and read it. It's an excellent book written by a wonderful metaphysical lady who taught people how to play the game of life, and how to reverse conditions by changing the quality of their inner conversations. It all begins with changing our attitudes of mind and heart. If you go around feeling very unhappy and wearing a sad face, people are instinctively going to move away from you. It's like Typhoid Mary: everywhere she went, somebody got Typhoid, so nobody wanted to meet Typhoid Mary. Well, there are metaphysical "Typhoid Marys" and "Typhoid Johns." Sometimes without realizing it, people go around saying, "Oh, it's terrible. It's awful today, and I'm sure it's going to be worse tomorrow. Everything is bad, and it's steadily getting worse." Well, if you want to sit in that arena, that's your choice. But if you do not want to sit in that arena, then you simply change the station. Change it from negative to positive. When you do that, it is as inevitable as night follows day that your life in all its aspects will change. That is an immutable law. Follow it, and change must come.

Yesterday I spoke with a man who was in a very depressed state of mind. Things are going badly in his marriage, and his work is also very difficult. I felt very sorry for him because he is extremely unhappy and discouraged; but I realized that I had to speak rather frankly, and maybe even bluntly, to remind him that he has dominion in his circumstances. He is so sure that everything happening to him is some kind of bad luck. And he was sure that more bad luck was on the way. He even fell off a ladder and hurt his knee. Then he got the sniffles, and a half dozen other unpleasant things happened to him. I said, "All right, as long as you want to string along with the idea that all this is simply bad luck, that's your business, and I can't help you. You have to *want* to change."

Are you satisfied being unhappy? Are you satisfied with the despondent conversations you have with yourself? Are you happy to go through the weeks and months simply groaning and howling about your troubles? Certainly you have some problems and setbacks. I grant you that. But you have to get up on your feet, so to speak, and fight this fight; and you do that quite simply by going within, because that's where the fight really is.

Now, everybody wants to say it's out there: "My wife did it. My boss did it. Aunt Martha did it." It's always somebody else that did it. But the truth of the matter is that, really, *you* did it. Why? Because you opened the door to negativity, and it came right in. You don't have to give it an invitation. Just open the door, and POW, it comes right in! Your negative thoughts act like a magnet, attracting more negativity, and pretty soon those thoughts snowball into a horrible day just filled with one unhappy or frustrating event after another. So we have to be careful what we attune ourselves to.

I find some television programs delightful. I'm not a Puritan, and I don't expect everyone on TV to be praying on every program. I don't think life is quite like that, so I am not averse to watching a program that has some action in it—provided it isn't outrageously violent. If I turned to a program that was too violent, I would simply turn it off. I would not listen to it. I would not watch it. Why? Because I don't want that kind of garbage dumped into my "inner." I don't want the tape recordings of my mind repeating garbage I have seen on TV or heard on the radio.

When we are met with a need to create change in our lives, that's an opportunity to practice being strong and positive. If you need another job, visualize the most fulfilling job you can think of. Know that just as you are seeking a new and wonderful job, there is someone out there who needs a wonderful person like *you*. Now, how are you going to bring about that new and wonderful job? You simply make the decision to tune in to the Infinite. You declare that somewhere out there is a person or company that needs you, and you ask that you and that person or company be brought together. You declare that it is a happy occasion indeed, because you are creating a way to sustain yourself. That's what we do: we float it out to the Infinite, and we don't tell God how to bring it about. We don't say, "It's got to come this way. It has to be this company or that person." Don't pay any attention to the "how" or "who" or "when.' Know that your good comes to you indirectly and in total fulfillment. Visualize and feel yourself in the kind of position you want. *Feel* yourself alive and active, sensitive to the environment of a job you would really enjoy. *Feel* that it's a job that is very good for you, that is already yours, and it will come.

Tuning in to God is, I believe, the most important and powerful form of prayer we know. When we become still and begin to contemplate and meditate upon immortal truths, they become very real to us. They grow and become such a part of us that we are literally made immune to the negative. If, on the other hand, we tune in to the negative, we become sensitized by that force. We certainly don't want to do that. So, inasmuch as you have the right, the power, and the duty to do your own tuning in to life, make sure you always tune in to the highest and most beautiful. Tune in to God, and do it first thing in the morning through quiet meditation. Give a little time to meditation and contemplation, and do it every day. Ten minutes out of twenty-four hours isn't too much to ask.

Later on you'll want to meditate longer because it is such a beautiful and fulfilling state. It's so relaxing and health giving, so energizing, that you will want to do half an hour. And soon you'll find that half an hour is nothing. In a few years, you'll want to extend your daily appointment with God to an hour, or even an hour and a half. Within a short time you'll celebrate special occasions like Christmas and Easter with a full day in meditation. You'll look forward to your meditation time each morning because you'll find that you are going deeper and deeper within—tuning in to that infinite quality, that area where silence dwells and where the voice of intuition speaks directly to the heart of your being. We all want that. We all want calmness, serenity, love, harmony, and beauty, and we all want clear and unfailing guidance. But we have to reach in for it. We have to be still enough to woo it, as it were, right into our consciousness and being.

So, good friends, be careful what you tune in to. It's your choice. Don't blame NBC or CBS or anybody else, because you don't have to watch anything you don't really want to. Don't blame anybody if you are constantly carrying on negative inner conversations. And be careful not to toss aside meditation and other techniques if they don't bring an immediate result. It's not instant soup or instant coffee. It takes a little while to calm the mind. Don't say, "Well, I don't know, this stuff is all right I guess, but it sounds a little 'Pollyanna-ish' to me. I tried it once, but I still don't know if I'll get that job." Well, of course, the minute you start thinking like that, the man doing the hiring will feel your doubt and negativity, and mentally he's already tossed your resume in the circular file. Go into the personnel office with such confidence that they will feel very lucky to have you. You know, it sounds very boastful, but you really have to present yourself as the wonderful being you are. It's not egoic pride; it's pride in knowing who you really are: a son or daughter of the Most High, and heir to the kingdom of heaven.

I remember a time many years ago when I needed a job very badly. I was very young, and never in my life had I done the type of work which involved accounting. When I went in to talk to the boss, I not only brought with me the attitude that this guy was lucky I was there, but I told him which shift I would accept and which shift I would not accept. Now, I don't recommend doing *that*! Be a little more humble. But I got the job anyhow.

You see, if I had gone in with my hat in hand, begging, "Please, Sir, would you be so kind as to give me a job? My pet cat is starving, the rent is due, and things are really bad. Oh, it's just terrible, and if you could just see your way to give me any kind of job . . ." what do you suppose the man hiring would have said? We have to let go of all doubt, fear, and self-deprecation, and realize that it is a very serious, wonderful, and beautiful thing to attune yourself to God. It is very simple to reach in and allow the divine vibrational impulses to become so profound an aspect of your being, that a kind of divine alchemy takes place within your inner temple. The inevitable result is a transmutation of energy and power, and a shift to right thinking and positivity that will surely bring about wonderful changes in every aspect of your life.

So rejoice and be glad, and let the words of your mouth (be careful about them) and more so the meditations of your heart (look in on them once in awhile) be perfect in the sight of the Lord, and then you will be standing on a rock of truth that knows no defeat.

Dear friends, remember that your whole attitude toward life can be entirely changed by a conscious and dynamic thrust of will in the direction of divine attunement. Daily place your hand on the dial of your life and tune it with assurance and faith, always and only to that which is positive. If you catch yourself slipping a little—drifting into the static of complaining, murmuring, and being negative—move the dial back. With just a flick of your mental wrist you can change your life. Just think of it: each one of you in this room today can change your relationship with your family, yourself, and God by the simple practice of tuning in to the all-pervading Spirit of goodness. Thank you. *Amen.*

In the Beginning

Heritage House Presbyterian Chapel, San Francisco, CA
July 26, 1981

"In the beginning was the Word, and the Word was with God, and the Word was God. The same was in the beginning with God. All things were made by him; and without him was not any thing made that was made. In him was life; and the life was the light of men. And the light shineth in darkness; and the darkness comprehended it not." (John 1:1-5.) *Amen.*

Heavenly Father, help us to take these words very deeply into ourselves, that we may always remember that You made everything; and that when You created the vast and ever-expanding universe, You declared it to be good. Therefore, if everything You made is good, then good must prevail. And if there be anything unlike good, it is of man's origin. It is not of You, the eternal Father, and therefore it is not real. *"In him was life; and the life was the light of men. And the light shineth in darkness; and the darkness comprehended it not."* Father, as we take in these words from the wonderful gospel and teaching of Your beloved disciple, Saint John, give us a sense of their deep spiritual meaning. Amen.

Dear friends, today we have read from the first part of the Gospel of John. You know, I don't think enough sermons are preached on this text, because if there were, people would begin to realize more than ever that the Christ principle resides within them. If mankind could only realize that every human being who walks upon the earth plane is a son or daughter of the Heavenly Father, and a brother or sister of Christ, there would be no more quarreling, no more wars, and no more strife on our planet. For good cannot strive against itself. Most of the strife and discord that prevails in our world has come about because, in a certain sense, we have denied the truth of man's divine nature.

Now, this scripture says, *"In the beginning was the Word, and the Word was with God."* Jesus the Christ is always described as the incarnate Word. The Christ principle abides within the bosom of the unmanifest Father, beyond vibratory creation, and it was made manifest on the earth as the incarnation of Jesus the Christ. I think this is probably the most important line in this part of the Gospel. We are told in another part of the Bible that when God had completed His creation, He called it good. It is essential that we who call ourselves Christians emphasize the reality of good rather than filling our lives with every imaginable thing that is not of the light.

In the mind of God, as well as in the consciousness of the prophets and saints throughout the centuries, all things that were made were called good. The blessed ones see evil nowhere; they tell us that evil is in the eye of the beholder. So, if you are seeing evil, begin to change your mind about it. Little by little, you will come into conscious identification with this utterance of Saint John in Chapter One when he said that all things—see, he didn't exclude anything—he said that all things, including you, were made by Him, and He called them *good*. Now, that's a pretty good starting place for teaching children. The whole idea of ancestral or original sin is a rather large burden of guilt for little ones to carry around without having the vaguest idea of what evil they committed. Isn't it better for youngsters to know that they were born of love and goodness rather than from shame and sin? When you teach a child that their true nature is divine and good, it is a wonderful gift that will impress and sustain them throughout their lives.

Now, we all know that we are in the classroom of the earth experience, learning and growing in an imperfect world. Once in a while we have to meet trials and unravel problems. How are we to handle the really tough challenges that occasionally beset us in our lives? It is through the grace of God, and by our own understanding of the deeper spiritual meaning of the scriptures, that we are able to successfully meet and walk through the challenges of life. When you dive deeper, you begin to realize as never before what Jesus came to teach: namely that the inner you, the real you, is divine and good and one with the Father. Jesus said that it is given to those who dive deep within to know the mysteries of the Kingdom of Heaven (or expanded awareness), and to others the truth is given only in parables. Now, most of us have heard and read this ancient gospel of Saint John many times, beginning in Sunday school and continuing throughout our religious studies, but we have not really understood it or taken it deep within. This text is a source of true liberation if we totally accept it and apply it to our lives. So let's take a fresh look at it. With new vision, let us see the reality and purity of its true meaning, and then take it home and meditate deeply on it all through the week.

Understanding this teaching, you can apply it to the most prosaic aspects of your life. Suppose you're having a bad day and you develop a headache, a stomachache, or some other malady. Now, God didn't make that headache, but He did arrange your body in such a way as to signal you when something is wrong. If you want to, you can deal with your pain strictly on the physical level by running for an aspirin; or you can deal with it on a spiritual level by going within the temple of your inner self and finding the cause of your headache and asking for it to be healed. The more you do that, the more you spiritualize your life. Each time you overcome some little problem, you become stronger and better able to handle a big problem when it comes along. By practicing in this way, you see, you come closer to embodying the direct teachings of the Christ.

You know, Jesus was not a learned man in the worldly sense. He had no university degrees, and no trace of a Harvard accent. He spoke to his followers with great simplicity because, in general, there was a lack of education among the people. There were no newspapers and certainly no Internet, television, or radio. Books were very rare, and were read only by a select few in the priesthood. This did not mean, however, that ordinary people were not intended to learn and understand. Jesus often said that the unlettered understand the true message of the Christ in the simplicity of utterance, while the learned philosophers oft-times obscure things beyond recognition. Down through the centuries, theologians have been so busy philosophizing, revising, and presuming better interpretations of what Christ said, that very often his words and teachings have been veiled of their true meaning.

Jesus delivered a simple and direct message. He said that in the Christ presence is life, and that that life is the light of man. He tells us that we are children of God and heirs of Heaven. He tells us that we are brothers and sisters in Christ. It is very hard for most of us to accept these statements because if we do, we think it means we will have to give up everything we enjoy in the world. Don't let your fear of "having to be too good" stop you from accepting the invitation of the Christ. Don't forever postpone the divine confrontation. You don't have to walk around in sackcloth and ashes in order to know God; you *can* have a free and beautiful understanding of what Christ meant, and still enjoy that martini (not six, but one) before dinner.

Remember when Jesus was traversing the Holy Land among the Pharisees, the intellectual elite of the time? Oh, they tried to put him down, saying, "He's only a carpenter, what does he know? Don't pay any attention to him. Listen to us; we have the message." Well, Jesus said, *"I am the way, the truth, and the life."* (John 14:6.) He also said, *"I am the light of the world."* (John 8:12.) How simply he tells us that the light, which is a symbol of God, lives in him and in the consciousness of every living being. He knew the "I-AM-ness" of his own being. He knew that the Christ spirit (within himself as Jesus the man) is *real*, and it is within each and every one of us. As I have said many times—and I repeat it very often—the only difference between Saint Francis, Saint Paul, Saint Teresa or Saint John, and you or I, is that *they knew who they were*. With a deep intuitional sense, they had a positive acceptance of the all-pervading light that dwelled in them. That's "the light that shines in darkness." In other words, Jesus was saying that *you*, too, are the light of the world.

What did the Master mean when he said that *"the light shineth in darkness,"* but *"the darkness comprehended it not"*? He was talking about those who were unwilling, through intellectual vanity, to accept his simple statements of profound truth. They didn't want a carpenter teaching them. They wanted somebody high in the echelon of the priestly aristocracy of that time, and so they would not listen. They really were in darkness. For it is the darkness of man's intellectual pride, you see, which obscures the light. So even though the light was shining in their midst, they did not recognize it. They were too busy building scholarly paraphrases, which they felt were much better than what the teacher of mankind was saying.

Sometimes man gets in his own way and trips himself up with intellectual vanity. If we would only sit down and read this simple utterance in the Gospel of Saint John, and accept it at face value, our whole life would be changed by a kind of internal divine alchemy. When one observes and practices the teachings of the Christ, an inevitable divine transmutation takes place, and we are moved from the baser level of consciousness and limited understanding to a higher consciousness in which we recognize the presence of God and the inherent goodness of our own nature.

Although we don't always behave like it, we *are* brothers and sisters, siblings of Christ. And, like him, we are filled with light. The darkness will never totally understand the light because, you see, it is the opposite of light. As we go back into antiquity and read some of the teachings of the Old Testament and other great scriptures from different parts of the world, we find that they all describe God as light. God is spirit, omnipresent intelligence, and supreme good. If you want to be saved, then come into conscious identification and harmony with this light, which is *already within you*. You don't have to look for it anywhere outside.

See, Jesus made everything really very simple. Most of mankind is looking for some kind of philosophy and teaching, but they are looking for it way out there somewhere. With our marvelous and sophisticated technologies, we peer into the ramparts of infinite space, searching for our source and meaning in the billions of galaxies beyond our visibility and comprehension. We think the truth must be out there, that God must be out there, and that the law must be out there. We're all looking for someone to point the way for us, so we go to preachers and practitioners, ministers and priests, rabbis, rishis, and swamis.

Now, I know we need our teachers. Most of them are very good, and they do point the way for us. Certainly, I wouldn't be standing up here talking to you if I didn't agree that ministers and priests have some purpose. But the great democracy of the spiritual trip returns again and again to our consciousness: namely that *you* must accept the absolute truth of your being. You must accept the love and wisdom that God is trying to give you. No one can do that for you. Christ said that you are a temple of the *living* God and that the spirit of God dwells *in you*. It can't be any simpler than that. So don't go looking for complexities and mechanical ramifications of what spirituality is all about. God is light, and that light of consciousness is everywhere, but most especially within your own heart.

God whispers to us in the stillness, in the silence. If you are running around talking all the time and cluttering your mind with inner chatter and contradictory ideas, you will never hear those whispers from God. If you are constantly going from one teacher to another, saying, "Oh, he tells me this, and she tells me that, and they say something else," you might end up in a tower of Babel: a tower of confusion. But if you sit down with the first chapter of Saint John and meditate on it as a reality—not just some nice poetic statement—you will realize that it is an immortal truth. It is the essence of reality and of our universe. We are well advised to read this scripture again and again: *"In the beginning was the Word, and the Word was with God, and the Word was God."*

The symbol of Christ is the Word incarnate. This should give us the direction we seek for liberating ourselves from all the trials and tribulations that beset us in our world. We look around and see all kinds of dreadful things, and we ask, "Did God make *this*, or *that*?" God made all things, and He called them good. When your mind becomes single pointed and rests upon the sustaining Infinite with absolute courage and reliance, then you will realize these truths for yourself. Sit quietly, even if it is only for fifteen minutes, and allow the consciousness of God, the light of God that is already inside you, to fill up your body temple. You will find that it is very healthy to do that.

Today many doctors are finding positive results in their work with terminal cancer patients and people with other life-threatening illnesses by teaching them to meditate three times a day. You see, not only does meditation quiet the emotional anxiety that accompanies illness; it fills the temple of your being with the blazing light of Spirit, wherein nothing unlike truth can exist or persist. As you come into increasing understanding that this divine light is the light of man, you will find liberation from so many of the ills that befall you.

The first thing you will notice is that you are being healed from a kind of systemic restlessness that may have been with you for many years. Next, you will find that you are thinking more positively and seeing solutions to your problems. Soon you will notice that you are sleeping better and that you awaken feeling refreshed and enthusiastic about your day. Little by little, you will begin to feel a deep quiet and peace in your soul. And finally, you will become aware of a general state of joyfulness that stays with you even when you are confronted with the vexations and trials that come along with everyday life on the earth plane.

God came to bring peace into the consciousness of mankind. Can Christ and his opposite dwell in any temple at the same time? Certainly not. So if you are habitually thinking about things that are unlovely, and if you are constantly talking about things which are negative and harmful, you are turning off one light after another, and you are banishing the spiritual light of God from your temple. Just become quiet and listen to the still small voice that whispers to you in those moments of silence. Then you will begin to perceive the deeper mystical meaning of the great and simple message, which is Christ.

Read the beautiful words in Chapter One of the Gospel of Saint John—the beloved disciple who sat so close to the great teacher of humankind. John tells us, in very direct and marvelous ways, how we simple ones can come into attunement with Christ. With that attunement, we begin to see only the good. This doesn't mean that you won't be aware of the negative aspects of life, or that you should live in some kind of ivory tower. It doesn't mean that when something bad happens in the world, you should say it isn't real or it isn't happening. Wars and injustices are very real when they happen, but those things are not Divine Reality. They are the actions of those who have refused the light. Darkness and light cannot coexist. Begin with the self; and remember that you have a choice: *"Choose you this day whom ye will serve,"* (Josh. 24:15.) the dark or the light.

It is wonderful when you can enter a huge auditorium and listen to the Word being given out by famous pastors or preachers. Many of them have a special gift for teaching and inspiring us, and they do a great job; but we alone are responsible for taking in and accepting the truths found in scripture. This morning our text says, *"In the beginning was the Word, and the Word was with God, and the Word was God."* The Word, remember, is the Christ principle, which abides in the Father and was made manifest on the earth plane as the incarnation of Christ. It is this principle that we must bring into our own lives, as sisters and brothers of Christ, because understanding it brings true freedom. To be freed of something means to be liberated. So if you want freedom and the liberating presence of God, then read about it in the Gospel of Saint John. Then meditate upon it and fill yourself with the consciousness of love, peace, power, and joy—for that *is* the spirit of Christ, which dwells within you. Thank you. *Amen.*

Fear Not

Heritage House Presbyterian Chapel, San Francisco, CA
August 16, 1981

"I will bless the LORD at all times: his praise shall continually be in my mouth. My soul shall make her boast in the LORD: the humble shall hear thereof, and be glad. O magnify the LORD with me, and let us exalt his name together. I sought the LORD, and he heard me, and delivered me from all my fears. They looked unto him, and were lightened: and their faces were not ashamed. This poor man cried, and the LORD heard him, and saved him out of all his troubles." (Ps. 34:1-6.)

In this psalm there is a great deal to be learned about trusting the Lord and about the abolition, shall we say, of fear. Those who really understand the reality of the indwelling Christ and the triumphant omnipresence of good know for certain that they will be delivered from all fears. If you want to know the power of fear, all you have to do is turn to the book of Job. What does he say? *"The thing which I have greatly feared is come upon me."* (Job 3:25.) This statement gives us a marvelous illustration of faith in reverse. If he had used that same faith in a positive way, he would not have ended up feeling desolate, covered with boils and overcome by terrible physical, mental, and emotional problems. See, Job gave too much emphasis to fear, and he forgot that God was accessible within the temple of his being.

What does Jesus, the great teacher, have to say about this? Well, he says, quite simply, that we must have absolute faith. He gave us the most perfect example of faith when he taught us to pray *believing* and to know that when we are afraid, we can take refuge in the sustaining, protecting Lord. In Job's declaration we learn a mighty spiritual lesson: that fear can be an awesome and destructive force when we let it have full reign. We know that fear can literally destroy us when we give our energy to it. When we focus on fear, we augment it and give it enormous power over us.

In today's beautiful text it says that when you seek the Lord, He will hear you and deliver you from what is fearsome. Isn't that beautiful? *"This poor man cried, and the LORD heard him, and saved him out of all his troubles."* Now, we all have little gremlins of fear that creep into our consciousness from time to time. There is hardly anyone who is not occasionally beset by mild fears, and sometimes even by very big ones. Faith is the answer, and absolute trust in the omnipresence of good is the cure. Realize that no matter how awesome and terrible the world might be, there is no place you can go where God is not. In the scriptures we read time and again about heroic personalities who moved through great trials with an immovable and steadfast faith in the presence and power of good, which is Christ within. The story of Daniel in the lion's den is just one of many that reveals to us the tremendous power of faith.

You know, fear can actually destroy people. Some years ago a wonderful spiritual teacher told me a story that took place during the building of the Panama Canal. At that time there was an outbreak of yellow fever that killed thousands of people. A team of medical doctors was called in to explore the nature of this terrible disease, and what they found was very interesting indeed. Upon careful medical inspection they discovered that many of the people who died of what seemed to be yellow fever were shown to have no yellow fever at all. If these people did not die of yellow fever, what did they die of? They died of fear—fear of contracting the deadly yellow fever. This story clearly illustrates that if we are not careful we can become so caught up in fear that it begins to master us; it can even kill us.

When people accept the idea of the inevitability of failure with the problems of life, they limit the possibility of ever overcoming and realizing the full measure of their own spiritual harmony and well being. There are great creative powers and abilities residing within the subconscious mechanism of our nature. That subconscious power can slay us or save us; it depends on what emphasis we give. This is what

Christ really meant when he encouraged us to think and believe in his marvelous statement of cosmic truth, *"Thy faith hath made thee whole."* (Matt. 9:22; Mark 5:34 and 10:52; Luke 17:19.) If we are not using the power that is available to us, we're missing a great deal. We're bringing our lives down to a very limited scale indeed; for as Christ taught us again and again, the limitation is ours. *We* set up the restrictions. But in truth, there are no limitations except those we set for ourselves.

I have known people who were literally at death's door, but they determined not to pass through it. They stood steadfast, trusting the healing power of the light which pervades every part of the universe, including the consciousness of man. You see: God is spirit, and *you* are spirit. Within the quietness of the self, that spirit apprehends the very nature of deity and gives playful reverence to its presence within your being. Jesus said that we are temples of the living God, but for centuries we have glossed over that. We can't quite believe him, but we really are temples. This body temple that you inhabit is temporary, but the real you is made of light. That is your spiritual body: your astral form, which is very much like your physical body only made of a finer fabric. Your spiritual body is ongoing and eternal, and participant in the divine life of God. Jesus reminded us constantly of our true identity, and he assured us of the omnipresence of good.

As we read the New Testament we cannot but notice all the marvels and wonders that happened whenever Jesus was around. He was able to do things which the villagers called miracles. These simple people stood in awe of Jesus and called his works marvels because they could not understand. These divinely natural occurrences were outside of the ordinary confines of their limited knowledge. But, you see, a miracle is not *super*natural at all; a miracle is a divine law operating an octave above ordinary physical laws. Jesus had total realization of the divine consciousness within him. Because he knew his Father as a real and immanent presence within him, he could truly say that he was a son of God.

A loving father always answers the cries of his child: *"This poor man cried [out for help], and the LORD heard him, and saved him out of all his troubles. The angel of the Lord encampeth round about them that fear him, and delivereth them."* (Ps. 34:6-7.) Now that phrase is interesting to me because it talks about fearing the Lord. That's not the kind of fear I was talking about a moment ago when I spoke about the people who died from the fear of yellow fever; that's a very basic kind of fear. Fear of the Lord means having profound reverence. We are told, "Fear the Lord." What does that mean? Translated into English, fearing the Lord means having a deep, abiding, and powerful reverence of God, or the omnipresence of good.

When we develop true assurance of universal good and take hold of it, we are leaning upon the sustaining Infinite. Then what we used to call miraculous, those things we have regarded as very remote and improbable, begin to happen regularly. Why? Simply because we have let go of the ordinary mortal sense of fear, and have put on the protective armor of invincible faith. Now, I know we are all beset with anxieties, worries, and apprehensions every now and then, but we have to realize that fear is *faith in reverse*; it's the negative kind of fear. You don't need that in your life; you don't need to give any energy to the negative. You will live a longer, happier, and more harmonious life when you truly begin to accept the liberating and transforming power which is the Christ presence within.

The greatest miracle, even beyond the miracle of physical healing, is the transformation of consciousness within humankind. It is a miracle of alchemy when we ordinary mortals, through the grace of God, are suddenly lifted up in consciousness to a place where we can see more clearly and can apprehend the reality of Spirit. Here we realize that when we take one step toward the Infinite, God has already taken three steps toward us. So whenever you are tempted to be fearful and uncertain, know that you always have available to you within, without, and all about, the profound and abiding healing presence of God. Accept that and make it part of your life; then your journey through this incarnation will be more fruitful, more harmonious, and more fulfilling.

God created us in His own image and likeness. He is immortal, universal, and all-powerful intelligence and love; He is the supreme spirit of good. Every human being is implanted with that same spirit through the breath of life, and that spirit unifies every one of us with the Christ consciousness. The saints and sages, mystics and prophets of every century have all had a certainty that transcends faith. They no longer believe, they *know*. As I say so often, the difference between us and the holy ones is simply a matter of degree. We are working on our faith and refining our soul qualities, but the great ones—those spiritual giants who have lived among us throughout time—are flawless examples of what it means to be lifted up by the realization that they are one with their divine source.

Jesus said, *"If I be lifted up from the earth, [I] will draw all men unto me."* (John 12:32.) Well, he draws all people who will understand and accept his truth. God isn't going to draw us up by the hair of our heads. We have to rise up, accept, and make a commitment to the immutable truth of our divine nature. But that's very hard for most people, because they "know" they are imperfect, fallible, and have so many faults. We think, "Oh, how can I measure up to anything like that?" Try, and let God do the rest. He will not fail you; He will deliver you from all of your doubts and fears.

So, dear friends, turn to your Bible this week and read Psalm 34 again. Then sit down, quiet yourself, and go within to receive the inspiration of the Holy Spirit. It is in the quiet of your heart that you will hear the inspiring whisper of eternal truth, not when you are sprawled trancelike in front of the TV or yelling your head off at a football game. God has promised us that He will be with us, and He will deliver us from all that we have feared most. He will give us the energy and the courage to rise above all our problems, for God is truly merciful, and He realizes that we are but little children growing into noble and exalted souls.

Many people are unable to accept the fact that the same power and love that poured through Jesus is available to us today. Too many people believe that financial freedom, harmonious relationships, perfect health, and spiritual illumination are very far away. They forever procrastinate the divine confrontation by imagining God off in some far-flung heaven world. But Jesus made a great point of saying, "No, don't look here, don't look there, for *behold* (whenever he wanted to make a big emphasis, he said 'behold'), look and see…the kingdom of heaven is where? *Within you.*" (Luke 17:21.) For ages people have turned away from that and refused to accept their true identity. It is time to stand up and claim your divine inheritance. Claim your oneness with Christ and place your hand in his. Become one with his spirit, his light, his love, and his miracle-working power. Then you will know, in truth and in deed, that you are a son or a daughter of God, and an heir of heaven with Christ. Thank you. *Amen.*

A Recipe for Happiness

Heritage House Presbyterian Chapel, San Francisco, CA
October 25, 1981

When we read through the pages of history, we cannot find a time when there were no wars or rumors of wars. We are aware of more wars going on now because our modern avenues of communication are much more immediate and efficient, and there is much more information coming to us from around the world. If a little fire starts over here, we know about it right away; and when another blaze begins over there, we know about it instantly. Years ago, we wouldn't have known about either of these events for days, if not years. Because there is so much we hear about, and because it is fired at us so rapidly, it's easy to get a little overwhelmed. But we are not helpless. We can affect our world as we balance and focus our minds in a positive direction. Imagine how much the world would change if each one of us became a living candle lit upon the darkness of the world stage. All our candles combined would ignite a great light that would envelope this entire globe.

Now, don't say, "Well, I'm just one little person. Who am I to make a difference in the world?" Don't let yourself be discouraged into thinking, "Who is even going to notice my little light, and how could my single prayer make any difference at all?" If everybody thought like that, there wouldn't be any light at all. But if everybody lit a candle, there would be a great luminosity, and that light would throw its incandescence upon the very recesses of our souls to bring about the good that we have denied, or temporarily forgotten.

Dear friends, remember what Jesus said in Chapter Six of Saint Matthew about trusting in God and leaning upon the sustaining Infinite. Now, when he says we should be like the lilies of the field and the fowls of the air, to take no thought and never worry, he doesn't mean we should all be lazy and do nothing with our lives. He is trying to point out to us that when we trust in God, things come to us aright. He is teaching us that we should not be disturbed or dismayed about how we will be provided for because, you see, God knows our needs. The very fact that you are living here in this beautiful place at this wondrous time in history is a sign of God's special benevolence. And so we want to learn a lesson from that, of not being *unduly* disturbed about what we need. We must never lose sight of the fact that you and I, and each one of us, can definitely and positively contribute to the betterment of the nation and the world by our attitude of mind and heart. We mustn't give any energy to the negative and the fearful. I know this is a tall order sometimes, but we have to try, because when we align ourselves to the energy of goodness, it has a powerful and tangible effect.

Once in a while we have to remind ourselves from whence cometh our supply, our good. The real source of our good, our abundance, our health, and our joy is not an outer appearance but an inner reality. When we rehearse that a little bit, we begin to realize that in spite of having gone through a lot of travail and challenging problems in our lives, we are still here, going strong. And in general, things are (thank God) very good with us. By meditating a little every day upon God's light and goodness, we shall come to lean trustfully upon His infinite love and compassion. Each one of us can be a positive force for good by coming into alignment with the powerful energy of God's goodness. Our very thoughts and feelings extend out from us and touch everything and everyone around us. So let us give no energy to troubling and fearful news. Let us remember instead that we cannot go where God is not.

You see, when we get nervous or disturbed, we relegate God to a place somewhere far away, unreachable and unattainable. We mustn't do that. Instead, we should occasionally turn to Matthew, Chapter Six, and let the message contained in its beautiful poetry about the lilies of the field fill us with a sense of renewed well-being. That touch of God's love is everywhere around us, but sometimes we forget to look for it. What is the beauty that surrounds us in our world but a smile of God? The mesmerizing prophets of gloom that appear as various forms of communication and media have dimmed our awareness of the omnipresence of goodness. It is crucial to our well-being that we begin to think about what we can do to defend ourselves against this barrage. We must steadfastly declare, *"As a man thinketh in his heart, so is he."* (Prov. 23:7.) Do you want to think baddies and bummers, or do you want to think goodies and light? You have a choice.

It's very human and natural to become worried about events taking place in the world today, but we must have an abiding faith that even if things get very badly out of order, it won't last too long, and there will be a shift back to balance. I have great faith in the fact that as individuals we *can* make a difference in the world. As individual sparks of the Infinite, we can light a candle within the temple of our being, and we *can* do something to bring about positive change. Isn't it better to light a candle in a dark room than to curse the darkness? The only solid fact of self-protection is to lean upon the sustaining Infinite and contribute to the energy of positivity in a world of growing darkness.

Recently, one of our church members gave me a beautiful little recipe for happiness that she had cut out of a magazine. I think it's nice to share these little pieces and poems, especially during trying times. The first ingredient in this recipe is, "Commit something positive and lovely to memory each day." That's such good advice. Pick out a little poem. It doesn't have to be seventeen pages long, just three or four lines, but it must be something beautiful that feeds the mind and soul. You know, the act of memorizing a poem, passage, or song exercises your brain cells and keeps you young, energetic, and involved. When you intentionally plant beauty and goodness into your consciousness, it serves to uplift you, both now and in the future. We can imbed constructive and optimistic ideas into the subconscious mechanism of our being by committing something lovely to memory every day. Those positive impressions and images that you take into your mind have a wonderful way of jumping out at just the right time to support you when you need them.

The second ingredient in the recipe for happiness is, "Look for something beautiful every day." Here we might heed the valuable thoughts of Goethe, the great German philosopher, who said that a man should hear a little music, read a little poetry, and look at a fine picture every day of his life in order to prevent the cares of the world from obliterating a sense of the beautiful—which God has implanted in the human soul.

The third ingredient is probably the most practical of all: "Do something nice for somebody every day." This simple recipe for happiness, based on beautiful thinking, is a valuable work of art. But instead of being stored away in a museum like most treasures of art, this little gem can be kept in your mental home where it is available to you at any time as a source of endless inspiration and satisfaction. The great Ralph Waldo Emerson said we should never miss an opportunity to see anything that is beautiful—for beauty is God's handwriting, a wayside sacrament.

Now, how many times have you walked past a beautiful painting in a hallway or some other place, merely glancing at it and thinking casually, "Oh, that's nice." Too often we are so preoccupied with our own cares and troubles that we don't even notice the beauty all around us. When we are indifferent to an exquisite and unique work of art, we lose the gift of awe. We may fail to appreciate, for example, how many thousands of brushstrokes it took to bring to life the beautiful inner vision of that inspired artist.

It reminds me of a story about Michelangelo. He had just finished a magnificent statue when some people came to his studio to visit him. They were sitting there drinking some wine, and one of his friends said, "This is the most beautiful work you have ever done." Michelangelo said, "But it's not finished." His friend said, "What do you mean, it's not finished yet? It is a marvel, a dream, a vision of perfection. What else could you do to make it more perfect?" The artist answered, "Well, right here, in the corner of the eye, it could be a little smoother, and here the line could be finer." His friend responded, "Oh, sir, but those are just trifles." The great artist Michelangelo said, "Yes, perfection consists of trifles, but *is* no trifle."

So when we look at a beautiful painting or hear a wondrous piece of music, we should recognize that such a magnificent work of art was born from a great and profoundly moving inspiration that arose from the depths of the consciousness of that artist. And if perchance you don't have a beautiful painting you can look at, go out onto the lawn on a clear day and look at the sky and the trees, and you will see the faultless work of the greatest Artist of all.

Now, when a magnificent work of art is accomplished, all cultured people immediately bow to it. We literally surrender to a brilliant work of art because we perceive in it a divine vision. We realize the immense amount of time it took for that sculptor, that painter, that musician, to perfect his art. It is all predicated on his or her clear and invincible determination not to give up their image and expression of beauty, not to give up that visual or aural perception within the temple of the Self.

Once in a while you hear a piece of music that is nothing short of a creative miracle. I was talking once to an atheist and I was telling him about spiritual things and some healings I had seen, and of course he didn't believe me at all. He said he didn't believe in spiritual things, that it was all nonsense and fraud. But he did say this: "Do you want to know what a real miracle is?" I said, "Yes, I'd like to know what your miracle is." He said, "Richard Wagner's magnificent opera, *Tristan und Isolde*. If you hear that opera played and sung gloriously, you have heard a creative miracle of total musical genius." Well, I had to agree with him, and I hoped that eventually I would be able to convert him to the idea that, like the miracles of music and art, God is working many other wonders through His infinite love and wisdom.

There are miracles in science and other fields, as well as in the arts. Just think of the marvels we have begun to observe with our sophisticated instrumentation and technology. What we have discovered in the last decade alone is far beyond anything heretofore envisioned by the most advanced scientific minds in the fields of astronomy and astrophysics. The universe is so incredibly vast that it boggles the mind. There are billions upon billions of galaxies in space, and the end is never. Before any of us were born, and even before the stars began to shine, God was, and God is. God is love, and His love is continuously manifested in His infinite creation. He created humanity, and all that has come into being on this and other planets. When we are taught the mysteries of God's loving power, goodness. and compassion, we begin to realize that we came upon the earth to reflect that divine love. That is our true purpose.

In India a story is often told about an old man who used to take care of the royal gardens on the beautiful estate of one of the Maharajas. He was a simple old fellow who used to go out and tend the plants at night, when the temperature was cooler. He would take little buckets of water and pour them on the shrubs and flowers. One night when he went out into the garden there was a very bright moon. As he looked into his bucket he gleefully said to his friend, "Oh, look, the moon is in my bucket." There were eighteen more buckets of water sitting there on the terraces, and as he peered into them, one by one, he excitedly said, "Oh look here, the moon is in this bucket too, and in that bucket over there, and in this one too." See, this dear and simple old man thought the moon had somehow gotten into each of his buckets. And just like that, each one of us is reflecting the divinity which has made us, which sustains us, and which transcends us. By attuning ourselves with that divinity, it is reflected in our hearts, our thoughts, and our world.

And so, dear friends, let us stand unshakeable in our courage, and walk with the certainty that God's power will protect and take care of us in a troubled and changing world. Let us remember that we *can* contribute to the healing of planet earth and the resolution of its problems by remaining above and beyond the contamination of great mental negativity. Negativity widely spread over millions of people is more destructive than an atomic bomb because, you see, thoughts and feelings are enormously powerful.

It is our duty then, as good people of God, to try to come closer to a sense of His continuing compassion and unending love. Then we will find that we are not only feeling better ourselves, but we are contributing to the well-being of the whole. Contribute what you can, and give of yourself. Offer your consciousness of the divine. Take hold of it and let it work its way with you. It is God's purpose, you see, to bring out the divinity hidden deeply within the consciousness of each and every one of us. Jesus knew who he was. He was the Christ. He knew his divinity and he urged upon all people everywhere to come closer to that divinity—which he declared for you too, if you would only have faith and work at it. Then, indeed, life's journey becomes much easier and more beautiful.

As we become senior citizens (and I did that an awfully long time ago), we should feel that these are the best days of our lives, for they are the sum total of all our experience. It's easy for us to think that by now we should be making fewer mistakes; but of course, even when we do not intend to make mistakes, we make them anyhow. We try not to, but because humans are fallible, we do make mistakes. We are very fortunate that we can lean upon the teachings and experience of Jesus and the other spiritual giants who have gone before us, for in following them we are able to transcend the obstacles and clouding issues in our lives that seem to turn day into night.

When we are pressured by these difficulties and challenges, we must realize, "This too shall pass." In any case, we must have a solid conviction that even if the whole globe should blow up, we may take refuge in knowing that we have a home not made with hands: a home eternal in the infinite heavens. Of course, I don't mean to say that we should bury our heads in the ground and not read the paper or listen to the news. Not at all. But we must remember that we have available to us a spiritual science, a marvelous and enduring philosophy that can liberate us from a thousand concerns. We need to know what is going on in our world, but we should see it all as the dream and drama of life.

The other day a lady told me about a relative who was recently healed of terminal cancer. The doctors had completely given up on him, and had told him to go home and smoke, eat, and drink all he wanted to because it wouldn't make any difference. But this man gathered his faith and his thought power, and he made a mighty determination, "No," he declared, "I'm not going to accept this deadly prognosis. I have faith in God's miracle-working power. I have heard about the power of the mind, and I know that it *can* and does work." He had read accounts of marvelous healers who had made it work a thousand times, and he was determined that he would make it work for himself. And he did.

Today there are many doctors working with so-called "terminal" patients, teaching them how to step aside from their daily activities three times a day in order to sit quietly and deeply relax both body and mind. While they are very still, they are told to visualize themselves, on the screen of the inner mind, as completely whole and healed. The medical profession has been astonished by the rate of success with these cancer patients and others who had been called "terminal." It is truly marvelous to see medical people leaning into the spiritual dynamic in order to accelerate the healing process. But spiritual people have known about this process for many years. Teachers and practitioners from religious traditions throughout the world have reminded us of the infinite and all-pervading power available to us now and always.

So, dear friends, let us remember that each and every one of us can be a positive force for good by turning away from the demons of doubt and fear, and coming into alignment with the powerful energy of God's goodness. Our very thoughts and feelings can create a world of happiness and good will, or of sadness and disharmony. What we think and feel is an energy that extends out and touches everything and everyone around us. As we work with this energy, individually and collectively, we realize that we really *can* have a conscious impact on the world. Then it becomes easier for us to make a commitment to sending light and love out into the world. So let us do that this week. Let us set aside a little time every day to send love and harmony to the people in every village, every town, every state, and every country—whether you like them or not. Then you will be participating in God's divine life. Then you will be doing a beautiful work that will make everyone feel better, including you.

Remember the simple recipe for well-being and happiness and practice it every day. Commit something positive to memory; look for something beautiful every day; read a little poetry, listen to some beautiful music, and look at a lovely work of art so that the cares of the world may not obliterate the sense of the beautiful, which God has implanted in the human soul. Thank you. *Amen.*

· PART TWO ·

SERMONS ON SAINTS

John as a Franciscan friar

Spiritual Inventory (St. Francis)

Unity Temple, San Francisco, CA
January 31, 1982

Good morning, dear friends. Today we are going to talk about the practical application of taking a spiritual inventory. I think religion should be a very practical thing—something that we thoughtfully apply daily, weekly, monthly, and yearly.

When we speak about taking inventory, we usually think about business. Looking inside the stockroom and tallying up what is on the shelves is an easy way for a business to determine what goods and supplies they have on hand, what they are a little short of, and what they have run out of. Taking inventory also lets companies know what is selling and what is not selling, what is working and what is not working.

All the big department stores take a regular inventory—corporations do it, the government does it, and even small businesses do it—so why shouldn't we take an inventory of ourselves? If we are keeping our interior house in good order, we should occasionally look into the well stream of our own spiritual dynamics to see where we have progressed, and where we have not progressed. Now, this doesn't mean that we should concentrate solely on the negative side of the ledger, making very sharp discriminations and listing every bad thing we've ever done in our lives; nor should we focus solely on the right side of the ledger, bolstering ourselves by listing only the very good things we've done. Both of these, you see, would be extreme. We want to take a balanced look at ourselves.

The practice of conducting an honest, unbiased, and unemotional accounting is very helpful as we travel the road toward spiritual emancipation and union with the Divine. Self-examination and meditation are the vehicles that lift us from one form of consciousness to another, and help rid us of the habits and tendencies of our lower nature. The currents of transformation will eventually ferry the natural man from beasthood to godhood, but that could take an awfully long time. We can move that evolution along by consciously drawing in the power of God, and by asking that our hearts and minds be lifted and illumined. In this way we may make an intelligent and beautiful inventory, a truly spiritual inventory.

The first thing to do before beginning your spiritual inventory is find a nice quiet little place where you will not be bothered for a while. Sit down and begin to breathe slowly and deeply until your mind feels very quiet and your body becomes very still. Then, start to observe yourself and your habits to see if you are developing into the person you really want to be.

As you look over the ledger of this past year, remember that God is supporting you in your desire to grow, not chastising you for any shortcomings you may find. Be very careful not to become too cast down when you recall those times when you really missed the mark, when you see a blotch or two on the negative side of the ledger. It is also important not to get overly puffed up about the good things that might appear on the positive side of the sheet, because no matter how good you have been, you can be a little better. We are always growing and becoming. The saints are people just like you and me; we see in their lives inspiring examples of the kind of progression and transformation that is really possible for us.

Everybody loves Saint Francis of Assisi. He is a wonderful example of someone who was transformed from a very egotistical and worldly youth into a very wise, down-to-earth, humble, and joyous man. He sought the gift of spiritual elevation and presence of God with such tenacity that it literally transmuted (what seemed to him) a base ingredient into the pure gold of the Christ spirit. Saint Francis gave us a marvelous example of what can happen in human consciousness when we enter into a deep and dedicated search for the sublime and ultimate reality.

When he was a young man during the Middle Ages, Francis dressed himself in the most extravagant and beautiful attire of the day. He sported bright-colored waistcoats made of the finest silks and satins, and he wore the latest hairstyles. His father was a well-to-do silk merchant, so Francis lived rather like a trust fund kid, unburdened by having to work for a living. He was free to roam through the village, strumming his guitar and drinking nice red wine, and serenading his favorite *signorinas* under their balconies.

We think of these things as quite normal for the average young man in Italy or anywhere else, but this was Francis, before he became *Saint* Francis. He was young, and he didn't think there was anything wrong with the way he lived; and there really wasn't. But later on, when he became more thoughtful and began to turn his mind toward spiritual things, he naturally moved away from all the drinking and wooing of women.

One day Francis was sitting in a crumbling little church on the side of a hill, meditating on the presence of God, when he heard an inner voice, which said, *"Francis, rebuild my church."* Now, Francis was a simple and straightforward kind of saint, so he immediately went out and got some water, mortar, and stones, and began to repair the dilapidated walls of the church. Later on, of course, the Holy Spirit indicated to him that it was not the repair of the physical church that was meant, but the repair of the spirituality of the Church. Francis went on, as we all know, to rebuild and revitalize the Church by forming a Catholic order called the "Friars Minor."

By his recognition of the presence of God in all of Nature as well as in himself, Francis felt a kinship with the moon, the sun, the stars, and all the little animals. Today, followers of every faith throughout the world revere him. Images of Francis portray his kind and gentle heart and his love for all creatures. He is usually pictured with animals at his feet, his head tilted down, and his eyes gazing sweetly at a delicate bird trustingly perched on his hand. In Francis we have a beautiful image of someone who was literally transformed from the ordinary to the divine. He made a dedicated effort to change by offering all aspects of his lesser self into the transmuting fires of divine love. We can look to Francis and other spiritual giants to lead us to our inevitable transformation and liberation in the Christ spirit.

Now, in taking your spiritual inventory, you must not get discouraged or be too critical of yourself if you should find that you've been sort of lazy, or that you have not brought into your spiritual practice a proper dynamic approach, without which you know you cannot grow. It is absolutely essential to your growth that you work and practice. Do you want to sleep this incarnation out? Well, you can if you want to, but if you sit on the sidelines of your life like a wallflower, then you are wasting the gift of a lifetime. You need to be about your Father's business.

One of the first public utterances that Christ made was to his mother and father when he was teaching, answering questions—and lost of them. He said, *"Why were you looking for me? Did you not know that I must be about my Father's business?"* (Luke 2:49.) He was only twelve years old. So remember to be about your Father's business by daily keeping your appointment with Him. Daily enter the quietness of your meditation and gather in the power and love that will feed and encourage you as you go about the activities of your day.

As you peer into the nooks and crannies of your spiritual household, bring into focus those things you need to overcome the most. Where are you lazy and pessimistic? What failings and regrets do you still cling to? What bad habits and addictions do you still defend? When are you afraid? Where do you still hurt? Where do you armor yourself against the love that wants to heal and bless you with the joy of spiritual and human companionship? What injuries have you still not pardoned? What failures in yourself have you not forgiven? Do not pass over these hastily; realize that these patterns of thinking and feeling are the habits that obstruct your clear path homeward.

Saint Teresa of Avila, the great Spanish saint of the sixteenth century, was counseling one of her young novices who was pleading for forgiveness and relief from her sins. She said to the young woman, *"My dear, all of us are human and prone to sin. Just see to it that you don't let your sins turn into bad habits."*

Sometimes we feel very weak and unable to correct our faults. In that case, we must ask for what we need. Maybe we need strength in our weak places or humility where we are a little too proud. Sometimes we need more acceptance and forgiveness of ourselves or others. We can change ourselves simply by asking the great compassionate God to help us. In this way we can be set free of every impediment, one by one. Most of all, we must ask to feel the presence of God, and to be freed from any idea that we can ever be separated from His love.

A periodic spiritual inventory helps us transcend the limitations of our past and move into our glorious future. Fear not the heights to which the soul must aspire, and never think of how far you have yet to go. Just carry on, "steady as she goes," and do your very best. As we ascend the spiral staircase of wakefulness, marching ever onward and upward, we are lured into a true sense of God's presence and power. Then we can stand with Francis and Teresa and all the others for whom it is no longer just faith, for it has become a rich and ever-present knowing.

There are many troubles in the world today; it is a time of extreme distress and uncertainty, and many people are suffering through very hard times. This would be an awfully hard period to go through if we had no anchorage at all. Yet, there are people who think they can get along without God; they have turned their backs on God, and say He is dead because some of their prayers were not answered. A person is bankrupt indeed, without a sense of connection to the light of creation and the source of all being.

As scientists probe the marvels of the far-flung galaxies, they remind us eternally of the strange and marvelous nature of this universe, which God has made and which is vastly beyond man's conceptions. Even with the most sophisticated and complex technologies, science has not been able to grasp the mind of God, for the Infinite is so much greater than we can ever conceive. If we try to row our boats by ourselves, with no help from God, indeed we shall be overturned by the rough waters of life and may even crash upon the rocks of error. But if we willingly determine that the best way to live this life is to lean upon the sustaining Infinite, we shall indeed be able to withstand all the storms and challenges that life presents.

Now, leaning upon the sustaining Infinite doesn't mean you can be lazy, or lie down and go to sleep; and it doesn't mean that you park your brains outside the temple door before you go in to worship. The Lord Christ never asked us to do that. We mustn't abandon good sense when we attempt to deepen our sensitivities through meditation and other spiritual practices. If you find that you are a little bit slack on brains, then ask for help. The Lord of lights can help you keep your feet on the ground as He illuminates your mind and heart, and elevates your consciousness to areas you never imagined possible. So, leaning upon the sustaining Infinite means practicing and working to become one with the transcendental power that makes the impossible possible, and it means coming into attunement with that force of love which brings about a revolution in your consciousness and in the whole operation of your life.

Life should be a joyous journey, but for most people it really isn't. We should not rob ourselves of that joy by carrying around regrets and sorrows. I'm pretty sure there is no one in this hall who doesn't remember at least two or three incidents in the past that are still causing some regret or unhappiness. You reproach yourself, "Why did I *do* that? How *could* I have been so thoughtless? It was so wrong and I should never have done it." Even if it was a petty offense, it may be a lingering thorn in your sense of peace and self-appreciation. "I hurt Mrs. So-and-So's feelings, and she passed away before I could apologize. I wonder if she ever forgave me."

Perhaps you failed in a business venture, got rejected by a school, or maybe you were fired from your job. Someone you loved was mean or cruel to you, and you've never gotten over it; you've kept the door shut tight to the idea of ever loving anyone again. You haven't forgotten the day your boss denied your request for a raise, or the time your spouse forgot your anniversary.

Some of you are still kicking yourselves for going off your New Year's resolution to lose a little weight. You just gave up and dropped your membership at the gym, inhaled a few bags of M&M's, and gained ten more pounds. Then, there was that lady at the supermarket who stepped on your big toe, and you spent the whole month thinking about it. By the time February was over there were thirty-seven people you weren't talking to anymore, and you were stomping straight into March full of resentment, confusion, and a hardened heart.

That's what the negative side of the ledger looks like. We need to look at some of that and release all those little hurts and regrets of the past. We must learn how to liberate ourselves from all that weighty baggage. Why carry such a heavy load? Let it go! When God looks down from His supreme heights upon the soul of a human being, He is fully conscious of what that person has done to others and to himself. But the Lord of compassion does not brood over the sins that person has committed, nor does He dwell upon them with a condemning eye.

The real idea of sin, you know, in both the Old and New Testaments, is *"missing the mark."* It is a term that was used in archery, and it simply meant missing the target. Naturally, we don't *intend* to miss the mark, but all of us have missed the target, or *"sinned,"* uncountable times. The real sin, and the real question you must ask yourself as you do your inventory, is, "Have I caused hurt to anyone? Have I caused injury? And have I turned a cold and dead heart where I could have been loving and kind?"

Jesus said repeatedly, *"By this shall all men [and women] know that ye are my disciples, [namely] that you love one another."* (John 13:34-35.) This is the highest law for humankind. Therefore, when you are doing your inner inventory and a memory emerges that still carries a sting about something you did to someone in the past, or you remember something unkind that they did to you, say a little prayer of forgiveness for the one who hurt you, and mentally ask forgiveness from the one whom you may have injured. Bow to the Christ Spirit in them and send them your blessing. Do it mentally, and do it often, especially if you cannot contact them in person or by phone, or if they have passed on. In this way you will release *yourself* from the hurt that person caused you, and you will also release yourself from a sense of guilt that you may have kept deep inside for a very long time. Continue this practice until you feel at peace whenever you think of that person. In this way, you begin to liberate your consciousness.

You know, growing up Catholic, I practiced a tradition called "confession." Once a week, before you could take Holy Communion at Sunday Mass, you would go into the little cubicle called a "confessional" and kneel down in front of the priest. He would pull back a little sliding door to reveal a simple mesh divider, and he would hear your confession. You would say, "Bless me Father, for I have sinned," and then you would recount all your sins, one by one, and say how many times you committed each of them. "I was late two times; I embarrassed my little brother twice; I talked back to my mother once; I had four impure thoughts; and I stole three strawberries." (You know, this sort of ventilated your sense of guilt.) Then, the priest would say, "My child, I absolve you from your sins in the name of the Father, and of the Son, and of the Holy Ghost. Amen." According to Catholic doctrine, as an instrument of God the priest can forgive you, because in the Bible it says, *"Whose sins ye shall forgive, they are forgiven, and whose sins ye shall retain, they are retained."* (John 20:23.) God most definitely does forgive you, and much more often than you think. We must also learn to forgive ourselves, let the past go, and be the best we can be.

Now, giving up the past and forgiving our sins doesn't give us liberty to play loose with divine law, but we should become acquainted with the awe-inspiring nature of God's infinite compassion. So learn to let go of the sins you've committed, those things you've done that were unlovely; and release the hurts of the past, all those times you were rejected, denied, ignored, and unloved. Just let them go; it's all over and done.

As you review the past year, say to yourself, "All right, here we are at the beginning of a new year, and I'm looking back over the whole of last year. Am I really more conscious of God's power in my life now than I was last year at this time? I've heard a thousand sermons about God's endless love for me, and I've read twenty books about His power and grace, but have they really affected me? Am I any nearer to feeling God's presence as a tangible reality? Do I really know that I am loved, that I am one with Him?"

It is very easy to fall into the trap of passively listening and reading without giving equal time to actively thinking, meditating, and making changes in your behavior and in your responses to life. You see, we sometimes get a little bit of metaphysical intoxication. We read books and pamphlets, we listen to tapes and lectures, and for a few days we are inspired—but does it last? Does it bring about the kind of transformation we saw in Saint Francis? We like to hear the minister or priest speak on Sunday and at special conferences and workshops, but all too often what we hear doesn't really take root.

Remember the wonderful story Christ told about those who went out to sow the seed? Some of the seeds fell on rocks, and then dried up; and some fell on good, fertile ground and bore delicious, healthy fruit. (The Parable of the Sower: Matt. 13: 3-9, Mark 4:3-20, Luke 8:5-8.) In the same way, *you* have to be the soil that is prepared and ready to receive His wisdom-pearls into your consciousness. How are you ever going to change your life if you don't first change your mind, your consciousness?

You have to change your thinking about who you *really* are, *what* you really are, and *where* you really are. The great saint, Ramana Maharshi, instructed his spiritual students to ask this question, "Who am I?" With every answer they came up with he asked them to go deeper and ask again, until they realized their true identity in God. If you take a serious look at this practice, you may quickly conclude that such a question seems like a mountain that is too high to climb. But God always gives us the grace to climb the mountaintop, and to understand the laws which He has projected into human consciousness.

When you work with divine laws and become one with them, what happens? More and more as you practice, you experience harmony with yourself and with everybody around you. Then you find that, little by little, it becomes easier to avoid those occasions when you might get into a scrap with someone. Even though you may not be able to get away from certain people, because you have to live with them or work with them every day, you find that you are able to tolerate and understand the behaviors that used to bother you a great deal. Now you are able to let things go while you maintain your balance and harmony.

When you begin your meditation, send warm and loving thoughts towards any person with whom you have had any kind of negative or unlovely interaction. You'll be astonished at the miracle of transformation that this simple practice brings. A strange kind of divine alchemy begins to take place within you and the other person, and suddenly, without knowing why, that person doesn't dislike you as much as they did. And then, after a while, they might even like you. In the meantime, you'll feel better, and eventually you'll feel really good about them too.

I remember a time in my life when I badly needed a job in order to pay the rent. I signed up to do work I had never done before, because I needed the money so urgently. I felt that the manager of the office really didn't like me. Now, not everybody is going to love you all the time, but this man was often peering rather sharply at me, watching my every move, and sort of measuring and testing how I did my work. I began to think, "Wow, this guy really doesn't like me." But then I recalled the teaching of Saint Paul: *"I am renewed by the changing of my mind."* Well, just who can do that for me? Can I ask somebody with a magic hat to do that for me? No! The great democracy of the spiritual trip, as I always say, is that YOU DO IT. You give the emphasis and God helps you; then things really begin to happen in your life.

So I began to say a little prayer for this man, visualizing him and sending him light and sincere love. I would mentally say, "Mr. So-and-So, I bless you, and I call you my friend." It worked so well that he promoted me, and I became more or less the one he chose to train those who came in to do the work that I formerly had done. Now, if I had remained in the mortal mind, thinking things like, "He doesn't like me, so I'm not going to like him either," the two of us would have had sparks together. That would have been the end of my job, because he owned the business. Instead, I chose the loving spiritual way and overcame the situation. We became such good friends that when I moved on to a much better position in a place where he often came for social events, he would always stop by my desk and talk to me. Isn't that nice? See how the miracle of that transformation occurred? You can imagine how negatively it might have turned out if I had poured out the dynamics of hatred instead of friendship.

This kind of thing hits all of us at one time or another. We are constantly being bombarded by thoughts, both negative and positive, so if we want to change our lives and move into a better frame of existence it is absolutely incumbent upon us that we not allow the negative to take root. We must plant only good seeds, the seeds that Jesus spoke about, and let them sprout into beautiful manifestations of metaphysical triumph.

Now, there are people who don't like that word, "metaphysical." They don't like to think there is anything real in the meta-physical—that is, anything that has no material form or substance. They say, "That's all nonsense; it's too remote for me. I believe in being practical!" One man spoke those exact words to me. I said, "Well, if you really believe in being practical, you'll lean upon the sustaining Infinite, and you'll know 'from whence cometh your power.' You'll look over the problems of your life, relegate them to their proper position, and infuse them with the kind of dynamics that will make this life of yours a joyful journey."

Life should be happy. Now, I don't expect everybody to get up in the morning, giggling and howling and dancing on the ceiling, but we should wake up with pleasant, harmonious thoughts and ideas, and we should go to sleep feeling well.

I remember one time when I was working at that better job I had moved on to. It was a private social club for the rich and famous. There were a great many members of this club, and they all used to say, "John, you're always happy. Every time I come in here you're smiling and playful. Nobody can be happy *all* the time—what is it with you?" Well, of course I don't go around grinning and giggling all the time, but as a general rule I feel pretty good about myself and quite good about other people. If a problem does arise I meet it head on—sometimes not with great success, but when I remember to use spiritual power, then, indeed, I do have great success.

We all know by now that we are truly the authors and architects of our own lives; so as we look back over our shoulders into the past year and take inventory of the mistakes we made, let us remember to look neither with condemnation nor offhandedness. Let us determine that we shall not fall that way again, we shall not make the same mistakes. In that way we will certainly grow.

Now, if you walked in the door and tripped on the first step, you wouldn't like that. If you did it once and suffered the consequence, you certainly wouldn't do it every time you came in—otherwise people would think you were not very bright. So, as you go through life, look around and see where the obstacle is, and transcend it.

Lift yourself above and beyond every obstacle by the help of the divine and all-pervading presence and power, which is imminent within you as a temple of the living God. The minute you come to know yourself as a temple of the living God, life becomes a more beautiful expression. God intended it to be so. It is our mistakes, our lack of understanding, and our misinterpreting that contribute to the negative. But, in truth and in deed, Christ, the saints, and the inspired teachers down through the ages have constantly reminded us to lean upon the sustaining Infinite. When we do, we will make fewer errors.

You'll find that, with a little meditation, what seemed insoluble does bring about insights into how to solve your problem. Again and again insights arise from within you, and suddenly you realize that you do have the answer; the way to work things comes to you, easily and naturally. You know, you are not meant to handle all the problems and trials of life all by yourself. Do you think you can drive the whole cart of life, all alone? Of course not. You need help. We all need help, and we are all given help. God gave you your life. God *is* your life and your refuge, your problem solver and your prosperity. So lean upon Him and realize that, with Him, you can move your cart through life with a great deal of ease, vitality, and joy.

I think it is very sad that some people sort of sleep through life. They say, "You know, John, it's very hard. Things are bad all over, and I just know it's going to get worse."

You hear disturbing news on TV and from every avenue of receptivity, but you don't have to listen to it. You *know* where your power comes from. And, you know that you have a choice to make each day a happy, outgoing day—or, if you want, you can make it a very bad day. Don't we have an option?

God didn't say it was going to be perfect, and He didn't say we would have rose petals thrown in our path every day. We have many lessons to learn in order to refine our consciousness so that we will make fewer errors. We transcend the difficulties of life by elevating our consciousness to an area wherein we can simply step over the seemingly huge and terrible blocks in the road.

Now, I can just hear some people thinking, "But, I'm only one little person; how can I do anything by myself?" Remember that "God and one are a majority." God put the light eternal within our consciousness, and He told us that we are temples of the living God. That means that God lives inside us. So each time you speak something negative following the words I AM, you are sort of taking the Lord's name in vain. When you say, "I AM," be very careful, because there is an eternal quality of God in that expression.

Remember in the Old Testament, when Moses asked the voice that spoke to him from the burning bush, "Who is it that speaks?" What was the answer? It was, *"I AM THAT I AM."* (Exod. 3:2-6, 13-14.) God didn't say, "I WAS," but "I AM." So whenever we say "I AM," we must follow it with a positive expression of the quality of God. We must say things like, "I AM radiant, endless, vibrant, electric energy and youth in every cell and atom of my being." Or would you rather say, "I AM poor; I AM sick; I AM tired; I AM in pain; I hate everybody and I wish there were more people in the world, so I could hate them too!"

You see, you have an option. If you haven't been keeping good books on the inventory of your life, then you'd better look over your shoulder and find out how to do it in this coming year. You must realize that you are never alone, that God never abandons you, and that when you sit and meditate quietly and listen to the still, small voice—which is available and always near—then wisdom insights, I promise you, will come and help you solve those things which seem impossible—and you will receive the help you need in order to do things better. You will feel much more joyous and sure about yourself. You will feel more certain about your life here on planet earth; and when you graduate from this earth experience and enter the eternal realms of Spirit, you will feel good about that too. People who are filled with the certainty of God's presence have a more joyous and expansive life. They *know* where they are going, and they live lives that are filled with a sense of ongoing, both here and hereafter.

I heard a story this morning about a dear elderly lady who is very ill. Her condition is quite grave. I think she has decided that she would just as soon pass on, because she doesn't want to live in a body that is very badly limited. She said to a mutual friend, "I'm not afraid because I *know* where I'm going." Wow, that is quite a statement. Do *you* know where you are going? *Do* you?

I have great assurance about the eternal nature of life, and that assurance gives me a certain freedom—a liberating quality that brings me close to the presence of God. It is that presence alone which can liberate us from all that is unlovely or negative. God never said we would not have any negative experiences. If we didn't meet the test of those negative experiences, we would never grow. Often it is by moving *through* the challenges and obstacles that we exercise our spiritual muscles. This is how we practice and develop mastery of ourselves and of our lives.

A few weeks ago somebody sent me a sweet little houseplant. I don't know the name of it—but this plant came in a little pot with instructions to take the wrapping off, pour in a little water, and keep a bit of it in the saucer below the pot; and that's what I did. Well, almost overnight a little spray of green shot up. So, the next day, I poured in a little more water to keep it damp. It is now three feet high and has four blossoms, each the size of a dinner plate. It is absolutely marvelous, and it all happened within a very short time.

This morning I looked at it and thought, "My word, the marvel of nature!" How this thing grew from a tiny bulb to a little green sprout, and then gave forth these beautiful flowers in an absolutely gorgeous orange color . . . The whole thing stands majestically; and there is still more life coming, because I discovered another bud on it this morning. It is a marvel to see how rapidly it all happened. Well, I *expected* it to!

Do you know that plants and flowers have consciousness? If you don't like them, they don't grow well. If you like them and love them, they grow much faster. So you see: all is life; all is consciousness; all is God. In life everything is pervaded with the spirit of Christ, which is God, which is the Father of lights, which is divine love.

So, dear friends, lean upon the sustaining Infinite today and always. And as you peek into the books of the coming year and watchfully take your spiritual inventory, make great emphasis on the credit side. Every time you are tempted to be negative and blame yourself for past errors, every time you are unforgiving toward yourself and others, stop and change your mind. Nobody is going to do it for you. If you are unhappy now, you're going to have to get happy later—so spare yourself the wear and tear and the strain, and do it now.

Even though there may be things which are less than perfect in yourself and in your world, *decide* to be happy now anyhow, and then you will find that this year will be the best and most glorious year. You will have an abundance of whatever you need; you will enjoy a sense of freedom; and you will know a new and deeper joy. You will have a fresh view of life, a renewed vitality and sense of ongoing purposefulness; and at the end of the year, you will feel that you have really walked up the mountainside many steps toward a clearer understanding of God. Thank you. *Amen.*

God is Everywhere (St. Francis)

Heritage House Presbyterian Chapel, San Francisco, CA
January 31, 1981

Good morning, dear friends. This morning I am going to talk about a short passage from Psalm 31. *"In Thee, O LORD, do I put my trust . . . Bow down [and incline] thine ear to me; deliver me speedily . . . For thou art my rock and my fortress."* (Ps. 31:1-3.) Now, that song was written centuries ago, even before the Lord Christ came into the earth plane, but see how contemporary it is. When you read these beautiful words of David, you realize that indeed he did put his trust in God, and he followed the inner promptings from Spirit with an absolute submission to the divine will. David expressed a sense of certainty that comes only from first-hand knowledge of God's positive strength and protection. We cannot just parrot nice words that we hear someone say or we read in a book somewhere. We have to cultivate such a sense of being protected that eventually it becomes so strong that we can stand with David and say, "I put my trust in God. I know I am protected and safe."

We all want to feel that we are safe and secure. And many people feel the need for security now more than ever before. I suppose every generation thinks that, but right now none of us is too thrilled by what we read in the headlines. A pall of fear seems to hang over the world today, and many people are going around with a kind of general or profound uncertainty about our future on this planet. With all the social and political unrest, and the nuclear technology to go with it, many people have grave concerns for the continuity of everything that we know as our civilization: from our art and music to our philosophy and religion. Not to mention that our villages, towns and cities could all be destroyed in the flickering of an eyelash if perchance the unthinkable should happen. It's enough to make the staunchest optimist defect to the other side!

When I was a young man and first came to California, I was a little more of a worrywart than I am now. I suppose I've improved with age, but in those days I used to make all kinds of noises and grumblings, and get all excited about this, that, or the other thing preceding World War II. Today I am a little more confident because I have developed a stronger faith. This certainty comes from deep inside, fostered by my habit of coming into contact with the tangible presence and activity of God within my soul every day.

We can stand steady and peaceful amid the chaos of this troubled world because we are absolutely certain that we are one with divinity. Knowing, not believing, that God dwells in the deepest part of our being, and that the essential and immutable part of every self is truly divine, we can stand and say exactly what Jesus said, *"I and my Father are one."* (John 10:30.) *"He lives in me and I in Him."* (John 14:10.) But we can't just say it; we have to live it. We must know where our sense of security comes from: the all-pervading Father of lights, the Giver of life, the Beloved of the soul. It comes from the Essence of joy, the Hand of forgiveness, the Ocean of love. There are a thousand names for God, but none of them can truly reflect His vast and unfathomable nature. We can only glimpse the immensity of divine consciousness, and know that God is all that we can ever know or imagine, and more.

Our classroom of the earth experience is, by its very nature, a temporary and limited arrangement. Everyone who passes through the earth plane is learning different lessons; and while ultimately we all learn the same lessons, we sometimes seem to learn them in a different order. Some people on the earth plane are learning how to nourish and take care of their physical bodies, while others are healing the emotional wounds of the past so they can live and love fully in the present. Some people exercise the intellect and broaden their powers of reason, and some work to expand their scientific understanding of the outer material worlds. In due course we lend ourselves to a deeper understanding of the impermanence of material things, and the absolute permanence of those things which we develop within the self. Jesus was teaching us this lesson when he told the man to *"store up in the heart those treasures which cannot rust or be lost, nor be stolen by a thief."* (Matt. 6:20.) Now, just what *are* those treasures that do not rust and cannot be lost? They are the true and lasting spiritual (not material) treasures of the soul. They are the integral and eternal part of the real *You*, that dwells within this temple made of clay, the temple known as the human form.

God has set within each of us a light: a tiny part of Himself. Now, if you want to, you can turn that light down, or cover it up, or even turn it out. (Well, *almost* out, because you can never extinguish the light entirely; it is always there, even if it is sometimes veiled and difficult to see.) Or, you can turn that light up by spiritual thinking, and by meditating upon the eternal nature of the Sustainer of unbounded life. The very fact that we can conceive of God as *being* is quite a marvelous thing, you know, and it is unique in the human species. We are the only animal on earth able to envision, understand, and touch the qualities of God.

The ancients—those great and holy ones of various Eastern religions—have spent thousands of years meditating on the nature of things. They tell us that when we breathe we draw in not only oxygen, but also a substance known as *prana*. This is the essence of life, which is borne in on the breath; and of course, there are as many names for it as there are languages and spiritual practices. Martial artists use the word "chi" (e.g.: "Tai Chi"). It is variously called soul, life force, essence, current, breath, energy, or spirit.

Spirit is another word for God, and curiously enough, the Holy Spirit is also another word for breath. Breath is life, and without breath no life remains within the body garment. Scientists in universities around the world have discovered what these great spiritual researchers of the ancient East apprehended ages ago regarding the spiritual nature of *Homo sapiens*, this wonderful creature called the human being. Current studies of breath, brain, and consciousness are bringing about a synthesis of understanding between the medical sciences of the West and the spiritual sciences of the East. I believe that at long last we are beginning to find a marriage between science and religion.

There *must* be such a marriage, you see, because there really isn't any contradiction between the two. The time is right for this fusion of understanding to occur, particularly since modern technologies furnish the capability of measuring not only the psycho-somatic (or body-mind) relationship, but also the effect mind has on the body and environment through the functions of higher octaves of consciousness. Quantum physics, for example, is yielding some very exciting information about the nature of matter and, not surprisingly, it is exactly what the yogis have been saying for thousands of years: namely that all matter is empty space, and that it never dies; it only changes form. The sciences of mankind are growing and uncovering, one after the other, God's wonders and laws, yet they are unable to perceive or touch the Lawgiver with their material science.

In my early years I was a Franciscan friar. I studied in the seminary right up to the time when I was supposed to take my solemn vows.

There were many reasons why I left the order, but principally it was because I was following a profound inner prompting. Soon after I left the seminary I met the great world teacher and lover of Christ, Paramhansa Yogananda, and became very devoted to him and his teachings. I have remained a devotee of Saint Francis of Assisi—the wonderful holy man revered by people of all religions the world over—and that's why I talk about him so often in my lectures. Francis saw God everywhere and in all things. He even personalized nature and the forces of nature; and he wrote stirring poems about "sister death," "our brother the sun," and "the lady of the moon." Francis personalized these picturesque aspects of nature so beautifully because he understood the very deep spiritual significance *behind* what was appearing as a law *within* nature. He was aware of both the manifest and the unmanifest aspects of creation, and he held reverence for both the seen and the unseen.

There is a legend about Saint Francis and how he nearly went blind at one point in his life. Apparently, the way doctors treated blindness seven hundred years ago was almost worse than the malady. It was horrible what they did to poor Francis. They took a red-hot wire and ran a little line with it from the corner of one eye out to the hairline on either side of his head. When he saw them heating the wire, this dear, simple, humble little man of God said, *"Oh, brother fire, be kind to me."* He really felt that he could speak to the forces of nature as agents of God. Isn't that beautiful? Legend has it that he felt no pain whatsoever during the procedure.

Now, that's a charming and sensitive little fable about the holy man, Francis, and who is to say if it is true or not? The point is that he had such positive reliance on God as the supreme protector, deliverer, and sustainer that perhaps he really was delivered from all pain. We must always remember that we, too, can stay close to a consciousness of this divine presence in all things by daily reminding ourselves that we are *never* alone, and that we can reach out and touch God's presence because we are a part of His consciousness. God is spirit, and in order to touch that power you have to reach out in spirit. Then you can bring it into your everyday life and enjoy a conscious confidence in the Lord as your protector, sustainer, and deliverer.

Many years ago, I met a dear old woman who possessed the kind of faith that God asks of us: a tremendous and unshakable faith. One day, as she was coming down a long flight of stairs, she caught the heel of her shoe in the rug and tumbled all the way down to the bottom. I was so shocked when she told me about her fall that I said, "My word, what on earth was going through your mind as you went tumbling down like that?" "Well," she said very calmly, "I told myself that I was falling into God." She silently reassured herself, "I know that I cannot fall anywhere where God is not." It's incredible, but you know, she didn't even break a bone. She had a couple of minor bruises; that's all. I believe that when we put our faith where it belongs, truly inexplicable and marvelous things can and do happen to us. When, however, we are filled with fear, all kinds of things we wish wouldn't happen do happen to us.

I like to tell these little stories because I know you will remember them long after you have forgotten most everything else John Laurence has said up here from the rostrum. So here's another one:

A good friend of mine, a very spiritual lady, decided to serve during World War II by becoming a trolley car operator. In those days it was unusual for a lady to operate a trolley car, but she did. Everything was going just fine, and at the end of her workday she got ready to turn the car in at the barn, which was way out in one of the worst districts of the city. It was around two o'clock in the morning when she finished her shift, and as she was walking away from the barn, she noticed a ferocious-looking man following her. She became frightened because she knew something was terribly wrong, and there was nobody else around at that hour of the morning on those dark and dismal streets. She crossed the street, and the man crossed the street after her. When he got literally right behind her, she turned around with a fury and glared directly into his eyes and shouted, *"God is my life!"* I don't know what he saw in her eyes, or what he thought or felt, but the guy ran away as though the devil himself was after him! He flew away from her and touched her not. Now, you see, *that* was faith in action.

These little stories remind us that we have to verse ourselves in faith, and the basic field manual for developing this kind of confidence is your daily period of meditation. Even if it is only for ten minutes, sit down, let go, and let God. Then amazing things begin to happen in your life, which the uninitiated call "wonders." There really isn't any such thing as a miracle, you know, unless you call *everything* a miracle. Even the most extraordinary occurrences are not *super*natural; they are *divinely* natural. We simple ones call such things miracles, but they are merely the operation of spiritual laws within the higher octaves of God's awareness and understanding.

Before we close today, let's take another look at these beautiful words of the Scripture, *"In Thee, O LORD, do I put my trust . . . Bow down [and incline] thine ear unto me; deliver me speedily . . . For thou art my rock and my fortress."* The song we sang at the beginning of our service this morning is titled "Everywhere." This simple little song has relevance in the same way our reading does. The words are: *"God's love is everywhere; God's love is near. Whate'er the world may bring, naught will I fear. God's love is everywhere; He is so near. Whate'er the world may bring, naught will I fear. What can disturb me now, when Thou art near?"*

So, dear friends, let us re-read this lovely passage from Psalm 31: *"In Thee, O LORD, do I put my trust . . . Bow down [and incline] thine ear unto me; deliver me speedily . . . For thou art my rock and my fortress."* Throughout this coming week let us remember again and again the importance of leaning upon the great Shoulder of the universe. Let us remember that in the consciousness of God, we can never be forsaken. We will always be taken care of, protected, and strengthened. Meditate deeply and ceaselessly until your consciousness has merged with that tangible presence and activity of God within your soul. Then you, too, will declare with the authority of your knowingness, "I stand steady and peaceful amid the chaos of this troubled world, because I am absolutely certain that I am one with the Infinite." Thank you. *Amen.*

Tell It From the Mountains (St. Francis)

Unity Temple, San Francisco, CA
January 1981

Good morning, dear friends. Today our topic is: "Tell it from the mountains." Jesus was the supreme exemplar of understanding the nature and importance of an elevated consciousness, and he often taught from atop the hills in the countryside. Many people ask, "How do you get up onto the hill, and what do you do when you get there?" Well, the best way to get up onto the hill is to meditate deeply, giving yourself totally to the operation of the Holy Spirit. In this way, you see, in all humility, you begin to feel the presence of the Christ spirit within yourself.

Like Simon, who knew that before he died he would see the Lord Christ with his own eyes, every one of us may expect to be awakened by the spiritual presence of the Christ child residing within. The ordinary consciousness of humankind is belabored with various complexities and burdens of daily life. But when the divine presence is apprehended even a little bit, a slow and beautifully serene elevation of consciousness of the divine Self begins to take place. It is then that we receive spiritual insight and realize the truth that sets us free. Then we are truly standing upon a mountaintop of understanding, and we can surely "tell it from the mountains."

We have just celebrated Christmas, the season when the Lord of the universe comes to us clad in the humility of a little babe. Jesus said that unless we become as little children, we will not understand the mysteries of the kingdom of heaven (or expanded awareness). As we walk into the New Year, let us make a pledge that we will never let a day go by without entering into the deepest recesses of our consciousness. In the temple of the Self, let us so elevate our minds and hearts that we may perceive with the inner eye of realization the presence that is the Christ, the presence that *is* God. In order to do that, we must become still in mind and body, and just rest in the Lord. Now, that doesn't mean you should go to sleep. You simply let go and rest quietly and consciously, alert to the promptings of the Holy Spirit. When you do that, you see, you are making contact with a kind of intuitional guidance, which alone can bring you into attunement (or "at-one-ment") with the divine presence.

Today we often hear people say they have been "born again." It is an interesting phenomenon. I think you are born anew every day when you accept the presence and transcendent glory of the Christ child within the temple of your being. Just as Jesus was brought into the temple by Mary and Joseph, so must you be brought into the divine presence within the temple of your own consciousness. We cannot grow into a deepening awareness of the presence of God or ascend the hilltops in consciousness unless we become very quiet and go deep within. God is not to be found in the marketplace, nor in the excitement and divertissement of the world. God is found in the silence of deep meditation.

From time to time we have all been perplexed by some problem and struggled for an answer. Maybe it is a health challenge, a family problem, or a financial crisis. Perhaps it is an intellectual puzzle, or a spiritual quest. Whatever it is you are confounded with, you need to have an answer. What should you do? Pray. Go up to the mountaintop to be alone—far from the confusion, anxiety, and all the noises of the world that muffle the voice of truth. Ascend the mountaintop and enter into a quiet interior place: the secret place of the most high, where truly unbelievable insights will occur to you. I have talked to hundreds of people who have felt the inspiration of the Holy Spirit in the depths of their being, and have felt Its influence in the activities of their lives. This divine presence is real. You can actually feel it coming into you in a peaceful and easy way, bringing answers to your deepest and most perplexing questions.

One of the most glorious and transcendental accounts in all of the Four Gospels is the wonderful story of Christ's transfiguration on Mount Tabor. Like so many other biblical stories, it is set upon a hilltop. Jesus took two of his disciples up to the mountaintop and told them to stay there and pray. He also went forward to pray with deep earnestness. It is told that, as Jesus was praying, he was suddenly lifted up into the air. Appearing on either side of him were Moses and Elias. The garments of the Christ became blindingly bright and as white as snow. The two disciples were very afraid, for they had never seen such a vision, nor had they ever felt such a mountaintop experience. Compared to Jesus, his disciples were simple children, and in their simplicity they said to Christ, "It is good for us to be here. Let us stay here and build three tabernacles: one for Thee, one for Moses, and one for Elias." And Jesus answered, "No, we have other work to do among the people." And so, having granted them this magnificent experience of elevated consciousness, he walked them back down, shall we say, to ground level—to the level of ordinary consciousness, from which they could continue to carry out their normal day-to-day work and activities. But the impact of that divine experience never left them. It remained inscribed upon the sacred tablets of their inner being forever. And all of this happened on a hilltop.

Saint Francis is certainly one of the most beloved saints in all Christendom. His love of nature and his beautiful consciousness of the omnipresence of good were so astoundingly transparent and so childlike that they literally transformed people. He has a lot to tell us about mountaintop experiences, especially the marvelous and spiritually transforming experience he had on top of Mount La Verna: where he received the stigmata, or wounds of Christ.

The accounts of these experiences remind us of the absolute necessity of elevating the conscious self. See, if we never work at getting up there, how are we going to "tell it from the mountains"? We won't have anything to tell. Saint Francis told it from the mountains when he spoke of his peak experience on Mount La Verna, and what he told began to spread like a fragrance over the countryside. He spoke of the love of God, the love of Christ, the essentials of charity and humility—and, for him, the love of poverty. Remember, he had come from a life of luxury and now he wanted to give everything away to the poor. He had seen so much indulgence and waste among the rich of his day that embracing poverty was his way of going against the tide, and reminding people that rather than accumulating silks and gold, it was far greater to have an uplifted consciousness.

Once this holy man was elevated by the Holy Spirit, he understood his personal relationship to the Christ. And, seeing God in all things, he began to spread the gospel of simplicity, humility, and love. Francis perceived all as a reflection of the divine. He saw the same divinity in the birds, the flowers, the water, the sun and moon, and especially within the heart of each and every one of us. In all things Francis saw God, and he "told it from the mountains" with supreme eloquence.

Down through the centuries, many other saints and holy men and women have had that same mountaintop experience. When you read the lives of the saints you'll find that, curiously, they all had the experience of being lifted up to a state of consciousness wherein they were allowed to perceive the divinity of everything, including themselves.

Saint Teresa of Avila, the great Carmelite nun who lived some four hundred years ago, was a woman of enormous erudition. She was recently made a doctor of the Roman Catholic Church. Such recognition was well deserved, and I think four hundred years was an awfully long time to wait for it. She had these mountaintop experiences in her own consciousness very often. If we are to believe the record—and I do because so many people at the time attested to their authenticity—her consciousness was so engrossed in the love of Christ that she was often found physically levitating above the floor. Her constant contact with the power and love of the Christ presence within her own consciousness transformed and healed not only herself, but all those who came to her for advice.

Now, levitation is an interesting phenomenon, and we have a record of it in most religious traditions. What is fascinating about Teresa's phenomenon of levitation is that she never asked for it. She never really wanted it. She used to pray, "Oh please, *please* Lord, don't lift me up above the floor, because the sisters and the rest of our spiritual community get so excited about it that they are diverted from their own prayers and spiritual discipline." Here was a woman who was raised to the highest mountaintops of consciousness, as it were. She was so lifted into infinite inner space that she temporarily defied the gravitational pull, and was seen levitating above the ground at various times and in various places by untold numbers of people.

We have all heard of holy men and women who possessed such a deep and inspirational love of God that it changed them forever. You see, there is a kind of divine alchemy that begins to take place in the consciousness of the simple person who has suddenly found himself making a total, unreserved, and permanent religious commitment.

My mother once told me about a wonderful Irishman who had lived in the skid row area of Dublin, Ireland. He had become a drunk and a derelict and had fallen down about as far as he could when, somehow, through some divine grace, he was lifted up in consciousness from the gutter to a place where he could stand tall as a man. That was God's grace, but this man did his part too. And his miracle didn't stop there. He went onward from that place, never giving up, until his consciousness became a beautiful thing to see. His love of God and his profound gift of prayer touched all those around him, and he eventually became a holy man.

This is a beautiful example of the profound and marvelous alchemy that takes place within the consciousness when we allow ourselves to be lifted to the mountaintop by the all-pervading love that is the Holy Spirit. Here was a man the least likely to have that kind of experience. His transformation is a magnificent display of the absolute, infinite compassion of God. We must rely on that merciful and unqualified love. We must totally trust that we too shall be guided into a wonderful sense of the presence and sympathy of the Lord. Then we become one with Him. Where we go from there—how deeply we intensify our devotional push, shall we say—is up to us. If you want to be lazy and not pray, not meditate, you must not be surprised that God does not lift you up to the mountaintop. You have to move towards Him. You have to ask, so that you might receive. Every one of us should ask, at the very least, to have a deeper sense of commitment, so that every day we keep our promise to spend a little time on the mountain peak of elevated conscious attunement with the power of God. If you do that, this year will be one of profound spiritual awakening.

It really doesn't matter where you are now, does it? Start from where you are. I can hear some of you thinking, "That sounds nice, John, but you don't know how many mistakes I've made." Well, we all make mistakes. As the orthodox people say, we are all sinners. That means that all of us have missed the mark to some degree or another. We have been taught a very damaging, condemning connotation of the word "sin." People have been pounding the pulpits for thousands of years, telling us that we are "no good sinners." We got so used to hearing that we were bad, right from the beginning, that we kept on being sinners. Now it is time for a spiritual resurrection. It's time to drop that old conditioning, that imprint that made us feel so bad. It is time to remember the truth: that when God made you He called you a magnificent creation. He called you *good*. Your loving Creator takes delight in you, even when you fall short of the mark, for you are His beloved child. You are the apple of His eye.

So as you move into this New Year, awakened to the divine presence within, you cannot fail to understand and accept the importance of reaching the mountaintop. Your example will become a great sermon. You don't have to be an orator in order to "tell it from the mountains." You don't have to have a PhD in English literature in order to speak of God. Jesus had no trace of a Harvard accent, you know. Perhaps you are comfortable just speaking in the silence of your mind and heart. All you need is to be sincere, relaxed, and receptive to the ideas, answers, and promptings of the Christ Spirit within your consciousness. Then who you *are* speaks a great, great sermon.

In the early days of this country there was a traveling minister who moved around through the South, as preachers often did in those days. This fellow was a missionary, and he was so religiously bombastic that he practically tore up the pulpit every time he spoke. Now, the old pastor was sitting there in the front row, listening to all this Bible pounding, fire, and damnation. After the service the guest speaker walked over to the old pastor and asked, "Did you like the sermon?" The old pastor answered, "Yes, sir, I liked the sermon all right. But frankly, I'd rather see a sermon than hear one."

And so, dear friends, let us try to be a sermon that can be seen. I'm a big ham (like a lot of Irishmen), so you're going to hear a lot of talk from my pulpit, hopefully, all through this coming year. Speaking and ministering is my life's work. It's what I'm supposed to do. But in my relationship with the total Reality it is much more important for me to regularly ascend the mountaintop of spiritual realization. Coming out from the depth of my connection with God, my words might be more sensible and may carry more beauty and inspiration, and in that way people might be moved to do a little more meditating for themselves. Then, we will all *"tell it from the mountains."* Thank you. *Amen.*

Workers in the Vineyards (Mother Teresa)

Unity Temple, San Francisco, CA
September 29, 1981

Good morning, dear friends. The various and beautiful parables of Jesus are marvelously practical, and they teach us in such a direct and simple way that we can all relate to them with ease. Today we are going to read from Matthew, Chapter 20: *"For the kingdom of heaven is like a landowner who went out early in the morning to hire workers for his vineyard. And after agreeing with the workers for the standard wage, he sent them into his vineyard. When it was about nine o'clock in the morning, he went out again and saw others standing around in the marketplace without work. And he said to them, 'You go into the vineyard too and I will give you whatever is right.' So they went. When he went out again about noon, and three o'clock that afternoon, he did the same thing. And about five o'clock that afternoon he went out and found others standing around, and he said to them, 'Why are you standing here all day without work?' They said to him, 'Because no one has hired us.' He said to them, 'You go and work in the vineyard too.'*

"When it was evening, the owner of the vineyard said to his manager, 'Call the workers and give the pay starting with the last hired until the first.' When those hired about five o'clock came, each received a full day's pay. And when those hired first came, they thought they would receive more. But each one also received the standard wage. When they received it, they began to complain against the landowner, saying, 'These last fellows worked one hour, and you have made them equal to us who bore the hardship and burning

heat of the day.' And the landowner replied to one of them, 'Friend, I am not treating you unfairly. Didn't you agree with me to work for the standard wage? Take what is yours and go. I want to give this last man the same as I gave to you. Am I not permitted to do what I want with what belongs to me? Or are you envious because I am generous?' So the last will be first, and the first will be last." (Matt. 20:1-16.)

This wonderful message is not only about work itself, but about the man who is in charge of the vineyard—who, in this case, of course, is the Lord—and what he does concerning those who come at different hours to work. Today we hear a lot about labor all over the world. We in America know a great deal about labor. We even set aside a special day each year, Labor Day, for people to think about the importance of work in terms of the way it serves all humankind, and our local communities in particular. So it is interesting to me that two thousand years ago problems were much the same as they are today, because people in those days were the same as we are today. The resemblance is so remarkable that you have to chuckle a little, for isn't it true that today the same kind of murmuring takes place? People say, "Hey, look man. I worked eleven hours and I got a penny, and this other guy worked only three hours and he got a penny too." Of course, according to a union contract that wouldn't be tolerated; but according to the Lord it would, because He is thinking about spiritual values.

Work is a beautiful thing, so if you have a job you like, thank God for it. If you have a job you don't like, that can be a bummer. But whatever the job, we all need a means of support: a place in the market where we can earn the wonderful way of life we have come to know so well in this country. Of course, I don't suppose today anyone would be asked to serve in the vineyard for a penny; but then, things have changed a lot. And we don't need to think of work as necessarily something out in the soil in the vineyards or the gardens. We just give thanks for the chance to labor, and to be able to take care of ourselves and our families.

It doesn't matter what kind of work you do. Whether you are an astrophysicist, a musician, a garbage collector, or a doctor, you should do your work to the best of your ability. When you do your best, you acquire a certain inner peace and a sense of balance and harmony. The nature of this planet on which we find ourselves requires this of us, and we should do everything we can to make our work as pleasant and as light as possible.

For many years I worked in the marketplace. When I was at work I used to make a game of it. I used to be in show business, and I love to entertain people and make them happy—so when I went to work, it was show time. I would make it a point to be kind to people even if they were not very happy. After seeing me at my desk for eighteen years, one man said to me, "John, I come here all the time and you are always pleasant, you are always smiling. This isn't possible; you can't be happy all the time. Don't you ever get mad? I said, "Of course, we all do. But I don't want to hurt myself or anybody else, so I am going to make life a kind of a game. I'm going to make work a game." So when you do any kind of work, make it a game. Make it a pleasant day for yourself and for everybody else. How do you do that? Begin your day by tuning into the Infinite for at least a short period. In your quiet meditation before going to work, fill yourself with the vibration of harmony and love. Then you are ready to go out into the marketplace, amid the confusion and babbling voices and noises of the world.

The Lord has given us a way to tune in and come close to Him. When we do that, no matter where we are or what we are doing, we are able to fend off the jarring inharmonious vibrations we sometimes meet in our daily lives. If we don't align ourselves with that divine presence of harmony and love, then we go into the marketplace and are immediately jangled by some kind of discord. Now, suppose you go to work and right away you find that everybody is up in the air, turning somersaults about this or that. Are you going to join them and turn somersaults too? No, you don't have to do that. Be calm and keep all that noise an arm's distance away from you. You will find that by not joining the tumult, chaos, and disharmony that sometimes goes on around you, you will feel better and you will look much younger too.

Christ himself gave parables concerning labor, not only in Matthew 20, but in other statements during his public life. He gave us this immanently practical way of teaching and showed us that we must not be greedy. He taught us that if the Lord of the vineyard chooses to give equal or more to someone who has done less, we should not get upset or pushed out of shape about it. Let us simply say that He has a right to do as He will. In that way we save ourselves a lot of anguish. Jesus gave the example of the workers in the vineyard simply to tell us that we must not be greedy, and we must not murmur against the Lord of the vineyards at any time. We should be grateful that in His infinite compassion, He has given of His bounty to all.

Now, as I said a moment ago, there are so many different kinds of work. Some people are in clerical work, others are in the scientific community doing all sorts of interesting work, and then there are the medical people, philosophers, teachers and professors, parents, and so on. They are all laborers, every one of them. And so, no matter what you are called to do, you are indeed a laborer in the vineyard of the Christ; and you only have to continue to hold fast to that Christ consciousness, and make it a positive and dynamic factor within your own expression as a working being.

I'd like to talk a little about a true "worker in the vineyard." She is a simple, tiny lady known as Mother Teresa of Calcutta.* I'm sure most of you have heard of her and have seen her on TV. This wonderful, saintly woman has received all sorts of honors from her Catholic Church and from many others.

Mother Teresa is a living example of the right attitude toward serving and working for God. She literally brings Christ's love and spirit to God's most abandoned poor. Recently, she was invited to Washington, D.C. to have lunch with the president, who honored her work with the destitute and dying in the slums of Calcutta. This simple nun originally came to India to teach. After a number of years, she began to look with the eyes of divine compassion upon the countless poor and forgotten people of Calcutta. She saw that people were dying on the streets, with no one to care for them. They had no shelter where they could go to breathe their last breaths upon this earth plane. And so she asked permission from her superiors if she could discard her nun's robe and don a traditional Indian sari. She was granted permission. And so, clad in the simplest traditional clothing of the people, Mother Teresa went into the worst parts of Calcutta to serve Christ in this most difficult mission.

Of course, *she* doesn't think her work is difficult—she loves every minute of it. She tenderly picks up the destitute, the homeless, and the dying, and carries them to the motherhouse where they are cleaned, fed, and cared for. She rescues abused and abandoned children and takes them to a safe place where Mother's Missionaries of Charity give them the help they need. She makes sure that the lepers and others in their

* This talk was given in 1981. Mother Teresa died in 1997.

final hours are cared for lovingly, and she insists that their religion be respected. If they are Hindus who are about to pass on, she calls in a swami to help them make their transition. If they are Presbyterians, she calls a minister. If they are Catholics, she calls in a priest. Mother Teresa's ecumenical spirit and total service are often completely unrelated to the orthodoxy from which she came.

That all-inclusive love, dear friends, is real Christianity. This is a modern-day saint, working in the vineyard of the poor. It is a very hard lot, believe me. I think most of us here would be glad that God didn't call us to do the type of work that he called this wonderful woman to do, because what she does takes supernormal courage.

If you read much about Mother Teresa (and quite a lot has been written about her), you will be astounded at the miracle of Christ consciousness that transformed this sensitive, teaching nun into a fearless lady who goes to the streets with such spiritual power in search of the dying, the diseased, the starving, and the helpless. Few of us would be able to spend hours steeped in the stench of death, or the sourness that pervades the hopeless alcoholic. But Mother Teresa is in love with God, and she cannot do enough for her Beloved. Because she sees the face of Christ in every person, her natural human revulsion is transmuted into deep compassion. When most of us would recoil in disgust, Mother Teresa embraces God's distressed humanity with the love of a mother.

As word got out about the powerful work of the tiny nun from Albania, it didn't take long for this worker in the vineyard to begin gathering men and women around her, and soon she founded a religious order. Now there are centers all over the world where people who follow her direction and her spirit go into the worst places to help the poor, the dying, and the helpless. Mother Teresa teaches her nuns and co-workers to see the face of Christ "in his distressing disguise" in every destitute and dying person.

When Mother Teresa received the Nobel Peace Prize she gave the most beautiful and touching talk to the assembled intellectuals, and of course immediately afterward they wanted to give her a banquet. I think it was going to cost something like twenty or thirty thousand dollars. But she said, "Oh please, *please* don't have a banquet for me. Give that money to the poor." So they cancelled the banquet and gave the money to the poor and destitute instead.

Mother Teresa was honored by the Vatican, and so she went to Rome. She arrived clad in her three dollar sari and a pair of simple sandals. Under her arm she carried a little pocketbook, which contained about twenty-seven thousand dollars in collections for the poor. She was so unthinking about the money that she left it on the bus when she went to the Vatican. But, you know, God works miracles whenever Mother Teresa is around, so she got the money back.

She found her way into the palatial halls where the cardinals were gathered. What a sight it must have been: this small unassuming nun, wearing her three dollar sari and sandals, standing next to all the cardinals, dressed in their magnificent scarlet robes and *birettas* (or caps). Now, please understand, I'm not criticizing cardinals or anybody else. But just picture this great gathering at the Vatican, with these princes of the Church all dressed up in attire that perhaps no prince of this world has ever equaled—and standing there in the midst of them was this simple, humble nun who works among the destitute. I hope that some of those cardinals were awakened to the need for relieving the suffering of the impoverished, the sick, and the dying.

In this gentle little nun we have a striking example of the Christ spirit, right in our own time. Isn't that marvelous? We all read about the saints who lived hundreds of years ago, and they are inspiring. But it all seems so remote, so long ago. Here we have a living example of Christ love right in our midst—a simple lady who demonstrates that selfless love in the streets of Washington D.C. and the capitols of the world, but most especially in the slums of Calcutta. Mother Teresa sees God in every face. She sees the Christ in every suffering child. That's beautiful. That's what Christianity is all about. This wonderful saintly woman (along with all those who come from around the world to work with her) has the joy of working in the most difficult vineyard of all. This living saint has a great ecumenical spirit. She describes herself this way: "By blood, I am Albanian. By citizenship, an Indian. By faith, I am a Catholic nun. As to my calling, I belong to the world."

I remember a beautiful little talk Mother Teresa gave on television some time back. She was telling us about the conditions under which she works in India. She spoke about the kind and loving quality of the Indian people themselves, and she told a little story about a Hindu family with eight children who hadn't eaten for three days. When she heard about this family, Mother Teresa gathered some rice and went to visit them. She gave a handful of rice to the mother, who was of course delighted because it meant that her family would have supper that evening. The first thing this woman did was divide the rice in half, then she disappeared for a short while. When she came back, Mother Teresa said, "May I ask, where did you go?" "Oh," said the woman, "next door is a Muslin family, and they have not eaten for three days either. So I divided the rice and gave half to them." Now, that neighboring family was not of the same religion; they were just neighbors. But religion didn't matter. This simple woman just shared what she had with the people next door. Now, instead of running right back the next day and giving them more rice, Mother Teresa waited an extra day before she brought more food. She said, "I wanted them to have the joy of knowing how to share in Christ." That's beautiful, and that's what Christianity is all about. That is what labor is all about. And that is what our hands are all about: to work, to serve, and to become instruments of Christ's love.

In one of her recent talks Mother Teresa said that she *expects* to be taken care of, for she knows she will always receive what she needs. She expects a miracle—and she gets a thousand miracles, for the simple reason that she has the kind of faith in Providence that will never let her down in any way. She does not doubt for even a second. Even in the most forlorn or terribly destitute person whom she might pick out of the gutters of Calcutta, Mother Teresa said, "When I look at that one, I see the face of God." How many of us can do that? Isn't it beautiful that we have this simple little nun who is able to teach the whole world what the Christ message really is, and what it really means to work for God? What joy and luminosity there is in the consciousness of this dear one who is serving God in His distressing disguise of the poor.

Now, if you've ever seen a picture of Mother Teresa or have seen her on TV, you know that she will never win any beauty contests, and I'm sure she doesn't mind that at all. But when you look at that face with a thousand people standing behind her, you can see no other face but hers, because shining through that humble and homely countenance is a light that can only come from the presence of Christ within the temple of her being. So let us give thanks that we have a few "Mother Teresa"s in the world. And let us be grateful that they teach us something about the obligation, the joy, and the spiritual dynamics of working with and for God. Then we, too, can experience a miracle of love. Thank you. *Amen.*

Father, What Can I Do For You Today? (Violet Olive Johnson)

Heritage House Presbyterian Chapel, San Francisco, CA
February 21, 1982

Good morning, dear friends. Today we are going to read from Luke 7:6-7: *"Lord, trouble not thyself: for I am not worthy that Thou shouldest enter under my roof. Wherefore neither thought I myself worthy to come unto thee: but say in a word, and my servant shall be healed."*

In this scripture of Luke we see that very often, with faith, people are marvelously healed. It is faith that heals, and it doesn't matter whether you are Christian, Hindu, Buddhist, or Muslim. What we must realize is that we are never far from the Christ spirit, and that with the fingers of faith we can reach out in spirit and touch the hem of Truth's garment. Then, in truth and in deed, as ever was and always shall be, a great healing undiminished shall come unto your house and make you whole.

So don't be afraid to call upon the Lord with deep faith and ask for help. Ask God for a lot of things. I know we don't need too much encouragement there. I think God hears "Gimme this" and "Gimme that" more often that He hears other prayers.

I am tempted to tell you about a wonderful lady who came here from England. She was a Christian mystic who always meditated every day. She prayed for people and sent her word to heal them, and sometimes she touched them in person and they were healed. She was a marvelous lady whom I knew very well. I studied with her for some years.

She was a titled Englishwoman, and when she arrived in Los Angeles one of the first things she wanted to do (like we all did in those days) was to see where Mary Pickford, Rudolph Valentino, and other movie stars lived. So on her first morning in Hollywood she did her usual meditation and said her prayers, not only for herself, but for countless other people whom she was endeavoring to help. At the end of her prayer work, she said, *"Father, what can I do for You today?"* She told me later with a little chuckle, "I don't know whether the Father hears that kind of request very often. He mostly hears prayers of petition." So she went on her way and got into one of those huge limousines that take tourists around Hollywood.

There were about eight other people in this vast stretch-out limo. They drove through the fancy neighborhoods where all the movie stars lived, stopping at all the points of interest they had come to see. When they were on their way back to the station where they had begun the tour, this wonderful little lady heard an inner voice saying, *"This young man* (the driver of the limo whom she was sitting next to) *has finished his work for the day. After this, he intends to buy a gun. Then he is going home to kill his wife and his best friend. And then he is going to commit suicide."*

Well, you can imagine how this dear little soul felt. She only weighed about ninety-five pounds all her adult life, but she was dynamite. She was so powerful in faith that it was like atomic energy at work. She was struck by the message she had received, and she thought to herself, "What can I do? What should I say? What *has* the Lord asked of me?"

She was really quite anxious, so she waited a little while, settling down and quieting herself inside, and again she heard the voice on the inner planes telling her the same thing. She knew that she could not fail to answer the direction of Spirit, so she turned her head toward the driver, leaned forward, and whispered in his ear, "Son, don't do it. *Don't do it!"*

Well, the young man was so shocked that he almost lost control of the car. He pulled over and stopped the engine. When they got out of the car, he looked at her and said, "Lady, why did you say that to me?" She replied, "Well, son, I don't know if you understand much about prayer and spiritual things, but I have a very important message for you. I urge you to come and have a cup of coffee with me." He did, and she told him what she had heard in her inner being, and he admitted that what she had heard was true. She said, "Now really, son, are you going to commit two murders and a suicide? That would be so frightful, so terrible. How could you do that? If your wife really wants to be with your best friend, then give her a divorce; but don't commit murder." Well, she persuaded him totally, and three lives were saved.

There she was, this tiny little soul, hearing the inner voice of Spirit telling her something about the man sitting next to her, someone she had never seen in her life before. Indeed a miracle took place that day, and two murders and a suicide were absolutely ruled out. Now, that is a true story; I know the person it happened to. She was an eminently sane, profoundly spiritual, and wonderful lady who worked in love and Christ consciousness until she graduated from the body at ninety years old while sitting in her little chair giving counsel to a minister. Hers was a full and wonderful life—and it shows you that the voice of Spirit, the power of Spirit, is *right here*, not out there somewhere far away.

Jesus placed great emphasis on this point so that we would not imagine that Heaven, the Power, or the Spirit is far away. Remember, I tell you again and again, the kingdom of heaven is within *you*. You are the temples of the living God. Of course, people find it very hard to accept that because we are all so conscious of being imperfect. But truly, the miracles of faith, the miracles of prayer, are just as real, just as powerful, and just as living a reality right here in the twentieth century as they ever were in ancient times.

Today is the birthday of George Washington. It is a reminder for us to be grateful to the founding fathers for their forethought and spiritual intuition, which inspired them to put in place the many safeguards of the Constitution. Now, George Washington and those who brought about the constitutional guarantees, gave us the most beautiful, sophisticated, and noble document on government ever devised by humankind. I am sure that, to a great degree, it was inspired by God. So let us pray that the Constitution will always stand firmly, and let us acknowledge the right of each person's religious freedom.

I am glad to see that churches today are coming together in an ecumenical spirit of respect and open-mindedness. Yesterday I read in the paper that Pope John Paul II was in the Philippines, calling on all Christian bodies to come together and at least have dialogue to see what things they can agree on. Well, they can all agree on the power of the living Christ Spirit. Religions really do have much in common, and we should acknowledge and honor their various ways of expressing the One God.

Many years ago, I assisted a wonderful Methodist minister in his talks at the Humanist Society. He often had interesting and sometimes amusing things to say. He used to tell me, "You know, John, there are hundreds of denominations of Christianity, and the only thing they have in common is that each one is 'the only true church'!" Now, that's what causes the trouble, isn't it? What we should realize is that each person may claim the power of the living Christ, and let that power work in his or her life as it will. Isn't that better than quarreling and killing each other?

So, dear friends, let us all be conscious of this One Divine Spirit, and let us live and serve in the unity of good, the unity of light, which is the imperishable and all-pervading Christ spirit. Then, we will be like the wonderful Christian mystic who dedicated her life to praying for others and asking, "Father, what can I do for You today?" Thank you. *Amen.*

Give Thanks Unto the Lord
(Kathryn Kuhlman)

Unity Temple, San Francisco, CA
November 29, 1981

Good morning, dear friends. I am very happy to be with you again. As we approach Thanksgiving Day, which has become a marvelous tradition within the very soul of America, let us enter into the spirit of truly giving thanks. I often think of how incredibly abundant this land is, and how continuously and prodigiously we have been blessed. We have our ups and downs, but by and large, we always seem to come through those experiences stronger than before. It is wonderful that we have set aside a special day when friends and family gather around to enjoy a feast of the harvest. But the main idea of this tradition is to give thanks. God has showered a wealth of blessings upon our great country, and we should not neglect to give thanks, especially when half the world is starving.

We have developed an incomparable marvel of agricultural technology capable of feeding the whole world, yet countless people perish every day from lack of nutritious food. Small farms are being shoved out of the way by big corporate farms. Half the world should not be starving. The bounty of this country could prevent starvation both here and in other parts of the world, but human greed and spiritual ignorance perpetuate the imbalance of wealth we see in our world today. Nowadays, much of our food is modified by gene splicing, and grown with deadly pesticides. We have to read our food labels very carefully to see if they are free of harmful additives and preservatives. Thank goodness there are so many good-hearted people in the world who *do* care, who work to bring awareness to this problem and to change the laws. These generous and loving people have a natural concern for others, and it is unfortunate that they are so seldom recognized for their tireless and selfless work. When we work to serve others we do not always get thanked for it, but never mind about that. What is important is that we thank God for the ability to do our work in the world.

Thanksgiving is a time to show our appreciation for the gifts of life. It is a time to offer thanks for our family and friends, and for all the blessings we have received throughout the year. Gratitude is another word for love, and love is really just another word for God. Jesus taught us that the highest law of heaven and earth is to love one another, and you are following that law every time you show loving kindness to your fellow man. At Saint Anthony's kitchen here in San Francisco this kind of love is expressed throughout the year, and especially on Thanksgiving Day. This Thursday volunteers will serve turkey dinners to thousands of poor and hungry people in our community. Such service is an act of selfless love; and it is expressed every day at Glide Memorial Church, the Salvation Army, St. Vincent de Paul, and many other organizations across the country, where people in need are given food for the body and nourishment for the soul.

The Lord of love has the reputation of offering refuge not only to the distressed, but to everyone. Working to serve those less fortunate than ourselves is beautiful; but we must remember to extend the hand of loving kindness to *all* our fellow humans, regardless of economic, racial, gender, or religious differences. After all, what is the color or financial portfolio of the soul? Very often people find it easier to show kindness to the homeless poor than to their own neighbors. It is easy for them to give leftovers and castoffs to those who are less fortunate than themselves, but not so easy to give a smile and a helping hand to the person next door. So let us remember to be kindhearted and respectful to everyone, regardless of any differences we might perceive. That way we honor the divinity within every being, and we give thanks to the One who shines through all forms. That is what Thanksgiving is really all about; and because it is a form of praise, we should do it every day.

We have so much to be grateful for, and it is important that we pause often to appreciate all of it. We are so accustomed to a comfortable life that sometimes we take things for granted, including the beautiful environment in which we live. We often pay little attention to the beauty that surrounds us. As creatures of habit, we usually take the same route when we drive home from work. And many of us go through life on automatic pilot, totally unaware and numb. Pretty soon we find that we have fallen asleep to the splendor of nature that is the backdrop of our lives. So let us stay awake, and let us always remember to give thanks for the blessings of abundance that we enjoy in this country.

You know, expressing gratitude is really a form of praise. It is an attitude of mind, and it brings to the self a joyous upliftment. Things may be very difficult in your life at the moment. Perhaps you are burdened with physical, emotional, financial, or family troubles. Whatever challenges life brings to your door, you will find the solutions to them by diving deep within the Self and drawing upon the resources of divine consciousness. The answer to every problem is available to you. When you look for the good and attune yourself to that dynamic power we call God, you automatically transform your attitude from pessimism and hopelessness into a blazing faith of positivity. By declaring your oneness with that power, and by giving thanks for it, you become spiritually invincible.

In order to develop a deep conviction about the power of giving thanks, we have only to look at the magnificent example of the Christ, who always gave thanks *before* he worked a miracle, not afterwards. Why did he do that? As an act of perfect faith. He knew that his Father would always hear him, because he understood that his own individual consciousness is forever a part of universal soul-consciousness. So in the beginning, even before he touched the leper, and before he healed the blind, he gave thanks to the Father: the mighty power within that doeth the works. All of us can learn from the example of Jesus the Christ— the supreme teacher of planet earth—who went about the countryside demonstrating good will, right thinking, right action, and giving thanks.

Down through the ages, wise people have told us that we are the architects of all our tomorrows. Solomon wrote, *"As a man thinketh, so is he."* (Prov. 23:7.) In other words, whatever you habitually think about and see in your mind's eye, and whatever you repeatedly affirm and visualize, you bring into manifestation. Whether we know it or not, we are all creating and materializing our thoughts in this way *all the time.* Remember that thoughts are things, and they carry a powerful creative energy. Now, you may say that you don't want to suffer in poverty, ill health, or loneliness. But if you are constantly affirming, *"I'm broke. I'm not good enough. I'm too old. No one wants me. I know I'll never get that raise,"* you are radiating the *energy* of those thoughts, and that is the kind of energy that comes back to you. By habitually focusing on what you are afraid of, and what you *don't* want, you actually draw it to yourself. I call that faith in reverse. *"As ye sow, so shall ye reap."* (Gal. 6:7.) Did you know that the slow-moving energy of your own negative thinking can actually cause the cells of your body to contract and block the life force? The result of this cellular shutting down is fatigue, pain, and eventually, illness. So if you want to improve your health or change the conditions of your life, you must begin by changing your thoughts and attitudes.

Most of you are familiar with the power of visualization and affirmation. If you want to bring about the right desires of your heart, you can do so by consciously training your mind and emotions, by working with your thoughts. Perhaps you have a desire to better your life in some way. How do you do it? Begin to visualize your desired state, and feel as if your wish has already been fulfilled—as if you already have that new job, that improved health, that wonderful relationship. And now put in the secret ingredient, as Jesus always did. Begin to give thanks, not *after* you get your wish, but *before* you get it. Anybody can say thank you after they have been given a box of candy or some lovely flowers. But to thank God *before* your prayer is answered is an act of *perfect* faith. In this way, you are expressing an absolute certitude that what you ask of your loving Father, the Source of all good, will indeed be given. You are so sure of it that you give thanks *before* the healing, *before* the change, *before* the new circumstance has appeared. Now, some people may say, "Wait a minute. I can see right here that my arm is not healed. I can't say that my arm is fine when it isn't." Or they'll say, "Why should I say 'thank you' for this pain in my back?" Well, there is no problem too big or difficult in the mind of God, and the consciousness which holds all solutions is available to you at all times because you are a part of it. Trusting that the work of divine consciousness is always for good, you give thanks for it in advance.

It is very important to understand your subconscious mind, because it is the vestibule of all the marvelous mystical aspects of man. Your subconscious mind does not reason or engage in logical arguments. It is a servomechanism, and it does exactly what you tell it. It doesn't determine the right or wrong of anything because it is *in*ductive, not *de*ductive. Therefore, it can kill you, or it can heal you from cancer. So whenever you talk to your inner self during meditation, give thanks to the great indwelling Healer *now, before* the revelation or healing. Don't say, "I'm *going* to get better," because that is mañana, and mañana never comes. Say, "I *am* better in spite of every physical evidence to the contrary," and you will *be* better. Why? Because in the consciousness of God there is only harmony and wholeness. When you attune yourself to that consciousness of wellness, and give thanks for it, you are touching into the power *within* that becomes harmony and balance *without*.

I think the need to give thanks is an inherent aspect of the human spirit. It is a kind of spiritual generosity that is beautiful and gracious.

Often, however, it is something we neglect. It is very easy for us to give thanks when we win a million-dollar lottery, but we forget to thank God for His many tiny favors. Remembering the little things, and giving thanks for them, sweetens life and makes us more akin to our Lord and teacher. I truly believe in the miracle-working power of giving thanks, not just on the special day set aside for it once a year, but every day. *"O give thanks unto the LORD; for he is good: for his mercy endureth for ever."* (Ps. 136:1.) Those words of devotion are like an offering of the heart that is boundless and immeasurable.

You know, a lot of people never get down to the nitty-gritty of prayer until they are in big trouble. The minute something major assails them they call out the name of God. But it is very important to practice turning toward the Source of all existence and to offer thanks as praise *every day*. In this way, you see, you begin to live in conscious attunement with that never-ending power of good all the time, and that is such a beautiful thing. Then, if some problem arises wherein harmony ceases to exist, you don't panic. You lean upon the sustaining Infinite and rest in the arms of the Solver of all problems. As you bring your concern to the Lord, always begin by giving thanks for the resolution of the problem. All you need to do is become very still, and expand your awareness until you have the feeling that the problem is already solved; then, give thanks for the solution. That way, you see, you immediately elevate your inner self and consciousness to another octave wherein you can more readily make contact with the free-flowing power of God. When you do that, you will realize that nothing is impossible to those who seek the unseen Benefactor of mankind.

I had a wonderful teacher who used to say, *"Thank God we have eternity, because most of us are going to need it!"* We're all learning and growing here in the classroom of the earth experience, and sometimes we fail a little bit here or there. Isn't it nice to know that we have the eternal mercy of God? He is infinitely compassionate of our weaknesses and failings, and He knows what we need. He is always there to lift us up, no matter how many times we fall. But that doesn't give us license to be lax or lazy. It means that when we do fall, we rise more quickly, through an understanding of the spiritual nature of God as power and light.

I think it is important to ask the Father to give us the things we need, and I believe it is essential to use the power of thanksgiving when asking for the things we want. Everybody needs something, whether material or spiritual. I'm sure God would be surprised if somebody came to Him and did not ask for something. But as Jesus said, we must ask *believing*. When you need something, go to your loving Father *expecting* that He will give it to you. Don't beg, half-heartedly hoping that maybe, if He is in a good mood, He might give you what you ask for someday. A prayer of petition, by itself, can become an obstacle if it enforces the mind with the belief that you are lacking something. So when you have a need, approach the infinite and all-pervading spirit of kindness as a beloved son or daughter of God, regardless of how unworthy you *think* you are. In a mystical sense, all of us are sons and daughters of God. So when you need help of any kind—whether physical, emotional, financial, or whatever—begin by giving thanks that the miracle is *already achieved*. Don't wait until God proves Himself by dropping the package on your doorstep before you give thanks. That's being very stingy with your faith, *and* with your gratitude! Say thank you *before* the change comes about, *before* the healing happens, and *before* the uplifting of your consciousness takes place.

Now, you know, a miracle may not materialize in just the way you think it should, and you would be very wise not to spend a lot of time telling God how to do it. He can handle things much better than you can. Some of us (being the dear and simple souls we are) forget what we have been taught by the great masters, and we think that we've got to tell God how to do things. We think we have to tell God where the money is supposed to come from, when the healing should occur, who the person should be, and how the situation should turn out. Don't trouble yourself with that, and don't carry around the baggage of uncertainty, resistance, and doubt. You don't need any of that, because the infinite consciousness of God residing everywhere, but most especially within the temple of your being, is aware of you and knows your name. The loving God knows exactly what you need, and He knows how to bring it about in the simplest and most efficient way.

Now, we've been *told* that this is so. Jesus the Christ reiterated it a thousand times. But as the centuries have rolled by, we have become less and less interested in accepting the simple and direct word of God. Jesus said that it is the Father's good pleasure to fulfill every right desire of your heart. He said that as a son or daughter of God, and heir of heaven, you have divine rights and privileges. You are not required to suffer and struggle, wanting but never receiving, because you've been told you are a sinner, and you think you don't deserve. Hogwash! Relax your struggle and *let* divine consciousness fulfill your heart's desires. Lean upon the sustaining Infinite and *expect* a positive outcome.

As many of you know, I had a church in San Francisco for twenty-two years called "A Metaphysical Design for Living." On my pulpit I displayed a little sign that was beautifully crafted and given to me by a dear Christian mystic. The plaque was inscribed with gold letters that read, *"Expect a Miracle."* That was many years ago. Nowadays we see that phrase everywhere. You know, so many people plead and cry and pray for something, but inwardly they don't believe their prayer is heard or expect that it will be answered. I often wish I could really know how God feels when people pray to Him for something, while in their hearts they believe they will never have it. As soon as they ask for something, they hesitate and silently utter to themselves, *"Well, I'm asking God for this, but I don't really think I'm going to get it. I've done this, and that, and everything else wrong; and I don't think I'm worthy to have what I want."* Well, if you're going to wait till you're perfectly worthy, you might have to wait a long time!

The invincible force of the Holy Spirit operates in ways we can never imagine; and if we will only let go and let God, our miracles will truly come about. If we would only take God at His word! If we would only believe that He wants to take care of us and give us the kingdom of expanded awareness: the kingdom of Heaven! His very nature is love, and His powers are more real and tangible than anything you can conceive of in the material world. You say you have prayed, you have asked, but your answers don't come? Well, you cannot successfully pray for one thing while holding its opposite in your mind. You cannot say, "Dear Lord, please bring me a loving partner—*even though I* **know** *nobody wants me because I'm too old, too fat, too poor, and unattractive."* Hold in your mind the fulfillment of the wish as if it is already accomplished now. It doesn't help to be filled with anxiety and worry about how your miracle is going to come about. Let that go, and leave it up to the Bestower of wealth and well being. If you go around thinking negative thoughts and feeling bad about yourself and everybody else, don't be surprised if you develop some kind of illness or begin to be plagued by all sorts of problems and disharmonies. You do have a choice, you know. Life is full of options. Isn't it wonderful that we have so many choices open to us? Life's possibilities are unlimited.

It is by our thinking that we structure all our tomorrows. You can make your life something positive and beautiful, or you can make it a bummer. When you choose to be positive by developing an unassailable faith in goodness, you will find that life's journey will be much more beautiful. Don't let the little obstacles of life turn into gigantic hurdles. See them as a summons to turn within, for it is there that you will find fresh ideas and peaceful resolutions. It's like finding a pebble in your shoe. At first it irritates. After awhile, your feet begin to hurt so much that you have trouble walking. Finally, you can't move at all. Well, you don't need any stones to impede your onward march toward total liberation. You must learn to perceive beyond the realm of the five senses and look past the appearance of sin and suffering to the higher spiritual reality of goodness, ever-expanding life, and God's endless love. With unlimited spiritual consciousness, not with the limitations of the senses, you perceive the eternal and immortal truths that heal and transform in ways that are nothing less than miraculous.

Miracles of healing and transformation are available to us today, just as they were in the time of Jesus. In the same way that, two thousand years ago, the master worked his miracles along the byways of what we call the Holy Land, miracles of consciousness take place today within the souls of people everywhere. People have been changed, rejuvenated, uplifted, and even glorified to some degree, by taking refuge in the infinite river of grace, wherein they are raised from spiritual ignorance and indolence to a vital and positive faith.

It is difficult sometimes to maintain a positive faith and a feeling of gratitude, when every day on the news we are bombarded with startling and worrisome reports. When I see all those negative news flashes on television, I cannot but pause and give thanks for the fact that I have an abiding faith. Think what it would be like to go through these times with no faith at all. Wouldn't it be terrible if we had no spiritual resources?

I've met people who have no belief in God, and no faith whatsoever. They don't believe in prayer or divine power of any sort. They only believe in what they can nail down on the workshop bench, or in what the latest laboratory experiment has brought to bear on material science. Those who have no faith have very few resources. The intellect by itself won't do. I have known a number of brilliant intellectuals who had no faith at all. One of them said to me, "I wish I had your kind of faith, but I don't. I don't believe there is life after death, and I don't believe there is a power that hears or answers prayers." He told me that his life was terribly barren and that he was full of despair. Well, I can easily understand why such people lose heart and become depressed. They have no belief of any kind, and many of them have even lost faith in themselves.

So even if your faith isn't as rock solid as you would like it to be, give thanks to God that you do have some faith. And if you think you don't have enough, ask the Giver of faith to bless you with a little more. If you feel that your faith is a little shaky, do some spiritual reading on the side; and when you meditate, ask that your faith be revitalized. Ask that it be reborn in you as a vivid and powerful reality, just as it was when you were first introduced to the truths of your religion at your mother's knee. Recall the feeling you had as a child when you had an open and trusting heart, and revisit the intimate conversations you had with your Heavenly Father as you gazed into the boundless skies. Let yourself be renewed by the changing of your mind, and remember that God has given you the power of choice. You can be miserable and wish there were more unhappy people in the world so you could be miserable with them, or you can *decide* to be happy. You can choose to have a positive outlook on life, or a negative one. You can choose to develop spiritual consciousness to perceive God, both within and beyond His creation, or you can remain in the limited realm of the senses and struggle to comprehend the material world.

The parks of London used to have a tradition—I don't know if they still do—of allowing people to stand up on a box and speak out about the issues of the day, or anything else that was on their mind. It was a kind of pop-off valve for people, a way for them to ventilate their emotions or present their ideas publicly. You could hear all kinds of wild theories, including some outrageous notions of religion.

One day a Jesuit priest was walking through the park when he came upon an atheist standing on a soapbox, shaking his fists and thundering against God. The man accusingly proclaimed, "There is no God; it is all imagination! This whole universe is nothing but happenstance!" The good Jesuit had been listening to this tirade for a while when the speaker noticed his collar and immediately singled him out. "Ah, ha! It's monsters like you, Jesuit, who are taking money from people under false pretenses! You are nothing but a religious fiend, going around preying on innocent people! You know there is no God. It's all just happenstance!"

The priest listened quietly for a few moments, and then, looking at the man, he took out his watch. He said, "Say, brother, do you see this watch? I tell you that the wheels, the cogs, the springs, and the hands of this watch all come together by themselves, by happenstance, to tick off the seconds, minutes, and hours of the day." Well, of course, everybody roared with laughter. When they quieted down, the Jesuit said, "Such is the orderliness of God's creation, from endless space unto the smallest subatomic particles. Can you tell me, young man, that these intricate systems and myriad life patterns all came together by chance? Of course not, not any more than my watch gathered itself from the winds and became a reliable timepiece." The atheist was pretty well shaken by that, so he picked up his soapbox and ran off somewhere to think it over.

Now, there are people who try to impress others with their negative materialistic philosophy, but it's hard to understand how anybody can be an atheist amid the beauty, orderliness, and love that pervades and upholds nature. The splendor of the flowers and trees, the grandeur of the mountains, the wonder of planting and harvesting cycles, along with countless other miracles of life that take place across time on this planet earth, are a triumph of creation. All this, you see, is God's smile. So when you see these marvels of nature, take hold of them and bring them into your consciousness, and then give thanks. This is what is meant by giving thanks as praise—praising God for His beautiful creation—and giving thanks for the gift of life.

Master Jesus, through the example of his life, showed us how to become perfect by turning away from that which is negative and addressing that which is positive. Always work to change the negative into love, and always change darkness into light, because light is just another word for God. When you have light in the center of your consciousness, then those things you were unable to grapple with before become patently clear. Now, that doesn't mean you will never have a trial. It doesn't mean you will never have an illness. And it certainly doesn't mean that a white-winged cherub will swoop down and sprinkle rose petals along your path every day. That isn't the way it's supposed to be. We're supposed to grow by flexing our spiritual muscles, through the tension that creates heat. Heat creates sparks. Sparks create light. Light is one with God; and so are we, as we work and grow in the classroom of the earth experience. It is our duty to learn our lessons gradually and thoroughly as we dance through this great drama of life.

Throughout his life, Christ showed his concern for us in so many ways, but perhaps the most touching is the care he took to satisfy the simplest and most prosaic needs of mankind. In the Lord's Prayer, Jesus says, *"Give us this day our daily bread."* (Matt. 6:11.) You can hardly get more basic than bread. And yet today, with our growing knowledge, technology, and philosophic sophistication, mankind needs something much greater and deeper than physical bread. Our needs may seem greater today, but in fulfilling them, we must take the same attitude Jesus did when he spoke to his Father. We must remember that the same perpetual stream of good that flowed through Jesus flows through us today. The beloved Son of God said, *"Give us this day our daily bread."* He didn't beg, "Oh please, Father, if you could just spare me a little crumb. *Please,* oh *please* just give me some bread." No, Jesus knew himself to be a true son and heir of heaven, so he asked like a son would ask a loving father, *expecting* to be given bread. A lot of people are afraid to do that. They think it's too audacious, or not quite proper. If you really believed what Jesus said, namely that you are sons and daughters of a loving God and heirs of heaven, then you would stand tall and walk confidently toward the Father and ask Him to give you what you rightly need; and you would expect to receive it. Then you would thank Him for the care He has shown you, and for His never-ending abundance. So do that, and give thanks that you have what you need now, no matter what your need is. Then you will see that this wondrous power really works. Don't worry about *how* it works.

In chapter twelve of Luke we are told, *"Take no thought for your life, what ye shall eat; neither for the body, what ye shall put on."* (Luke 12:22.) Well, it's awfully hard to take no thought when you lose your job, when your child needs an operation, or when the price of gas continues to rise. But God is mindful of His own. He never fails to answer our prayers, even though He sometimes answers them in ways we don't understand. He will always deliver an answer to your prayer, but it may not come in the way you think it should, or in accordance with your timetable. And though you may not like the way God answers your prayer, it is always for your ultimate good. For example, by enduring a challenging or arduous situation for a certain period of time, you may grow spiritually. You may discover a strength and sense of determination you never knew you had—and through your fortitude, you may gain courage, wisdom, and compassion. By persistently dealing with a difficult problem, your development might actually be accelerated. Eventually you will come to understand that what you have been given to do is in itself the answer to your prayer. Ultimately you will claim your freedom. Then those things that once gripped your mortal body and mind will begin to drift away. They must leave, you see, because they are not part of your true identity. They are not part of the higher reality of the Christ spirit.

And so, dear friends, throughout this Thanksgiving week, let us remember the beauty of God. And let us give thanks for our bountiful planet earth. I just returned from Washington, D.C., where the trees were ablaze with orange, yellow, and red colors. They were just gorgeous. Soon the leaves will fall off and become part of the replenishing earth carpet. In the spring there will be a complete rebirth, and a total renewal will take place. If you stop and think about it, the cycles of nature are nothing less than miraculous. Every autumn, tiny little seeds are scattered about by the wind, and pretty soon spring comes along and gorgeous flowers start popping up all over your garden. We sort of take that for granted, but we really shouldn't. So, as you go about the activities of this week, stop for a moment here and there to draw in the pure loveliness of the flowers and other beauties of nature, for they are a sweet smile of God. When you get up in the morning take a moment to watch the sunrise, and in the evening, pause to drink in the sunset.

You, too, are constantly being renewed, right down to the cellular level. You can recharge and revitalize not only your physical body but your whole life, as you learn to ask confidently for what you need. And then relax, let go, and *expect* your miracle. Now, some people say, "Maybe miracles happen to other people, but that's because they have more faith than I do." Well, that's not exactly true. People who have no faith at all have gone to holy shrines and have been healed.

Now, I don't think miracles are popping up on every street corner, but I do think that those who lean upon the sustaining Infinite find that even the transformation within their consciousness is a miracle. I'm sure you all remember the famous healer, Kathryn Kuhlman. She was really a wonderful lady. I corresponded with her for years, and I sat with her six different times, both here in San Francisco and in Los Angeles. Though countless miracles took place in her presence, she never claimed to heal anybody herself. That was the secret of her success. She was totally non-egocentric about her work, and she said: "It is marvelous to see the wonderful physical healings that take place under the power of the Holy Spirit. However, even more wonderful than the physical healings, great though they are, is the transformation of consciousness in those people who feel the touch and inspiration of divine power." I did quite a bit of research on Kathryn Kuhlman and her ministry. Nearly every person she touched was healed in some way, and they all went away giving thanks because God had blessed them through her.

I think spiritual healing is a wonderful thing and I'm very interested in it. It was perhaps the most powerful of all aspects of the early Christian movement, and there is no reason that it should not be so today. Don't say, "Well, of course, that was when Jesus was physically on earth." Jesus, the reflection of the Christ consciousness, came on earth for all people and all generations. In every era, people are healed when they reach out in receptivity and touch the hem of Truth's garment. Jesus commended the faith of such people. He was wonderfully compassionate, and he was a marvelous psychologist. He realized that some people had no faith at all. So what did he do? He engaged them in some tangible action in order to stir up their faith. For the blind man who had no faith, he mixed spittle and mud and touched his eyes with it; and the man saw. Now, obviously, the mud didn't do it. Jesus knew that because the blind man was so full of doubt, he needed to feel that something concrete was being done for him. Jesus told another person to go and bathe in a certain pool, that his leprosy would leave. Then he told the man to go and show himself to the priest. And so it was, again and again, that miracles came about. Christ could have touched these people and healed them instantly, but in their limited understanding, they needed something material and practical. That healing power, dear friends, is as immense and available today as it was in the time of our Lord, but we have to come into attunement with it. We do that through daily meditation and prayer.

I'm sure you all meditate . You must keep your appointment with God every day! How else are you going to hear the "still small voice"? When you meditate, remember to allow at least a little time to giving thanks for this marvelous planet on which you live. As I said, giving thanks is a form of praise; so as you come into the vibration of God's ultimate and omnipresent good during your meditation, do as the great David did when he sang his wonderful Psalm: *"O give thanks unto the LORD; for he is good: for his mercy endureth for ever."*

No matter what is happening in your life, give thanks that it will soon be improved. Then you will become spiritually invincible. By attuning yourself to the consciousness of wholeness, wellness, and harmony, you become one with that dynamic source of all power, which is God. Now, don't think that I am standing up here speaking from an ivory tower about a lot of nonsense. Don't let the "doubting Thomas" in you say that this is just a waste of time or that it hasn't any truth. Not at all. It doesn't matter how bad things have been in the past, or what kind of change you are looking for in your life, your personal world can be transformed by nourishing the fire of thanksgiving as praise.

There are thousands of case histories of people who have been lifted up from the most depressing aspects of life. People who were living with literally nothing—enduring the most deplorable physical, financial, emotional and mental conditions—have been totally transformed by the positive radiance of faith. So don't wait until next Thanksgiving to operate on the wavelength of gratitude. Get in tune with it now and practice it all during the year, even when those little things happen that occasionally make you feel that life is a bummer.

Why would you want to cart around those heavy burdens? Let them go. Just toss them aside and refuse to carry them with you. I've known people who go around every day carrying a five hundred pound backpack filled with thirty years of regrets, hatred, self-condemnation, shame, grudges, guilt, resentments, and sorrow. What a heavy load that is! Holding on to all those grievances is a sure way to close yourself off from the divine radiance that roots out evil and heals all ills. You block the flow of joy and well being when you constantly rehearse the memory that somebody did this or that to you—somebody said something cruel—your lover rejected you—the supermarket cheated you—the bigwig passed you over for that raise—your best friend betrayed you—your mother or father was toxic in one way or another. . . . For heaven's sake, *let all that go!* Clear the decks, and begin to bring about newness of life through the uplifting and transforming power of gratitude. Anchor your soul in the awareness that God is the ever available, ever present, invincible force of good.

It's important, as we discussed today, to give thanks not just for the amazing miracles of healing, but even for the littlest things in life. Give thanks that you are well and that you have a roof over your head. But most of all be thankful for the gift of life, and for the ability to know that God *is*. As you endlessly pursue the love of God and the service of your fellow man, you become very much a part of what religion is all about. For *religio* means to bind back to the first cause: to become one with God. Then you can stand as a good citizen in the court of the world and acknowledge a supreme and all-pervading power divine. Give thanks that through the simple act of prayer you can feel that divine attunement, which transforms the ordinary mortal into something very nearly divine. And have the decency to give thanks to God: the origin and soul of all things.

So, dear friends, Thanksgiving week is your week for expressing gratitude. This is your week for giving thanks for your home, for good food, for loving friends and neighbors, for peace of mind, and for the deep realization that *"the Lord is good, and his mercy endureth for ever."* I hope you will have a wonderful Thanksgiving, and I hope this year will give you a thousand new things to be thankful for. God bless you all. *Amen.*

I Will Lift Up My Eyes (Kathryn Kuhlman)

Heritage House Presbyterian Chapel, San Francisco, CA
January 31, 1981

Good morning, dear friends. Today we read from Psalm 121: *"I will lift up my eyes to the hills, from whence cometh my help."* As students in the classroom of the earth experience, we can never hear these assurances often enough. With repetition these great spiritual truths are impressed upon the inner nature of our being and thus become part of our spiritual consciousness. Then, when trials and tribulations come, as they do from time to time, we will know *from whence cometh our help.*

Now, what does it mean: *"I will lift up my eyes to the hills?"* Does it mean that you should lift up your physical eyes to the hills? Perhaps, but I think what is implied here is spiritual elevation and a conscious identification with the all-pervading truth, love, mercy, and healing power, which *is* God.

As Saint Paul said, we humans live at the basic, ground level of consciousness, and we see only dimly. When a dear one passes away, we say, "Oh, poor Mr. So and So is gone; he has fled from our view." In our limited vision he has indeed fled from our physical sight. But Christ promised us that there is no death. Saint Paul said that when we leave this physical plane and enter the next expression of life, we do so clad in a body made of finer stuff, a body made of light, and we retain an ongoing consciousness of our individual being. So, even though we may not yet see clearly the vast and unending life that is promised us, it is important for us to commit to the daily practice of turning our eyes upward to the hills of elevated and expanded consciousness, from whence cometh our help. Let us do this especially during those times of difficulties and stress.

It is so easy to move away from these beautiful teachings that most of us were raised on. We have to be reminded to practice them and apply them in our day-to-day lives. We have to practice beginning each day with a fresh excitement, and a sense of play about life. Taken this way, life is more enjoyable and meaningful. Now, of course, not every day is going to be beautiful. Sometimes there are floods or droughts, earthquakes or fires. Dreadful things do come upon us, and we wonder, "How can all this be happening?" Here in California, for example, we recently experienced the devastation of severe flash floods. Many people had to stand by helplessly as they watched their $400,000 homes slowly slide down the hills into ruin. Things like that are indeed very hard to bear. And while all of these people were deeply affected by their material loss, some of them came to the realization that material things are just that, *material* and therefore impermanent. Only that which is brought about in the temple of our consciousness can sustain us in the here and now, and in the hereafter.

Every day we are bombarded with bulletins of catastrophes, and daily our newspapers deliver photographic commentary on the ravages of different wars. It is natural for us to fret about these things. We're inclined to say, "Oh, isn't that awful. Isn't that terrible." Well, I tell you, the only way to deal with these things is to follow the advice that a friend of mine gave me way back in 1937. At that time I was working with a very fine gentleman in a government office, and there were a lot of dramatic things going on in our world. Being the outgoing emotional type, I often liked to jump up on my high horse and rant about the need to get things changed. This man observed all the anxiety I was taxing myself with, so he said, "Look, young man, when you see a troubling situation, ask yourself this question: 'Is there anything I can do about it?' There are only two answers: yes or no. If the answer is yes, go ahead and do everything you can. If the answer is no, let it pass. If you carry something within you that you can do nothing about, it becomes a great burden to your soul. That kind of burden, you see, eventually weighs down and crushes what should be an exuberant and wonderful life. You don't need that kind of pressure on your soul."

That was the best advice I'd ever been given, and it remains so to this day. When challenges and difficulties come along, dear friends, ask yourself the same question. If there is something you can do about a situation or a problem, then by all means do it. If there is nothing you can do, let it go and free your heart of any unnecessary burden. The important thing in every contest is to know whether to act or to let it pass.

Now, some things can be helped only through prayer. I have great faith in the power of prayer. I have experienced the working of wonders through people who possessed great faith. I have also observed miracles in the offices of spiritual practitioners, nuns, priests, yogis, rabbis, and housewives, and on several occasions I witnessed undeniable healings during the public services conducted by great healers such as Kathryn Kuhlman. All of these people possessed a profound faith, and they inspired that sense of belief and expectancy in the people who came to them for help. Their faith and attunement with divine power was so dynamic that definite and verifiable physiological changes actually took place.

Prayer is dynamic; within prayer there is a great invisible power. When combined with a positive outlook, this power can dramatically affect changes in every area of your life. It doesn't matter how old you are, things can still change. It is never too late to be renewed by the changing of your mind. Change your mind from worry, doubt, and fear, and begin to lean consciously upon the sustaining Infinite. Lift your eyes to the hills and realize that help is on the way. And, most importantly, cultivate a deep and unshakable certainty that there is absolutely nowhere you can go where God is not. When you have developed that kind of confidence and conviction your whole life is certain to change for the good because the inharmonies of worry, fear, doubt, and unwellness simply do not belong to the realm of God's omnipresent good. When you attune to God's realm everything that is *not* a part of that realm must be transformed to that which *is* a part of it. Then you will experience for yourself the wonder and transformative mystery of divine love and healing.

Dr. Alexis Carrel was born in 1873 and died in 1944. He was a medical doctor, scientific researcher, and Nobel laureate who helped to develop the pump which made heart bypass surgery possible. Carrel was a confirmed agnostic in 1902 when he visited the healing shrines at Lourdes in France. What he experienced in Lourdes was so powerful that it brought about his conversion and he became a devout Catholic. God is infinite and all-pervading consciousness, and every one of us can touch into this Christ power and be healed, whether we are Catholic, Buddhist, Hindu, or Baptist. On the train to Lourdes, Carrel happened to be seated near a young woman who was very ill. Her name was Marie Bailly. She was twenty-three years old and dying of tubercular peritonitis. Doctors in Lyon had refused to operate on her because they didn't think she would survive the procedure.

Dr. Carrel observed her closely throughout the night and it was his medical judgment that her condition was hopeless. As this young woman was being carried off the train up to the grotto, she was literally dying. Her stomach was terribly swollen and full of tumors. She had not been able to keep any food down for at least five months, and she was desperately weak. After waiting a long time in line, she was taken to the grotto where she was washed three times with holy water. They were getting ready to dunk her in one of the baths when Dr. Carrel shouted, "Oh, no, don't do that! You cannot do that! She has a terrible fever, and the bath is icy cold; these waters will kill her!" Well, they dunked her anyhow—and by four o'clock that afternoon she was well. She slept beautifully that night, and the following morning she got up, dressed herself, and began eating and talking to people as if she had never been sick. Two days later she boarded the train by herself and went back to Lyons, where she continued to improve day by day until she was completely healed.

Dr. Carrel was so stunned by what he saw at Lourdes that when he went home he began to delve deeply into the questions that medical science has not been able to answer, into what science does *not* know. The result of his research was a marvelous book that he called *Man, the Unknown*. In it, he concluded that the extraordinary facets of human consciousness and personality engender a kind of atmosphere in which the miraculous becomes almost ordinary.

Now, as a young doctor, Carrel was taking a big chance to write such things that were so far outside of standard medical thought. He could have been branded as some sort of fanatic and been thrown right out of the profession. But somehow, by the intensity of his sincerity and the power of his intellect, people upheld their respect for him. Carrel eventually became a renowned medical scientist and his work has influenced healing professionals all over the world. As an older man at the twilight of his scientific investigations, he wrote a couple of other little books. One of them was called *Journey to Lourdes*. In it, he said that one can be healed even if he or she has no faith. He said that it is enough just to be *near* someone who is filled with the living presence and power of God.

Remember the marvelous healings that occurred during the early Christian movement? Thousands of people were inspired by the words of the apostles who walked with Christ, and countless miracles took place. People were inspired and open to receiving that power of the living Christ. As Dr. Carrel said, just by being near someone who is so attuned we can pick up the extraordinary vitality of their living faith. Carrel writes of one instance in which a person with very little faith was kneeling next to someone who had enormous faith. Somehow, through the mystical power of prayer, a miraculous healing was brought forth in both the believer *and* the doubter. That magical quality and spiritual essence of divine communion seems to communicate itself in a subtle way, and very often miraculous healings do occur. In *Journey to Lourdes*, Carrel writes that he actually saw cancerous tissue disappear before his eyes. He called it an instantaneous healing. He said, "I know this is medically impossible, but I saw it happen."

Now, these are beautiful and wonderful stories, and they should encourage us because they are happening today, not two thousand years ago in the time of Christ. We must remember that miracles are still going on today. They didn't end when the Master Jesus left planet earth. Remember, Christ said that even though he would no longer be visible to our physical sight, we could do the same things he did if we believed in him. So people who have tremendous faith in the healing power of the Holy Spirit and who dedicate their lives to working with Spirit are able to transform and totally liberate people from all manner of physical, mental, emotional, and spiritual inharmonies. In the presence of these healers of immense faith and power countless people, including medical doctors, have been cured from so-called incurable diseases.

When you have a powerful faith you can really change things, and if things seem to be impossible according to medical science or other worldly information, don't let that disturb you too much. We love and respect our doctors. Most of them are wonderful people, and we couldn't do without them. On the other hand, they are *practicing* from their limited knowledge; according to that incomplete knowledge they sometimes tell us that no healing is possible. When spiritual healing takes place and a patient does get well these physicians cannot understand how it happened. So, while we respect the scientific knowledge of our medical doctors, we must understand that their knowledge is imperfect and incomplete. Even as we allow ourselves to be helped by them, let us never accept a diagnosis of doom. Instead, let us turn toward the unlimited healing power of God, for Whom there are no incurable diseases and no problems too difficult to solve.

When I was a young man I had polio in my right foot. The doctor said, "You'll never walk without a crutch; never." I said, "Balderdash! I'm not going to buy that." I always was a rebel. . . So after awhile I threw away the crutch and the doctor said, "You'll never walk without a cane." (I had a big sturdy cane that I carried with me at the time.) And again I said, "Bull feathers!" (or something stronger!) and threw away the cane. Now, even though medical science said I shouldn't be walking, I've been doing pretty well all these years without a crutch or a cane. I had my seventy-fourth birthday last week and I'm still running around quite capably on my own.*

Some of you in this congregation are much older than I am, and much wiser, too. Many of you have been around the block more times that I know anything about, but I can still tell you this: the great and living power of conscious identification with God through the act of prayer is literally invincible when it is structured in such a way that you literally *expect* a miracle. Now, if I hadn't expected to walk again, I wouldn't be walking. But I decided that I was not going to accept the materialistic dogma of defeat. Instead, I was going to elevate my consciousness and *lift my spiritual eyes to the hills from whence cometh my help,* my sustenance, my joy, my peace, and my power. All of these things come from the upliftment of consciousness.

It is very important that we practice uplifting our individual consciousness, and then apply it on a larger scale. Why not address your consciousness to something of a national or global nature? If you're

*This talk was given in 1981. John Laurence left the body in 2003 at the age of ninety-five.

going to ask for a miracle, it might as well include the whole world. Why stop at the borders of our country? Let's not be pikers when asking for miracles.

Now, I can almost hear you thinking, "Well, it's one thing if you've got something wrong with your foot, and through divine determination you are able to throw away your cane and walk on your own, but it's quite another thing to have an affect on the whole world." If you are tempted to feel very small and helpless, saying, "Oh, I could never do anything about *that*," realize than you *can*. You can do this much: you can give the divine energy of your prayerful reaching out, and in this way your single prayer becomes an enormous dynamo for change in the world.

Imagine the incredible power that such spiritual light would engender if thousands of people were to apply that energy for good on this planet. Nothing less than a total world shift would take place. When vast numbers of people together hold thoughts of love and then send that focused energy to a difficult and negative situation, the effect is phenomenal. What was once called impossible becomes entirely possible. This is not some sort of Pollyanna propaganda. For those who think something is impossible, it is. But everything is possible if we train ourselves and build our faith and thought power. Faith brings to us a sense of attunement to God, and a certainty that He is always there with enough power to bring about the divine state of goodness, wellness, harmony, and abundance, which is our natural state.

Faith is the most marvelous gift, and if you think you don't have enough of it, ask for more. You know, God appreciates it when you ask for deeper faith and enhanced spiritual awareness. So, if you feel that your faith is a little weak, then talk to the all-pervading and all-loving One and ask for an increase in the eternal flow of mountain-moving faith. By lending that energy to the happy aspects of life and by withholding it from the negative, you not only help to improve things in your own life, but you also become a force for improving things on a larger scale.

Every day I address myself to a positive approach to life. During my daily meditations I give thanks for an ongoing, happy approach to life, because I think we have to make a statement of faith. Now, I realize that not every day is going to be filled with dancing and singing. There will be days when life presents little problems. But if you have already given yourself to a positive approach to life, when problems do arise you will take the option of being positive, rather than slipping into the valley of negativity, darkness, and unhappiness. So make your statement of faith and *"Choose you this day whom ye will serve."* (Josh. 24:15.) Are you going to choose the dark or the light, the negative or the positive?

So many of us say, "I wish I had lived in the time of Jesus; I would have known him, I would have been a great disciple." Well, you don't know; you might not have known him at all. It has taken some of us a very long time to understand what the Christ spirit is really all about. But now that you do know the Christ spirit you must direct yourself each and every day to the positivity and the joy that *is* his spirit. Smile a little bit every day, and even if you don't like some people, be nice to them anyhow, because Jesus said, *"By this shall all men [and women] know that ye are my disciples, [namely] that you love one another."* Loving one another just means treating other people as you would like to be treated. Then you are fulfilling the law and the prophets, for this is the alpha and omega, the beginning and the end, the true teaching and message of the Christ Spirit of love. (John 13:34-35.)

I'm going to end my talk today by reading a little poem that was given to me by a gentleman I'm very fond of, Tom Torrington. He is a very refined man who is always impeccably dressed and groomed, and he is always very polite to everyone. He is a seasoned opera singer with a wonderful voice, and he sings like a young Italian tenor. He is also a proficient and talented pianist, and he can play anything you name in any key you want. He just turned ninety-two and yet he still runs around like a schoolboy. I was worried about him when I heard that, during his daily walk through the neighborhood the other day, he was hit by a car. He had just stepped off the curb and was about to cross the street when a car came sailing through a red light and hit him. He was knocked over onto the curb and had to be taken to the hospital in an ambulance. But, guess what? The next day he was up singing and dancing in his studio, as cheerful as ever.

Mr. Torrington is a wonderful example of someone who operates with a firm and positive approach to life, and that's what keeps him so young and vibrantly alive. He is very playful and I feel like a kid when I'm with him. I'm no spring chicken, but next to this ninety-two-year-old I'm a mere whippersnapper of seventy-four! The other day we were talking about how singing brings such a wonderful upliftment of spirit, when he spontaneously recited this poem:

"A song is no song till you sing it,
The bell is no bell till you ring it.
And love in your heart wasn't put there to stay;
Love isn't love till you give it away."

After he recited this little poem, he wrote it down on a piece of paper and gave it to me because I liked it so much. I don't know if he composed it or if he got it somewhere,* but to Tom Torrington, that's the way life is. It reminds me of how good old Walter Cronkite used to end his nightly news programs. He would always say, "And that's the way it is." You have a lot to do with the way life is for you by your choice to be positive or negative. It's as simple as that.

I think God wants us to be positive because, unless we ourselves are lifted up in our hearts and elevated to a higher position where we can express our spiritual consciousness, we cannot help others. Can a person lying in the street with only five cents in his pocket give you a thousand dollars? If you have no spiritual resources how are you ever going to give counsel and healing energy to others? Think of all the talented individuals who possess extraordinary gifts of art and intellect, who are completely destroyed because they cannot have what they want. They don't know how to get what they want and they are devoid of spiritual power simply because they will not listen to the principles which Jesus and the saints have taught so clearly.

What is it that these spiritual masters have been trying to teach us? They have all told us, very simply and directly, that in order to live with ease and harmony, with good health, abundance, and enduring love, we must lift ourselves out of the dark realm of ignorance and impossibility into the consciousness of light and wisdom and the perception of all possibility.

And so, dear friends, make the decision today that you are going to renew yourself again and again and that you are going to begin each day with fresh and vibrant thoughts. Begin each day with inventive ideas and say yes to living fully, holding nothing back, as though you are going to live forever. For in truth, we do live eternally in the omnipresent, infinite life of God. So let us meditate on Psalm 121 throughout this coming week: *"I will lift up my eyes to the hills, from whence cometh my help,"* and

---

*The poem was an adaptation from *The Sound of Music's* "You Are Sixteen (Reprise)" by Oscar Hammerstein.

let us pray thankfully every day that we know from whence cometh our good. Let us always remember to lift up our consciousness to the endless realms of our heavenly Father, from whence cometh our help—from whence cometh all good and all love. And remember, love is not really love until you give it away. Thank you. *Amen.*

Practicing the Presence (Brother Laurence)

Unity Temple, San Francisco, CA
February 28, 1982

Today I am going to talk about practicing the presence. The presence of what? you may ask. The presence of God; what else? No matter where you are, and no matter what happens to you, God is always there. You cannot go where God is not. He is infinite, eternal, and all-pervading. And He lives especially within the temple of your heart.

The word "heaven" is a literal translation of the Greek word *Oranos*, which means "expanded awareness." So don't look up in your attic, and don't look down in the basement to find the Kingdom of Heaven. Don't go anywhere; because heaven resides right here in the very midst of you, in the very temple of your being.

When I came in this morning, I met your pastor and had a few brief words with her. As we spoke, she spontaneously said, "Well, John, we know that all is in D.O. All is in 'Divine Order'." She didn't have to stop and think about what she was going to say. She didn't have to get out a book and thumb through it, searching for something meaningful to quote—scratching her head and saying, "Now, let's see, I wonder what it says here in this book." No, those beautiful words just popped right out of the fullness of her heart. Why? Because in every moment she is attuned to the Christ consciousness, and she prays without ceasing.

That's the attitude of ongoing prayer Saint Paul meant when he wrote, "Pray without ceasing." (1 Thess. 5:17.) See, when Saint Paul said to pray without ceasing, he didn't necessarily mean "on your knees." You don't have to kneel down on the cold hard floor for seventeen hours every day in order to "pray without ceasing." You can live a joyful, active, and fruitful life, and still practice the presence of the Lord. You can be inwardly attuned to the consciousness of God in every moment of your life, no matter what you are doing in your outer world. You can walk around downtown, shop at the Macy's "White Sale," visit with friends, clean your house, or sit at your computer—and still, you can be praying inwardly.

When Saint Paul wrote that we should pray without ceasing, he did not mean that we have to struggle and suffer. He simply meant that we should constantly cultivate a positive, joyful, peaceful, and loving attitude of mind and heart. That is what is meant by continuous, ceaseless, ongoing prayer. Believe me, when you cultivate that attitude, your life will be much better and brighter.

Today there is so much negativity all around us. It is natural and understandable that people sometimes get a little shaky about what they hear on the radio and what they read in the paper. Are you going to let those things dim the Light Eternal, which dwells within you as a burning candle of positivity and joy? Are you going to snuff out the Light that can bring to the darkness what it needs so much? I can hear some of you mentally declaring, "No way!" But that's exactly what you do every time you give energy to fear, lack, self-doubt, and condemnation—to resentment, and a thousand other negative thoughts.

You do have alternatives, you know; you can *decide* to be happy or not. If you want, you can go around being cynical and depressed, repeating every disapproving and disparaging word that pops up in your mind, or that you hear on the radio or TV. Every day you hear people talking like that on the bus or on the subway, but you don't have to join them. Don't give any energy to that kind of pessimistic talk, because if you do, you will soon be so filled with negative energy that you will lose your balance and your joy, and then your immune system will break down. The first thing you know, you'll come down with the flu or a nasty cold, and you might even develop some sort of chronic illness that is much more serious and hard to shake off.

We must be very careful what we say out loud, what we express in our actions, and even what we allow into our thoughts and inner conversations. *"Out of the fullness of the heart the mouth speaketh."* (Matt. 12:34.) We have to remember that what is in the heart, and what is expressed on the lips, will become reality in the universe of our being. Keeping this in mind, we will speak only that which we want to create in our experience. So throughout our work-a-day week, let us be mindful of this wonderful gift: this marvelous power that is our divine creative consciousness.

Always remember that no matter where you are or what your circumstances, and no matter how grim things may look, you have the choice either to accept the negativity that inevitably arises, or to reverse the coin and determine that you will be positive and uplifted, by practicing the presence of the omnipresent Christ consciousness. Affirm within yourself, this very day, that you are not going to remain in the old habits of attitude that have kept you separate from the love, the confidence, and the joy that you know are your true self. Decide right now to carry the torch of luminosity as an ambassador for God, and a true son or daughter of the Christ light. Remember who you really are, and claim your divine inheritance so that you may walk through the world with your head held high. Then, like the saints and sages throughout the corridors of time, you will realize the divine nature of your true being.

And so, dear friends, let us learn to insulate ourselves from the negativity that seems to pervade our world these days. We want to keep that flame of divine continuity burning within the temple of the self, so that we may make our contribution to the Christ light. In the world, this flame is the light of compassion and understanding. It is a positive approach, and it is an ongoing love for all. When we continually practice the presence of God, the whole of our consciousness is leavened and changed. It is uplifted and transmuted by a kind of divine alchemy: that which was once base metal is suddenly transmuted into pure gold.

Let us turn now to a wonderful soul who lived in the seventeenth century. Brother Lawrence was a simple Frenchman who, at the age of eighteen, went to war, fought, was wounded, and finally returned home. This young man had developed a profound spiritual consciousness; both his mother and father were deeply religious people who encouraged devotion in him. Somewhere along the line, Lawrence determined that he would become a monk. He was quite unlettered, so he didn't aspire to the priesthood. But he knew he could become a brother in the Carmelite Order, and so he did.

Brother Lawrence entered the monastery, began reading books, and conscientiously followed the disciplines. He said his prayers diligently, knelt properly at Mass, and did all the other duties that were given to him throughout his early religious training; and still he remained unchanged. But one day he was suddenly awakened to the divine breath of heaven, which came like a radiance into his consciousness. In his utter simplicity, Brother Lawrence began to realize that religion was indeed nothing more, and nothing less, than practicing the presence and power of God immanent within his own being. Brother Lawrence became a holy man, a saint. And he wrote a number of letters to the faithful, as well as to people outside the Church, encouraging them to pray and meditate, and concern themselves with the dynamics of practicing the presence of God. He knew from his own experience that this was a sure, simple, and direct way to God Himself.

Brother Lawrence realized that in order to know God, you don't need a PhD from Harvard, a Doctor of Divinity, or anything but a sincere and devotional attitude of mind and heart. I'm sure that if Brother Lawrence walked in here today he would say something about D.O., because he was always thinking about Divine Order. He knew that it pervaded the universe, from the smallest aspect of matter to the most vast and infinite galaxies. He knew God as both transcendental and immanent, and totally available within the hearts of even the most simple, loving, and devout souls who practice constantly, and remind themselves of the Lord's presence and supreme power and love.

You know, over the years I've given a number of talks about Brother Lawrence. In fact, just the other day I came across a program from a talk I gave about him in 1950 at the old Metaphysical Library in San Francisco. Last night I was reading a little book about Brother Lawrence, and again I was moved by what this simple little saint from the seventeenth century had to say. His words are so beautiful, so uncomplicated, and so applicable today. He points out in his little book* that while practicing the presence of God is *simple*, it is not the easiest thing in the world to do. Why? Because too many people get all mixed up and distracted by theology and doctrine. They are so busy intellectualizing about God, trying to fit God into some encapsulated formula that they can hold and maneuver into their limited understanding, that they miss finding and really knowing Him.

For the most part, the men and women who became saints were not theologians. There are some exceptions, of course; but by and large, they

---

* *Practicing the Presence of God* by Brother Lawrence.

were people who found God, not in some theology, but in the very midst of their own hearts. They were not wondering how many angels could stand on the head of a pin.

In the Middle Ages that was a big thing, you know. You weren't in the group if you were not speculating on such things. Today, fortunately, we don't care. I'm sure that if we wanted to count them, we would find an infinite number of angels, but we're interested in something immensely more practical and down-to-earth. If there is anything to metaphysics, it is that it is immediately practical and down-to-earth. Look at how many people today have come to realize that everything they ever sought in their lives was already right there inside them, but they just didn't know it.

Most of us believe in these teachings, but Christ and the saints *knew*—and this knowing allowed them to exercise that miracle-working power: the wondrous force of love, through which all manner of diseases are healed. As I say so often, the difference between a knowing saint and a believer is simply a matter of degree. Let us give thanks that we are capable of becoming, like the saints and sages, intimate knowers of God.

Jesus always gave thanks *before* he brought about a miracle. He said, *"my Father is greater than I,"* (John 14: 28.) and *"[the Father] doeth the works,"* (John 14: 10.) So take that in, and don't forget to give thanks in advance when you need or want something. Give thanks all the time, even if you're not asking for anything. Give thanks to God that you are alive and aware, that you can know Him.

It's easy to give thanks *after* a miracle, but if you say, "Father, I thank Thee *in advance*, for I *know* that You always hear me," you begin to awaken within yourself an awareness of the presence and transforming power of God. It's right there inside you, and you *can* access it. You don't have to cross your fingers, mutter unpronounceable foreign syllables, choke on incense fumes, or sit all day with your eyeballs crossed and your legs locked in a pretzel. You don't have to reach up and stretch out to the far-flung galaxies in hopes that maybe someday, somehow, your prayer signal will be clear enough that God will respond. You need not go anywhere to find Him except within the silent temple of your own being.

If we will take Christ at his word and move in a more positive and loving direction, we *will* grow and become. We can find no better or simpler technique for realizing our true self than daily working with the consciousness of God and practicing His presence. *Practicing* the presence means doing it very often at first, then most of the time, and eventually all the time. It means that when you see something very ugly happening in the world, you remind yourself that God is there too. Even in the midst of the seeming unlovely, God *is*; for God is in everything, and everyone. So let us always choose to see the good in every situation.

That reminds me of a story of two men who were leaving a railroad station one night in Chicago. There was a long line of people waiting for taxis, and since the two men were going in the same direction, they decided to share a cab. Like most railroad stations, this one was situated in a poor and rather run-down part of town. It was raining as the two men came out of the train station, and the rain accentuated the gray and dreary atmosphere of the scene. But as they were waiting for their taxi, the rain cleared and the sky opened up a little.

The two men got into the cab, and as they drove away, one man looked around, snarled, and said, "Oh, isn't it awful! Just look at the mess this rain has caused, with all that mud everywhere, that smelly garbage, and those homeless bums!" But the other man leaned out the window and looked up at the heavens. With a gleam in his eye and a smile spreading across his face, he said, "Yes, but look how the rain has washed the sky. And see how many stars are out tonight. How beautiful."

See how differently those two men looked at their world? You do have a choice: You can look down into the gutter, or you can look up at the stars. It's up to you. God does not coerce you. He gives you intelligence to find your way, and He gives you His grace to help you grow and become.

In one of his essays the great mystic Emerson said, "Nerve thyself with incessant aspirations." Now, Emerson was really quite a guy, and we would be well-advised to listen to him. So when you practice the presence of God every day, many times throughout the day, say a few little aspirations of love for the supreme and all-pervading spirit of Goodness. It's very important and very healthy to do that.

In ancient Rome there was another man, Cicero, who said, "Ye who suffer, know that ye suffer from yourselves." He wasn't a religious man; but just as King Solomon wrote centuries earlier, Cicero understood that, *"As a man thinketh in his heart, so is he."* (Prov. 23:7.) Again and again, down through the centuries and right into modern times, we are reminded of the immense and limitless divine power which is already there, right within us. So give thanks for whatever it is you want and need. Are you the man or woman you would really like to be? If not, visualize the person you would like to become, and send that image and feeling out into your universe. Having been conceived and born within the self—the temple of light and the presence of God—it must return to you as a living reality.

And so, dear friends, in these days of turbulence and uncertainty, let us turn with a deep devotion to our spiritual principles. As we carry out the many and varied daily activities in our business and home life, let us constantly remind ourselves that God is in the midst of it all. Brother Lawrence said that practicing the presence of God isn't easy, and it doesn't come about in three days; it takes a little time. But, he promises, if you are persistent, the rewards are enormous. It won't be too long before you will begin to see the power and majesty of God in every aspect of life—within, without, and all around you—but always as the One, the Same, the Eternal.

All of us here truly believe that God *is*, and we know that He is to be found not only in His manifest universe, but most especially within the humble temple of our own being. Repeat this, recite it, and chant it every day. Make it a practice to utter many little aspirations to remind yourself that God is everywhere. Then you will not only *believe* it, you will come to *know* it as a living truth that will fill your heart with peace and allow you to rest easy amid the changes and challenges of your life.

In India, the mystics and saints have made a great study of the power of sound and the spoken word. They have cultivated a profound knowledge of the spiritual dynamics of repeating seed syllables that imprint one's consciousness with the presence and power of God. They have something called *mantra yoga* in which the aspirant repeats mentally or out loud, through prayer or chant, the name of God as *AUM* (or *OM*). That's how they "practice the presence" in the East, and that's their wonderful religion. In the West we can do it too, by saying over and over (as Saint Francis did), "My God and my all." Say it, chant it, sing it, and dance it. Then you will transcend your difficulties. You will find liberation from all the ills that have beset you, and you will see yourself as that which you truly are supposed to be—or rather, that which you truly *are*.

Thank you, dear friends. May you practice the presence and truly realize the power of the Christ Light within the very center of your heart. Call forth that radiance and let it blossom in you; let it strengthen you, heal you, and love you. Take it with you, use it every day, and *know* that you can never be where God is not; for He is everywhere. Thank you. *Amen.*

A Modern Mystic (Padre Pio)

Celtic Catholic Church, San Francisco, CA
October 24, 1982

Today I'm going to talk about Padre Pio, a Franciscan friar who is internationally known as the greatest modern mystic in the Catholic world.* I first learned about Padre Pio in 1919. A wonderful Franciscan priest, who was my spiritual director at the time, had gone to San Giovanni Rotondo to meet the great mystic. During Holy Mass, my director observed Padre Pio's stigmata and received his blessing. One of our friars had also been close to Padre Pio, serving his Masses, so I had a little insight into this great man's spiritual power long before he became world famous.

Now, I'm sure you all know that the stigmata were the wounds of Christ, which were inflicted on his hands, side, and feet as he was crucified. Over sixty Catholic saints have borne these same wounds, or stigmata, on their own bodies. The first of these saints, and probably the most well known of them, was the beloved Francis of Assisi. His wounds were seen by the leaders of the Roman Church and by countless ordinary people in his time.

Francis is universally revered because he dazzled everyone by the simplicity of his message. He had a great yearning for contact with the Lord Christ, and he achieved such a degree of identification with Jesus that he literally walked around as a living crucifix. That was eight hundred years ago. It is therefore interesting, I think, for us to realize that during this modern age, there lived in our midst a man who was very much like Saint Francis: a great devotee of Christ, who also bore the wounds of the stigmata.

Padre Pio was a Franciscan Capuchin. You may know that the Franciscan Order is divided into three parts. The so-called Black Franciscans are those who have a rather mitigated rule; the Friars of the Observance wear the brown robe and cowl; and the Capuchins who, because they were living as hermits in the mountains at the time of the change of habit and didn't know anything about it, continue even today to go around in the original simple gray habit and cowl attached to their tunics.

---

* Padre Pio died in 1968.

I am reminded of a story about these three habits of the Franciscans. On the seven hundred and fiftieth anniversary of the death of Saint Francis, a beautiful painting of him was commissioned by the Franciscan leaders in Rome. The artist duly arrived on the scene and was met by one of the superiors of the Black Franciscans, who said, "Of course, you're going to paint Saint Francis in our black habit." The next day came the Friars of the Observance, and they said, "No, no. You must paint Francis in our brown habit, with the cowl and the white cord tied around his waist, just as he wore it." A little later, a Capuchin leader came in and said, "Oh no, sir. You must paint him in the Capuchin robe, because that is the one Francis *really* wore." Well, what could this poor artist do? He painted a beautiful picture of Francis lying on his bed, and on the door of his little cell hung *all three of the habits—he* could make his choice!

So now we turn back to Padre Pio. Our modern world, so filled with noise and stressed by materialism, is the last place we would expect to find a mystic with the extraordinary qualities of a saint like Francis. Like others before him, Padre Pio's love of Christ was so great that he too was visited by the phenomenon of the stigmata. Francesco Forgione (as Padre Pio was named at birth) was born on May 25, 1887 into a family of simple, illiterate farmers in Pietrelcina, a small town in southern Italy. His parents were very devout. The whole family attended Mass every day and recited the rosary every night; and even though his father and mother could not read, they memorized the holy scriptures and told Bible stories to their children.

From a young age, Francesco was set apart from the other boys by his peculiar devotional nature. He claimed to have visions, ecstasies, and divine discourse; and soon the priests began to realize that here was someone who was destined to serve the Church. Francesco was attracted by the nearby Capuchins. And so, when he was just fifteen, he applied and was accepted as a novitiate at Morcone, where he completed his program of study and became an ordained priest at the age of twenty-three.

Padre Pio's health was rather poor, and it was strongly suspected that he had tuberculosis. He was given permission to live with his family, but he still wore his Capuchin habit. In 1916 Padre Pio moved to the Capuchin Friary in San Giovanni Rotondo. He remained in that community, with seven other friars, until his death. In 1918 he received the stigmata.

Now, we are told that one day Saint Francis was out in the countryside, kneeling in prayer, when suddenly he beheld a crucified angel floating in mid-air. At that moment he received the stigmata. Well, Padre Pio's story is similar. He was saying his thanksgiving in the choir stalls after Mass, and was deeply absorbed in the most extraordinary meditation and love, when all of a sudden, without warning, he let out a piercing cry and fell to the floor. One of the friars ran in and discovered Padre Pio lying unconscious in a pool of blood. Pio was bleeding profusely from his hands, side, and feet. As dramatic as that event was, it was only the beginning of this poor man's incredible difficulties.

Many people had heard about the stigmata of Francis and other saints in centuries past, but now they had a live stigmatic right there in San Giovanni Rotondo, the little Capuchin monastery in a mountainous region of southern Italy. Eight hundred years ago, people marveled at the stigmata of Saint Francis and left him alone, but this was the modern day. Padre Pio's superiors had to bring in all the medical boys to see what they could do about his stigmata. Doctors, archbishops, and cardinals were called in, and they applied all possible nostrums, healing devices, and whatnot. All they really ended up doing was torturing this poor man, irritating the excruciating marks on his body and making them worse.

Finally, after a number of doctors from Rome and other places had come to observe him, and attempted to ameliorate his condition, his superiors said, "Heavens, leave this poor man alone—you're torturing him." So he was left untreated and unhealed. He was told only to wear a small pair of mittens with holes in the fingertips so that he could perform his duties. The marks of the stigmata were not visible except when he said Mass. During that time he often took off the mittens.

You see, those marks upon this holy man were clearly indicative of the tremendous devotion he had toward his divine guru, the Lord Christ. Padre Pio's meditations were so intense, and his identification with Christ so personal, so vivid and ecstatic, that the manifestation of stigmata took place and remained until his death.

Not infrequently, Padre Pio's simple everyday Mass (not a special and more elaborate high Mass) would take about an hour and a half. He would start the Pater Noster and suddenly go into an ecstatic state, wherein he remained absolutely immoveable for twenty or twenty-five minutes. Then he would come back into body consciousness and proceed with the Mass as designed.

Many people observed Padre Pio levitating during Mass, and they would gather around him as closely as they could in order to observe this extraordinary occurrence. Now, Christians aren't the only people who have been seen levitating. Some Hindu yogis levitate, and there are reports of people in many other religious traditions who have also been found levitating and manifesting all sorts of supernatural phenomena. All these things, you see, are a beautiful confirmation of the living truth that comes into the lives of true devotees of God. Such occurrences are evidence that we are more than our physical bodies, and that we are made in the image and likeness of God; for God is spirit.

Like so many other great mystics, Padre Pio had several marvelous "gifts of the spirit." If you study mystical theology, you may know about a phenomenon called *bilocation*. Bilocation is the extraordinary gift whereby a holy person may be seen quite vividly in more than one place at a time. Padre Pio was known to have visited people in various parts of the world, without ever leaving his little room in San Giovanni Rotondo. It is recorded, for example, that he attended the canonization of Saint Thérèse of Lisieux (affectionately called "the Little Flower"), and that he was greeted by many people at the Vatican and Saint Peter's Cathedral at that time. Normally he avoided shaking hands as much as possible—as you can imagine, because of the painful wounds on his hands—but it is said that on this occasion he greeted people at the Vatican warmly, and had cordial conversation with them—although he never physically left San Giovanni Rotondo! That is the gift of bilocation.

Everybody that came in contact with this saintly man was greatly uplifted. People were enchanted by the charisma of someone who daily experienced the living presence and divine consciousness of the Christ within.

I'll tell you a little story about a television newscaster in Nevada who was very devoted to Padre Pio. One day, when he was relaxing in his big leather chair, the newsman thought to himself, "It's been quite a while since I've seen Padre Pio. I must get over to visit him as soon as I can." That evening he went to the studio to give his newscast, and as he walked through the door, he was struck by the most terrible headache he had ever had in his life. The pain was so intense that it was impossible for him to do the program. He had no replacement for the broadcast, and he was becoming quite distraught. He thought, "What shall I do?" This man was at the point of yelling for help, when the door opened—and in walked Padre Pio! (But remember, in that moment Padre Pio was still in San Giovanni Rotondo in southern Italy.) Pio looked at the man, blessed him, and disappeared. Just like that, he was gone. The man's headache also disappeared, and he was able to give a beautiful reading of the news.

When the program was finished, the newscaster went back to his office and sat down, leaning back in his big leather chair. Reflecting on what had just happened, he made up his mind that he wasn't going to mention it to anyone. You see, even after such a wonderful visitation and healing, this man was thinking, "Oh, it was probably just an hallucination. Padre Pio wasn't really here; it was probably just a symptom caused by the intense pain of my headache." So he didn't tell anyone about his experience. A few days later he said to himself, "I've really got to go see Padre Pio," and he did. They were having a nice little chat in San Giovanni Rotondo, when Padre Pio looked at this man rather piercingly and said, "Be careful of those hallucinations!"

People would come to Padre Pio's confessional to recount their wrongdoings and mistakes, and ask for his blessing. Now, Padre Pio was full of divine compassion and love, and his whole mission was to bring people to the merciful heavens with an incredible faith in the spirit of the Christ. However, he wanted you to be accountable for your actions and *in*actions, so that you would change and grow. If there was something you should have told him about in confession but didn't—such as the sins you committed long ago and had forgotten about—he would narrate them for you and remind you of what you had left out! He could sometimes come down heavily on those who tried to fool him. In all of these extraordinary instances, what Padre Pio was demonstrating was the spiritual gift of true *clairvoyance*, or "clear seeing."

One evening a good Dominican friar decided to put aside his religious habit and don ordinary slacks and a Hawaiian shirt so that he could go out into the crowd. After a while, the friar noticed that Padre Pio's eyes seemed to be following him everywhere he went, but he thought Pio's gaze was meant for someone else. Finally, Padre Pio called to him, "You there. Come forward." The young monk approached, and Padre Pio, with loving kindness in his voice, said, "Sir, why don't you go back and put on your Dominican habit. You look much better in it."

I could go on and on, telling you stories about Padre Pio's amazing clairvoyance and other spiritual gifts. Books have been filled with them, and many other books are filled with accounts of his divine healings. There are innumerable cases in which devastating illnesses have been completely cured, including several cases of people who were healed of total blindness. There was one young woman in Sicily* who was born without pupils in her eyes. She still doesn't have any pupils, but since visiting Padre Pio she is able to read with 20/20 vision. Now, put that in your hat and see what you can make of it!

While he was alive, Padre Pio worked all kinds of miracles. He healed countless people of spiritual, emotional, and physical problems; and he did it with total ease and a deep sense of humility. That is the hallmark of the truly great. He claimed nothing for himself. He simply recognized that he was an instrument through which God was expressing Himself. Though he is no longer living in a body on planet earth, Padre Pio continues to answer prayers and heal countless people, for he is an unobstructed channel for the divine love which flows uninterrupted to thirsty souls everywhere.

When Padre Pio passed away in 1968, his body was placed in a little church where people could come and pay their respects. It had been his custom every afternoon to appear on the balcony overlooking the courtyard, where groups of people from all over the world would assemble to receive his blessing. Very soon after his death, a strange thing happened. As he lay there in the casket, the marks of the stigmata began to disappear from his hands. After the funeral services were over, and after they had buried his physical body, everyone who was in the courtyard that day looked up to the window—and there stood Padre Pio with his white hair and beard, giving them his blessing, just as he had always done. Padre Pio exemplified the living truth of the holy scripture which asks, *"O death, where is thy sting?"* (1 Cor. 15:55.) Surely, it *"is swallowed up in victory."* (1 Cor. 15:54.)

In addition to clairvoyance, stigmata, and untold healings, there are at least one hundred recorded instances of Padre Pio's bilocations. There is a remarkable and well-documented incident of his bilocation that took place during World War II. Padre Pio had told a number of GI's exactly which places would be bombed, but he assured them that San Giovanni Rotondo would be safe. The German military had dumped munitions there, and the townspeople were very afraid that their little

* Gemma di Giorgi.

village would be a target. Pio said, "Don't worry, they will not bomb this area." But the Allied planes came anyway.

One pilot was guiding his plane directly toward San Giovanni Rotondo, preparing to bomb this munitions town, when to his utter astonishment he suddenly saw a Franciscan friar floating right in front of his windshield, holding up his hands in a forbidding gesture. The pilot thought he was hallucinating. He was so dumbfounded that he aborted the mission and went back to tell his superior about it. Now, as far as *materia medica* was concerned, this was merely a psychiatric episode— but San Giovanni Rotondo was not bombed! The pilot came back later and said, "I must see this holy man, this Padre Pio, with my own eyes. I want to know for sure that he is the man I met in mid-air, levitating and literally forbidding me to bomb his town." He did meet Padre Pio and found that he was, without any doubt, the man who had flown in front of his airplane, preventing him from destroying a town and killing thousands of innocent people.

As if all these spiritual gifts were not enough, divine Providence also bestowed upon Padre Pio the hallmark of many great devotees, namely the *"gift of perfume."* Perfume literally pervaded his being. Perfume exuded from the wounds of his hands, filled his tiny room, and followed him out onto the balcony. One of the doctors who visited him was so intrigued by this phenomenon that he saturated a piece of cloth with the blood from Padre Pio's wounds and took it back to Rome with him. There it pervaded the whole clinic like delicate incense. Sometimes the fragrance was like violets and sometimes like roses, but it always filled and overflowed his aura with the "odor of sanctity."

Padre Pio was a true and faithful devotee of the Lord Christ. I brought a little book with me today, and I'll pass it around so you can all have a look at it. In the front you will notice a simple photo of Padre Pio that was taken in 1918, when he received the stigmata. It shows the blood stains on the mittens that covered his hands. His immediate superior had ordered the photo to be taken, so Padre Pio obeyed, but he really didn't want anyone to see his wounds. Later on the Church authorities changed their minds, and he was ordered not to show the stigmata to anyone except medical people. Only during Mass could the public see them.

Padre Pio was a man of very simple habits. He ate very little, but he drank a bottle of beer every day. That didn't do anything to his sanctity at all. He was a rather stout and sturdy man, and he often fasted. One time, following a nine-day fast, he was weighed. When it was found that he had gained three pounds, he said to his superior with a chuckle, "I guess I'll have to eat more in order to reduce." Padre Pio had a wonderful sense of humor, and despite the constant agony of his stigmata, he radiated joy and divine love to all.

So, dear friends, today we've had a tiny glimpse of this marvelous modern mystic, Padre Pio. His whole life was a beautiful demonstration of the gifts of the Holy Spirit—which are an eternal reflection of the truth, the power, and the luminous love of the Christ. I hope you will read one of the many books written about Padre Pio and learn more about him, for he is truly one of the glorious sons of God, for whom the laws of common nature do not always apply. He is an inspiring example of what wonders can happen when we offer ourselves as vehicles for God's miracle-working power of love.

Padre Pio shows us the way to God through his constant attunement, daily prayer, and meditation. By following his example of simplicity, and his unshakable commitment to living for God, we will quickly realize the same Divine Love that poured through Padre Pio beginning to flow through us. As we give ourselves fully to God, He happily uses us as vehicles for the awakening and healing of others. So let us give all that we are joyfully, and without shyness or reserve. Let us give all of ourselves—our talents, our skills, our experiences, and especially our love and blessings—so that we may grow and become like Padre Pio, and all the other saints throughout the centuries who have loved the world with God's love.* Thank you. *Amen.*

A Bridge Between East and West (Paramhansa Yogananda)

7th Avenue Celtic Catholic Church, San Francisco, CA
July 11, 1982

Good morning, dear friends. Today I'd like to talk about the incomparable yogi and saint from India, Paramhansa Yogananda. We all know the story

---

* Padre Pio was canonized as a Catholic saint in 2002.

of the divine Christ Jesus, the great guru of the West. And we know that his teaching was essentially about devotion, unconditional love, and service. From time to time, the Lord of all the universes sends into the world an illumined soul who is a reflection and living example of all the things that Christ taught two thousand years ago. Paramhansa Yogananda was such a soul. He was truly a beacon of wisdom, inspiration, and God consciousness.

Yogananda came to America in 1920, sent here by the lofty Himalayan masters in India. His purpose was to build a bridge of understanding between Christianity and the wisdom of the East. On the passing of this great soul, Shankaracharya, the spiritual leader of millions in India, said of Yogananda, "Only occasionally does God bring into manifestation a human being who has all the attributes and qualities of Divinity." In other words, Yogananda was someone who took the Christ at his word when he said, *"All the things I have done you also can do, and greater things, because I go unto my Father."* (John 14:12.)

In 1933 I had the great good fortune to meet this holy man, Yogananda, whose *Autobiography of a Yogi* has enthralled readers from all over the globe, and transformed the lives of countless true seekers. I give you my word that meeting this spiritual giant was the turning point in my life. I had never met anyone who possessed such love, such power, such humility, joy, and spiritual dimension. Here was someone who had all these divine qualities, plus the marvelous paranormal gifts we read about in the holy scriptures.

Yogananda never made a show of his miraculous powers; and whenever he did something the uninitiated would call "supernatural," he always asked people to please keep it quiet. To the people for whom he did work miracles, he said exactly what Jesus said, *"Go, and tell no man,"* (Matt. 8:4, 16:20; Mark 1:44, 7:36, 8:30; Luke 5:14.) because he didn't want those miracles to attract individuals who were only interested in supernatural phenomena. He didn't want it to be a big ego thing.

There are three occasions I know of when the great Paramhansa, brought people back to life who had been pronounced clinically dead. He did this with great humility and love, but also with a kind of authority that was born of the indwelling presence of God. Remember that Jesus said, *"It is the Father within that doeth the works."* (John 14:10.)

On one occasion there were twelve people at Yogananda's table, and they each had a little mug. Yogananda went to the refrigerator and brought out a pitcher of carrot juice, and said, "I want all of you to have some refreshment." He filled all twelve mugs from this one little pitcher and put the rest back in the refrigerator. Only one person realized what the master had done, and that was a devotee named Bhaktananda, who was living at the Yogananda center at that time.

One of the outstanding attributes of Yogananda was his devotion to Jesus. He told us (and I believe him) that there were many occasions when, on the inner planes, he received direct, spoken instruction from the Christ.

We in the West are apt to distrust people from the Orient, saying, "Oh, they're a strange bunch of people. They see all sorts of visions because they've been out in the sun too long, with Turkish towels wrapped around their heads." Not so. The wisdom of India was blazing hundreds of years before the Christian era; and, as Yogananda pointed out so eloquently, most of the teachings we find in the Four Gospels of the Bible are to be found in almost identical terms in the Bhagavad Gita and the Upanishads (scriptures of ancient India). But, of course, we're apt to be a little haughty in our claim that ours is "the only true Church." God is not a Methodist, a Mormon, a Catholic, a Hindu, a Baptist, or a Buddhist. God is the all-pervading Light and Truth, which are to be found everywhere—and especially within the temple of your heart. This is one of the important truths Yogananda consciously and continuously emphasized in his teachings.

Yogananda was a marvelous and wonderful man. He was able to organize a myriad of projects and handle all the details with complete ease; and sometimes he accomplished his goals in the most astonishing ways. His autobiography has been translated into more than fourteen languages, and it has caused a spiritual revolution in the heart of every person who has read it. In *Autobiography of a Yogi*, you will find a spiritual superhuman at work—a consciousness filled with profound wisdom, surging love, and overwhelming humility. At the same time, with the simplicity of a trusting child, the master spoke to God as his Divine Mother. And so, dear friends, if you have not read that book, I urge you to get a copy and embark on the most fascinating and thrilling spiritual adventure of your life. I have known this wonderful man since 1933, and I am persuaded that his understanding and love of Christ will make you a better Christian.

A wonderful Jewish lady—a practicing psychologist—once came to me for advice; and I gave her a copy of Yogananda's autobiography, urging her to read it. When I first mentioned it to her, she wasn't interested. She was worried that she would have to abandon her Jewish heritage. I said, "No, of course not. By reading the life and teachings of this wisdom-filled guru, you'll be a better Jew, and you'll understand your scriptures with a kind of illumination that has never been brought to you before." She stuck the book in her purse.

When she got home to her apartment, she took out the book and threw it onto the coffee table, where it remained untouched for three days. Every evening she would come home from work and glance at it lying there. She was magnetized by Yogananda's photo on the cover, and by his big dark eyes which seemed to follow her, no matter which way she turned. On the third night, she picked up the book and said out loud (as if she were talking to Yogananda), "Okay, okay. I'll read it!" So she did.

Now, this woman was already blessed with many wonderful qualities; but, believe me, after reading the book, she was awakened and beautifully transformed. You won't find a more devoted lover of God in any religious tradition than the one she has become. So Yogananda is not just for those from the East. We are apt to forget that, though Jesus is the guru of the West, he came into incarnation in an oriental body. It strikes me as interesting that Yogananda came from the East too. People often say that the arresting beauty of his physical being reminds them of Christ.

Yogananda, a fully God-realized man, possessed an astounding divine intuition, which illumined and brought new significance to the Four Gospels. He unraveled and explained rather obscure biblical teachings so that Christians everywhere could finally understand their true meaning. He taught the omnipresence of good, and the divine nature of our true being.

This is also one of the most important teachings of Christ, who said, *"Know you not that you are gods?"* (John 10:34. "Is it not written in your law, I said, Ye are gods?") and *"The kingdom of God is within you."* (Luke 17:21.) But we haven't believed him. Jesus said that the kingdom of heaven—of expanded awareness—is *within* you; so you don't have to look for it anywhere else. If you look for it outside yourself, you're in big trouble. Jesus *knew* he was the Son of God; and he claimed that Son-ship for himself, and also for you. People down through the centuries have shied away from the true meaning of what Jesus taught because, whether they were from the West or the East, they were afraid they would have to change. They were afraid that they would have to be too good. Realize that, truly, you are sons and daughters of God, and heirs to the kingdom of heaven. When you accept this truth, deeply and totally, you no longer need to cling to the dogma of sectarianism. And you begin to take heart in the ecumenical spirit present in the scriptures of both the West and the East.

You know, when Christian missionaries first went to India, they thought, "Oh, we're going to have trouble with these Hindus. They have nine hundred and fifty gods." Well, that's not true. The Hindus have *one* God, with perhaps nine hundred and fifty names! *"God is called by a thousand names; and by a thousand ways He may be found: the One, the Same."* That is what Ramakrishna, the great saint and leader of the Vedanta movement, said. And it is interesting to see that, if you look closely, there is also a marvelous ecumenical thought in most of the utterances of the Christ.

Sometimes it is difficult for us to find the truth. In a hard aristocracy, those who had authority would dictate to you what was true and what was not true. I would rather have truth for authority than authority for truth. But, of course, how do you find truth? In the West, we pray in our churches and we do good works in the world; but few of us think about achieving the kind of consciousness that Yogananda and Christ possessed, with the divine intuitional knowing of God as our true Self. Within our various denominations of Christianity there is often a lot of opposition, each one claiming to be "the one and only true church." People growl and fight each other, claiming that if one hasn't been dunked in the baptismal bath the right way (or at least sprinkled properly), they are going to burn in hell for all eternity.

The man who founded the modern Baptist movement, Reverend John Smyth, was an Englishman who had first been an Anglican clergyman, and then became a reader and intellectual theorist. He began what has become one of the largest Protestant denominations in America: the Baptist Church. With a very strong emphasis on baptism, he insisted that people be totally submerged in the baptismal waters. However, Smyth himself was never dunked.

Among many so-called loving and religious people, there are often big battles over doctrine and the correct way to be baptized. Down through the ages, wars have been fought over these things. Of course, this is all contrary to what Jesus said: *"By this shall all men know that you are my disciples, namely that you love one another."* (John 13:35.) We really haven't learned to love too well on this planet, have we? No human situation is perfect, because it is human. Until we graduate from "the classroom of the earth experience" and go to the higher areas of eternal learning, we will always see things dimly and fall short in our love. Only when we realize and embody the divine consciousness, and understand that our true self is the Self of God, can we fully express perfect and unconditional love for everyone, regardless of our seeming differences.

Jesus, the great guru of the West, knew that it was God within him that did all the works. He knew that his little self was nothing, compared to the great God that dwelled within him. That's why he spoke so often about stepping aside and letting God run the show. Jesus was the repository of truths, and he always claimed that he was lesser than God. *"Of myself, I do nothing. It is the Father within that doeth the works."* (John 5:20, 14:10.) He reiterated that again and again, and yet he fully recognized the power of God within himself. Before he left his body, Jesus told his people, *"When I am gone, you who truly believe what I have taught you will be able to do the things that I have done, in my name."* (John 14:12.) Why? Because Jesus was an awakened Son of God. He was at the center of a tremendous spiritual power. He has made the same claim for you; so you don't have to run away saying, "Oh, I can't do it. It's too hard. I'll have to give up everything I enjoy. I'll have to work too hard, and meditate too long. I'll have to be too good." Nonsense. Accept Christ at his word, as Yogananda did. The teachings of Yogananda are simple, direct, and marvelously illuminated Christian teachings.

When he first came to America, Yogananda was invited to speak in churches all over the country. He often attended conferences where twenty or thirty ministers would sit around a large table. In those early days, he was quite green about what went on in the theological temples of great wisdom in the West. One minister got up and began howling, pounding his fists and splintering the pulpit, sending everybody to hell. Yogananda asked, "Who is that man?" "Oh, that's Doctor Smith; he's a Methodist." Then somebody else got up and declared that Doctor Smith was all wrong. *"This* is the way it is!" Yogananda again asked, "Who is that?" "Oh, that's Doctor Jones; he's an Episcopal." This went on and on, with one speaker after another. Finally, Yogananda looked bewildered and asked, "What is all this doctor business?" "Oh, when you get a doctorate in theological seminary, it's called a D.D., which stands for Doctor of Divinity." Yogananda replied, "I think I would rather call it Doctor of Delusion."

In America we have more than three hundred forms of Christianity, and it's sad to say that often the only thing they have in common is that each is "the only true church." So we have to get over that idea and realize that the only true church is *inside of you*. It isn't a building or an organization, or some sort of elite fraternity with a special pin you wear on your lapel that says Presbyterian, Baptist, Mormon, or Catholic. These denominations are all good, and they meet the spiritual needs of the people at that level; but to truly be one with Christ, you have to admit the *omnipresence* of good. You have to realize that the eternal and ongoing wisdom of God expresses itself in many facets throughout human consciousness, and therefore we must not sit in judgment or condemn anyone who may be expressing in a way different from ours.*

During the Middle Ages, eighty thousand people were brutally murdered because they displayed a certain degree of extra-sensory perception. They were arrested and treated horribly, subjected to ghastly tortures, and then burned at the stake as "witches." And yet there is no monk or nun, pastor or priest, who doesn't develop a high degree of sensitivity if they meditate on God long and deeply enough. Whether you like to call that being psychic or sensitive, it amounts to the same thing. It is intuitional guidance: a direct and positive knowledge, given

---

* Most Christians believe that Jesus was uniquely divine: the "only-begotten Son of God." Yogananda interprets that term differently, explaining that the "Son of God" is the omnipresent Christ consciousness, hidden throughout creation. Since it is omnipresent there cannot be another like it, which makes that consciousness unique ("only-begotten"). However, because it is omnipresent, it exists in all people, any of whom may realize that Christ consciousness and manifest it in their lives as Jesus did.

Furthermore, to quote from Swami Kriyananda's *Revelations of Christ: Proclaimed by Paramhansa Yogananda* (pp. 363-64): "Christians as a whole have failed fully to understand how very impersonal Jesus was in all his references to himself. When, by contrast, he seemed quite self-assertive, it was always while speaking of the divine Self—as, for instance, when he said, **'I am the way, the truth, and the life: no man cometh unto the Father, but by me.'** (John 14:6) His meaning, in such statements, was cosmic. His reference was to the omnipresent Christ consciousness, which alone was truly manifested through him."

by God. If you meditate daily and practice prayer, it is inevitable that you will awaken and enliven the dormant faculties of your inner divine self. Gradually, little by little, your connection deepens, and you begin to exhibit one after the other of the "gifts of the Spirit," as outlined in the Bible.

What is religion? The Latin root *religio* means "to bind back to the first cause." What is the first cause? God. We seem to forget sometimes that God is spirit. Many of us were brought up to believe that He is an old gentleman with a long gray beard and a bad temper, who spends His time hurling thunderbolts and punishments at His creation. I think this is a very blasphemous way to view God. God is Light. He is Love and Wisdom, and Supreme Good. There are endless attributes of Divinity, and countless words to describe Him. No matter what your level of evolution, the omniscient and all-pervading Spirit of God is all that you can comprehend or conceive—and much, much more. So let us not put God in a little box of mortal thinking, restricting the availability of His vast and omnipresent spirit to those chosen few who have been properly dunked and anointed by the rituals and dogmas of man. Does it really matter how many angels can stand on the head of a pin? Who cares? It matters a lot more how you treat your brothers and sisters, and how you treat the planet we call home. If we would only meditate on brotherhood and forget that we have different theologies, the world would be a much better place.

God knows what we need, and He delivers it to us in ways that are easy for us to recognize and receive. Mother Teresa of Calcutta says that God brings Himself to us in various disguises. God knew that people in America would be more apt to listen to a man who had a university degree, was very handsome, and possessed a magnetic personality and a great sense of humor. So He sent Yogananda to awaken the West to the omnipresence of good. The beauty, power, and light of this master from India was so stunning that sometimes people literally could not stay in the same room with him. Sometimes people would be consumed in flames of divine love as the master entered into *samadhi*, or complete absorption in God. They simply could not sustain such intense and exquisite love. It was so lofty and indescribable that people literally had to get out of the room; they were unable to stand it.

But Yogananda was infinitely compassionate. He told people that, spiritually, they should make haste—but not recklessly. You cannot run two hundred watts through a fifteen-watt bulb. You have to slowly and gradually build your capacity to receive the influx of divine power. It doesn't come like instant coffee or soup. It must grow, slowly but surely, through discipline and the daily practice of meditation and prayer. Look closely at the eyes of the Master Jesus, who lived among us two thousand years ago; and then peer into the eyes of Yogananda, a fully God-realized master who lived among us in modern times for over thirty years. In the eyes of Yogananda you will see the eyes of Jesus the Christ, and you will begin to see the same compassion and mercy of God.

This beloved prophet and teacher consciously left his body in 1952, just after he had finished addressing a large crowd in Los Angeles. Twenty years earlier he had told his leading disciple, "In 1952, before a large concourse of people including many notables from India, I will leave this body garment, speaking about my beloved India. It will be at the Biltmore Hotel in Los Angeles." It happened exactly as he had said it would. His talk was brief, only about ten minutes or so, and he finished it by reading from his poem, "My India." Then he raised his eyes upward and sank gently to the floor. His body was placed in an open casket at Forest Lawn Memorial Park from March 11 until March 27, 1952. During that time, no mold was visible, and there was no drying up of the body tissues. Yogananda's body was free of bacteria, and there was no sign of physical deterioration, even twenty days after his death. The mortuary director wrote a letter stating that Yogananda offered the most extraordinary case in his entire experience. This state is called "incorruptibility." It is the state of sanctity found only in the purest and most elevated saints.*

---

* The bodies of a number of Catholic saints were also found to be "incorrupt" after their passing. Although highly advanced, they themselves would have openly stated that they were not spiritual masters. Nevertheless, "incorruptibility," as John Laurence said, is a manifestation of divine purity. Therefore, if lesser saints have manifested this divine attribute, one can imagine that enlightened masters might do so as well.

Jesus said, "One is your master, even Christ." (Matt. 23:10) Paramhansa Yogananda explained this passage by saying that, to become a spiritual master, one must merge with the light of Christ consciousness at the spiritual eye located between the eyebrows— thus uniting oneself with the reflection of the motionless and infinite Spirit beyond creation (the "Heavenly Father"), that lies hidden behind every atom of creation (the "Son of God"). The proof of this high state is the ability to enter the breathless state at will. All other miraculous manifestations may hint at spiritual advancement, but are otherwise inconclusive. Jesus, Yogananda, and others throughout history have attained Christ consciousness, and therefore are truly "masters."

So, dear friends, I could go on talking about Yogananda all day. I urge you to read his *Autobiography of a Yogi* and get in touch with his magnificent spirit and love, which are available to all. Though he has passed from our sight, he is ever near and available to us because, as he said, "For those who think me near, I am near." Like God and Christ, Paramhansa Yogananda is only a thought away, beckoning us to awaken to the truth of our being in God. Thank you. *Amen.*

The Search (Paramhansa Yogananda)

Unity Temple, San Francisco, CA
March 28, 1982

Today we are going to talk about *the search*. The search for *what*? Well, everybody is searching for something. Some people are searching for love and others are searching for gold. Many are looking for honor and glory, while a few seek power and control. The governments of the world seek ever-new means of becoming superior and dominant. Each one is searching for information that will advance their own scientific achievements, both on earth and as they probe the far reaches of the cosmos.

This searching quality of humankind is inherent in our nature; it is a positive aspect in us that brings about all progress and evolution. Not much would happen if we did not have this natural curiosity and appetite to know more, to reach out and grasp an understanding of our universe. When we lend our consciousness to searching for truth it becomes, as it were, like a ship of light—a steady compass that helps us navigate the rough waters of misunderstanding. It steers us in the right direction, toward all that is essential and good in our lives. Otherwise, what would a search mean?

Now, there are myriad things we can search for. Down through the ages man has been in search of the Fountain of Youth, the elixir of life, and the philosopher's stone. Remember Ponce de León? He searched all over, looking for the path to rejuvenation and youthfulness for all people, including himself. But he failed to find it because he didn't look in the right place—the Fountain of Youth is not to be found amid the palm trees, waterfalls, coconuts, and beautiful climates of Florida or

Hawaii, but rather within the very depths of the self. See, heaven is a state of being that is free from all care; it is a state in which you are joyfully alive in the eternal NOW. In that state you are vibrantly alive with all the attributes of ever-new life.

Maybe you're not searching for the Fountain of Youth. Maybe, like a lot of people, you are seeking lost treasure. I was just reading an article in the paper this morning about some people who recently discovered a sunken ship that is said to contain a great deal of gold. They are organizing an underwater expedition into the depths of the ocean in order to search for the sunken treasure. Now, we often hear that money is the root of all evil, but in fact, the scriptures never said that. There is nothing wrong with gold. It is only the inordinate *love of gold* that is wrong. Money itself is a symbol of God's supply, and we should never say anything about money that we wouldn't say about God. For some people this is, at first, a rather startling statement; but when you begin to analyze it, it is a very true statement.

Money is part and parcel of the inexhaustible abundance that life continuously supplies. It is a representation of the infinite stream of good that flows to both the material and spiritual worlds. Gold, in itself, is neither good nor evil; it takes on the quality of the energy you bring to it.

Whatever you believe about money will be your experience with money—or *without* it. If you believe that money is the root of all evil, you will never allow yourself to enjoy having money because a part of you will feel that having money is wrong. If you feel guilty about having money, you will find some way to block the flow of it in your life. That's just one example. If you believe the supply of money is limited or dependent on a certain source, you will probably begin to hoard and hide your money. Your belief in lack and limitation will result in less money coming your way. If, on the other hand, you hold the belief that there is an *un*limited and steady flow of God's supply of all good things, including the supply of money, then you will accept a steady stream of money into your life. Like everything else, money is a thought form; what you think *about* money is what your experience *with* money will be. So never say anything about money that you wouldn't say about God.

There is, in every one of us, a natural desire to reach out and explore the world in which we live. There is also a natural urge for us to discover who we really are and why we are in this world. But, just as Ponce de León was looking in the wrong place for the Fountain of Youth, most people are looking *outside* the self for the meaning of life. They are seeking God in some far-flung, mysterious, galactic habitat of heaven. That's not where Christ told us to look. Jesus said, "the kingdom of heaven (expanded awareness) is within you." He recognized the limitation of our understanding, and so he spoke very clearly, in unmistakable words. He told us that whatever we are searching for, we will find it by looking *inside*.

When we are young we begin our search for meaning and fulfillment by looking to the outer world. But when we become a little more spiritually mature, we get down to the nitty-gritty of the search for true fulfillment. We seek the real meaning of life, and we begin to dig for the deeper aspects of our true, spiritual self.

Perhaps you are searching for a job or career, a partner in life, or an improvement in your health. All these desires and aspirations are noble and lovely aspects of a rich and full life on planet earth. But each of us is on a bigger quest. Whether you know it or not, your real search is for your true identity and heavenly consciousness. Our most significant search is for an understanding of the deeper aspects of the spiritual Self. That is the truest treasure, and it can only be found by digging deep within the vastness of inner space.

Last Monday we observed a rocket ship lifting off the ground and entering the range of space above earth's gravitational pull. It is awesome to observe such engineering and scientific know-how. It is almost magical to watch the precision with which these instruments can launch a satellite into outer space, orbit it around the earth, and then land it on a tiny point of the compass. We cannot help but marvel at such technology, and applaud those who search for ever-increasing knowledge of the universe.

It seems we are driven to search the cosmos—and search we *must*. We must seek to uncover the laws and mysteries of the universe. But, as wise as man is, and search though he might—finding first one and then another of the awesome manifestations of God's creative nature, and the laws thereof—he is nonetheless not able to discover the Author of the universe—the Lord, the Creator of those laws—anywhere, except within the Self. The grand project for each and every one of us is to make that great and noble search within. Therefore, let us make our search for God the greatest of all missions; let us take a daily expedition into inner space, and there, through deeper and deeper states of meditation, discover not the self of matter, but the Self of Spirit.

All mankind seems to be lifted up an octave when great discoveries are made, and when great triumphs of science take place. We all stand in awe of man's mind, and we marvel at the wondrous things he is capable of doing. But this is only an infinitesimal outer reflection of what man can do when he begins to send the rockets of his consciousness into inner space. All the saints and sages, prophets, mystics, and mahatmas throughout time have sought deeply within the temple of their being for a definite and tangible contact with the all-encompassing haven of heaven. It is possible for us to discover the same eternal truths that these great ones found.

Those who practice meditation live with the newness of each present moment. When we are young, we are carefree, flexible, and very playful. Youth-consciousness always looks for the fun in life, and it sees the light side of experience. A young mind looks for what is new and exciting, and never gets stuck in a rut. A child adapts to change very easily. Children are supple and pliable, both in their thinking and in their bodies. They are never rigid in their thinking. And children are very quick to forgive; they seldom hold grudges.

Not long ago I heard a tape of a lecture given by a psychotherapist in San Francisco. During her presentation she told a story about her five-year-old son who was, as usual, having some difficulty getting himself dressed and ready for kindergarten. He was dawdling, like he did every morning, completely fascinated by every toy and object in his room, and his mother thought he was taking way too much time to get ready to leave for school. This therapist was, like all single moms, under a great deal of stress. That day she was in a hurry to catch up to her busy schedule, and she became impatient with her son. She was anxious and annoyed, and without thinking of the impact her words might have on her sensitive five-year-old son, she spoke with irritation in her voice, *"Tommy, if you don't hurry up, I'm going to leave without you!"*

A few minutes later, she heard the sound of her son's heart-wrenching sobs and the gentle sniffling of his runny nose. She turned and saw her little boy standing in the doorway—still not completely dressed, with one shoe untied and the other dangling from his little hand. Great big tears were streaming down his tiny face. His mother knelt down in front of him and wiped away his tears. She asked, *"Honey, what's the matter?"*

Tommy looked right into his mother's eyes and, in-between his sniffles and sobs, his little voice cracked as he whimpered, *"Mommy, if you leave me, I will still love you."*

See how forgiving this little one was? Even if his mother didn't love him anymore, he would always love *her*. Of course, this lecturer-mom lightened up the story and said to her audience, "So then I threw another $50 into his therapy fund!" But, for those who are searching for the fountain of youth, let them "become as little children": carefree, happy, flexible, and forgiving. Let them remain ever young in spirit, for such is the life of God.

I do hope you meditate or contemplate a little every day. There are many kinds of meditation and many ways to meditate. Do what is easiest for you, but do it, and do it every day. Go within, for that is where you will find what you are really searching for. What you have been seeking has been there all along. You don't have to add anything; it is already there.

Now, suppose you want to rejuvenate yourself like Ponce de León did, only instead of trying to do it from the outside in, you're going to do it from the inside out. How will you go about it? Well, the first thing you need to do is make a firm commitment to yourself that you're going to admit no negativity whatsoever into your consciousness. As soon as a negative thought arises in your mind, you're going to banish it. If you find yourself looking in the mirror and thinking, "Oh no, I'm getting old. See how tired I look. Everything is sagging. I look just awful; and I know I'm going to look worse tomorrow," then you have to stop right there and change your mind. That kind of pessimistic consciousness cannot but beget a mass of wrinkles! Through the operation of spiritual law you *can* transform yourself; you can change from an ordinary being into an extraordinary being. Remember: the same power that animates the lives of great saints is also at work in *your* life. Take ahold of it and let it work for you, just as it works for those spiritual giants.

There was a saint from India who lived and taught in America from 1920 until his death in 1952. His name was *Paramahansa Yogananda*, and he was more Christian than most of us. I had the privilege of meeting him for the first time in 1933, and then again some years later. My last contact with him was via a letter he wrote to me a month before he consciously left the body.

Here was a man of absolute purity, total joy, utter humility, and youthful playfulness. He radiated divine love to everyone, without exception. As we say so often, love is just another name for God, and when people begin to fill their consciousness with the loving presence of God, they become such a beacon of light that everyone and everything that comes within their orbit feels the impact of that love. Those who met this saint from India felt that kind of transforming love.

Now, I happen to think Yogananda was more Christian than most of us because he *lived* the principles of Christian love. He built a bridge of understanding between Christianity and the eastern philosophies, and that was an invaluable attainment that continues to serve both East and West today. He came to this country as India's delegate to the Congress of Religious Liberals, which was held in Boston in 1920. Many of you have read his magnificent book, *Autobiography of a Yogi*. If you haven't read it, run out right now and get a copy. It is an unbelievable and magnificent spiritual adventure that is simply wrought with unparalleled divine love, wisdom, and inspiration. Yogananda tells each and every one of us that if we search diligently within for that "pearl of great price," we too will find the divine aspect of our being—that consciousness which is already there, waiting for us to awaken to its presence.

Some people have enormous charisma; it radiates through their personality and affects a whole roomful of people. We look at people like Yogananda, for example, and marvel at the divinity that is expressed in him. What a marvelous example he is for us. I like to speak of him occasionally during my talks because I met him in 1933 and have remained very devoted to him. I was initiated into his techniques for spiritual development, and I've tried to follow his example.

In 1932, he said to one of his closest disciples, "When I leave this body temple, it will be in Los Angeles. I will be speaking about my beloved India before a vast concourse of people, including several notables from India." Well, what do you know . . . in 1952, just twenty years later, he was at the Biltmore Hotel, giving an address to that very concourse of people. Before he spoke, he sat and ate with his guests, and when he was called upon to speak, he did so very eloquently and beautifully. He spoke a little slower than he ordinarily did, and his words carried great importance and sincerity.

When he finished his talk, he recited a beautiful poem called "My India." As soon as he had uttered the last words of that poem, he slipped gently to the floor, having consciously fled his body. Weeks later, when people came from India to conduct the final yogic rites over the body of the master, Yogananda's face was soft and looked just like someone alive. There was no sign of decay or deterioration in his body, nor was there any odor.

Such incorruptibility is a symbol of God's imprint on the life and teachings of this man of divine love and wisdom, whose search for the Infinite brought him into a blaze of divine realization and glory. In this marvelous mystic from India, we have an unparalleled example of what it means to search for ultimate union with God, and to fully realize what is meant by Christ's command: *"Be ye . . . perfect, even as your Father which is in heaven is perfect."* (Matt. 5:48.)

And so, dear friends, let us focus our search in the right direction. Let our consciousness steer us like a rocket ship of light, steady and assuredly, into inner space wherein we will find the answer to every question and the fulfillment of our hearts' every desire. Let our search take us not into the outer world of temporary form and fleeting pleasures, but inwardly to the kingdom of heaven, where we will discover and dwell in the all-pervading reality of inexhaustible goodness, love without condition, and perpetual, ongoing newness of life. Thank you. *Amen.*

PART THREE

SPIRITUAL TALKS OF 1982 / 83

Reverend John Laurence celebrating his birthday with his "second family," the Viscogliosis, in the San Francisco Bay Area

Praise Ye the Lord

Heritage House Presbyterian Chapel, San Francisco, CA
March 28, 1982

Some of the writings of the Old Testament are among the greatest lyric poems of the world. Let's take a look at Psalm 106: *"Praise ye the LORD. O give thanks unto the LORD; for he is good: for His mercy endureth for ever. Who can utter the mighty acts of the LORD? who can shew forth all his praise? Blessed are they that keep judgment, and he that doeth righteousness at all times. Remember me, O LORD, with the favour that thou bearest unto thy people."* (Ps. 106:1-4.) *Amen.*

The first lines of Psalm 106 are an important reminder for us to sing out from within our hearts in praise of the divine. Praising is a great way to keep in touch with the omnipresence of good. *"Praise ye the LORD. O give thanks unto the LORD."* Jesus is the best example of giving thanks and practicing remembrance. The Master went about the countryside, healing all manner of disharmonies and diseases, very often instantaneously. Before he ever touched anyone to heal them, he always gave thanks in this way: *"Father, I thank Thee, for I know that Thou dost always hear me."*

The Lord Christ has given us a perfect example of what our spiritual attitude should be toward the all-pervading heavenly Father. We must not think of God as remote or far away. We should follow the simple and direct example of Jesus and never miss a day in which we practice the good office of praising God. Every one of us has a hundred thousand reasons for giving thanks. We must never allow our spiritual vision to become distorted by the annoying or frustrating things that occasionally pop up in our experience. Nor should we allow our positive mental attitude to be manipulated by what we see on TV. Much of it is pure bunk anyway, put there to keep us in fear. Instead of fretting and fussing about what you are being told on TV, hold onto this: *"Let not your heart be troubled, neither be afraid, for the spirit of God dwelleth in you. Blessed are they that keep judgment, and he that doeth righteousness at all times."* (Here John Laurence combines excerpts from several biblical passages: John 14:27, 1 Cor. 3:16, and Ps. 106:3.)

"Blessed are they that keep judgment." What does that teach us? It teaches us to be balanced in our judgment and to cultivate a spiritual approach to everything in life. It means we should be balanced in the way

we look at the earth, the cosmos, and the Divine Creator of all things. Every speck that exists participates in this wonderful gift of life. Every creature that lives in the billions of universes beyond our comprehension is a piece of God and a part of this magnificent reflection of the Infinite.

Now, this planet we inhabit is the classroom of the earth experience. Through the divine drama of our daily experiences, we are learning and becoming. Sometimes we breeze through our lessons, and sometimes we struggle, but the whole play of life is designed to help us awaken and evolve. As we turn more toward the interior life, we begin to develop higher thoughts, and then our outer experiences naturally improve. As we meditate we notice that we are gradually able to transmute the unlovely aspects of our personality into the more refined qualities of the higher Self. We find that by keeping our daily appointment with God through deep meditation and prayer, we become more patient and kind, more generous and joyful. Every time you bring a spiritual approach to the little trials that come your way, you are flexing your spiritual muscles and growing closer to liberation. Ultimately, you will realize your true identity in peace and joy, but you can't expect to see rose petals strewn in front of your pathway every day. That sometimes happens, but not every day is going to be filled with ecstatic "ah-ha" moments. You can't have cake, shall we say, all the time. You have to eat a little ordinary bread and butter once in a while.

On occasion, we do encounter things that cast us down a bit, but we mustn't remain in that downhearted place. We can pull ourselves up by calling forth a sense of gratitude. When you wrap yourself in the spirit of gratitude, even if you think you are just pretending at first, you will very quickly be lifted out of the doldrums into a genuine feeling of appreciation for even the smallest things—but most especially for the mystery of your inner being. Only in the deepest and most silent aspect of the Self can you hear the voice of God, who is the source of all joy and the remedy for all distress. For this we should be full of gratitude.

Most of us in this congregation have been brought up in the Christian faith. We have in the Lord Christ the imperishable example of right living, right acting, and right thinking. Now, most of the world's religions, ancient or modern, Eastern or Western, all say pretty much the same thing when it comes to managing the mind. King Solomon wrote, *"As a man thinketh in his heart, so is he."* (Prov. 23:7.) In that statement, we realize that we have options in the way we think, and we have choices in what we do with our life. In any moment we have the possibility of good or ill health, happiness or unhappiness. If we wish to be happy and well, then we must plant seeds of happiness and wellness. We must not be like dry leaves in the wind, pushed around by every negative thought that arises.

We have to remember that no matter what happens in the physical world, there is a reigning power within, and that Divine Spirit can never be defeated. When you can expand your awareness of the body beyond its limitations and infirmities, you will see that you can enlarge your perception of life beyond all its limiting conditions. In your moments of quiet contemplation, see if you can move beyond the flesh into the domain of spiritual consciousness. That is the way to turn away from fear and instability and regain your equilibrium, no matter what is going on around you.

A lot of people go around thinking, "Oh, such terrible things are happening all over the world, and all around me too. I feel so depressed about everything." Well, you don't *have* to feel depressed about things. You can if you want to, but it won't help you or anybody else. It will only make things worse. You aren't going to look very nice either. And when people pass you in the corridor or on the street, they're going to say, "I wonder what's wrong with Mr. So-and-So. He looks so glum, as if he's carrying the whole world on his shoulders."

You know, the consciousness of your inner self is always reflected in your outer appearance. Your moods and energy are reflected in your aura, and your energy field affects other people around you. You don't have to look at yourself very much during the day, but other people *do* have to look at you. Wouldn't you rather reflect beautiful soul qualities than walk around with a sour face, radiating melancholy and gloom? People around you at work or in the supermarket have to endure that heaviness every time they look at you.

Now, I don't mean that you should run around wearing a silly grin and giggling all the time. Nor am I suggesting that you suppress your real feelings, or wear a phony mask of happiness if you truly feel unhappy. What I am saying is that inasmuch as God gives us trials, He also gives us options to deal with them. The wise person goes within the Self in both his joys and his sorrows. The choices people have made are written on their faces. Some people habitually reflect happiness and a kind of simple gladness. Even with all the ups and downs of life, they reflect a basic serenity within the temple of the Self. This state of calmness and confidence is available to all of us, no matter what our past experiences or present limitations. It comes about naturally through meditation and prayer work, through reading the scriptures, through being awake on the interior side of life, and by keeping the company of other positive and inspired people.

There is an old saying, "The coward dies a thousand times, but the hero dies but once." Fears and uncertainties are very real sometimes, and they certainly do bedevil a person who lacks courage and stamina. If you carry around feelings of apprehension, anger, doubt or distrust for a prolonged period of time, those feelings will most certainly bring about inharmonies in your life and dis-ease in your body. So whatever your spiritual roots or religious persuasions, know that you have options. If you are smart, you will choose a positive approach to your earthly experience.

Undeniably, we are living in one of the most precarious times in world history. We have the technological capability of annihilating our species and our entire planet. So if there was ever a time in history when we needed the inspiration of all that is beautiful, inspiring, uplifting, and optimistic, it is now.

Let me tell you about a wonderful old teacher and healer I knew many years ago. This man was probably the greatest healer I ever met in my life, and his entire life and ministry were filled with the divine office of selfless service and a dedication to the tireless work of helping, uplifting, and healing the constant stream of people who brought their heartaches, sufferings, and spiritual thirst to him.

How could he possibly do all that work if he didn't know the true Source of his energy and strength? See, we cannot give what we do not have. You cannot go to a pauper for a ten-thousand-dollar loan because he hasn't got it; he needs a loan himself. You have to go to the right Source for your material needs, and for spiritual wisdom.

This wonderful healer was a master of the Self, and he is a marvelous example for us. His life was beautiful in every respect, and his departure from the earth plane was a graduation into the astral, heaven world. He left the body literally at his own time and under conditions that he predicted himself. There was no death for him, you see, only a change of environment. Jesus constantly reiterated the cardinal principle of practically all religions that have ever been, and as far back as the Book of Job we hear it said, *"If a man die, shall he live again?"* (Job 14:14.)

The Bible gives us many marvelous examples of what to do, and also some very striking examples of what *not* to do, if we want to live a life of balance and serenity. The story of Job tells us something very important about the power of the mind and the power of choice. Of course, the picture of Job is a grim one. There he sits, covered in sores, profoundly dejected, and what does he say? *"All that I have feared has come upon me."* (Job 3:25.) Certainly his prospects looked pretty bleak, but good ol' Job had a lot to do with what happened to him. You see, he did have options. In a certain sense we all have the capacity to create circumstances within our own personal universe, as it were. If there is some area of your life you would like to improve, take a look at the options available to you, and then make a decision that from this day forth you are going to make a positive change in that area. Decide *right now* that you are going to put into practice what you have studied and learned, and what you know to be right.

I have been around for a long time, and many things have happened to me in these seventy-four years that have occasionally caused me to feel a little downcast. During those times, I have often been tempted to feel that I had a right to be annoyed or upset because someone had done some wrong to me. Now, I could have gone on with that kind of thinking, digging myself deeper and deeper into a hole, but I realized that I always have a choice in how I feel. When a troubling situation arises, I know I can harness the power of the mind; so I stop and say to myself, "Look, if I'm going to be miserable *besides* having this thing happen to me, then I'm losing on all fronts. I'm not going to let that happen. I'm going to change my mind right this minute and not let this experience floor me."

Nobody said it was going to be easy. How can we learn, how can we grow, without a little friction? See, friction makes heat, and heat makes fire: within, without, and all about. Sometimes a little friction helps us exercise the muscles of the mind. It helps purify us, and it helps us to learn and grow. Friction teaches us to make the right choices. The foremost choice for us is to enter the stillness of our own inner temple of God—for whenever we enter the luminosity of God's presence, all sorrow is destroyed, all broken places are mended, and we are lifted up to a clearer vision of our true self. The real task for all of us as we travel in this wonderful caravan of life is to surrender the little personal self to the divine and infinite Self, recognizing our oneness with the Father.

So, dear friends, let us remember to do those things that will help us realize our oneness with that divine Presence and Power. In the stillness of our own inner temple of the living God, let us always remember to give praise and thanks. Then, with the psalmist, we may joyfully sing: *"Praise ye the LORD. O give thanks unto the LORD; for he is good: for his mercy endureth for ever."* Thank you. *Amen.*

Thy Gentle Presence Silences All Fear

Heritage House Chapel, San Francisco, CA
April 25, 1982

Song text: *"Teach me, oh love, to know that Thou art power; that every hour Thou art there. Thy gentle presence silences all fear. Help me to know love healeth every ill. All hate and fear be stilled."*

Psalm 118 is so applicable to current world conditions that we might imagine it was written last week. *"O give thanks unto the LORD; for he is good: because his mercy endureth for ever. Let Israel now say, that his mercy [doth indeed] endureth for ever. Let the house of Aaron now say, that his mercy endureth for ever. Let them now that fear the LORD say, that his mercy endureth for ever."* These words are a call from David—the prophet, singer, and poet—for his people to remember the eternal and ongoing mercies of the Heavenly Father, no matter what is going on in their lives.

When we take a look at what is happening in the world today, it is easy to lose sight of the divine truth that God is nothing but goodness and that His mercy does endure forever. In many parts of the world today people are "rattling sabers, shouting, and making noises," as it were; but we must remember that transcending all this strife is the eternal and all-pervading Spirit of good, which is the power of God's eternal love and mercy. So let us keep that in mind as we read our morning paper and listen to the nightly news. Let us be aware that God is not far; He is very near at hand, and He is not responsible for any of the evils we see in our world today.

The question inevitably arises: Why does God allow the evils of war and destruction, starvation and disease, prejudice and inequity? How could a loving God permit the kind of domination and imbalance of wealth that has taken hold of this world?

There are enough resources on our planet to feed every person, and we have enough know-how and technology that not a single child should be suffering from lack. God offers us an infinite and never-ending supply of everything we need. He has nothing to do with the lack and injustice we see in the world today. People are suffering solely because of spiritual ignorance and the failure to love.

When you carry the belief that there is not enough for you, you become greedy. When you feel that you are powerless, you seek to control and dominate; and when you feel that you are separate from others, you become self-centered, selfish, and callously unaware of the needs of other people.

Our world is suffering the effects of flawed thinking and coldness of heart. It is not that *God* doesn't care; it is that *people* don't care. God has given us the gift of free choice—and along with that He has given us a magnificent creative power, a power to manifest our every thought. If we want peace in the world, we must change our thoughts and open our hearts to the fact that each and every person on this planet is a beloved spark of the Infinite, and as such, every person is entitled to the freedom and unlimited possibilities that are inherent in the very nature of divine life.

Truth is not divisive. God does not reserve His love for the literate, the wealthy, and the powerful. Light is available to all; and when there is light, all social and political darkness is transformed into harmony, justice, health, and prosperity. The light has nothing to do with the sufferings of mankind. It is our individual and collective *obstruction* of the light that is the cause of all suffering on this planet. If you and I, and everyone else in the world, would dedicate even five minutes a day to entering the silence and filling ourselves with the light of peace, and then sending that peace outward on wings of love, it would touch people everywhere. It would become a powerful force for reconciliation and harmony in the world.

In every one of us resides a divine spark of the Infinite. Such prayer, going out to the world, could not but light a candle in the temple of every living soul. If that could be done (and I know it can be done), we wouldn't be reading so many horror stories in our press. When we abide in the consciousness that *"God's mercy endureth forever"* and that *"every hour Thou art near,"* we set an example for people everywhere. By our thoughts and actions we encourage a peaceful way of living and a nonviolent, respectful way of handling problems, rather than a warlike way.

Now, I'm going to leave for a moment our wonderful prophet David back in the antiquities of time, and turn to the song I sang this morning. In this text there is a powerful message about the importance of transmitting the transcendental power of love. There is a kind of divine alchemy that takes place in the consciousness of people everywhere when they begin to realize that God is not a far-away force, but a power residing within.

Today I sang, *"Teach me, oh love* (meaning God), *to know that Thou art power."* Now, if you want to worship the god of fear, then you are worshiping two gods; and you're certainly not fulfilling the law, are you? For there is only one God, and that is the God of love and goodness. When you know that God is all the love and all the power you need to fulfill every need and desire of your heart, then indeed you are on very firm spiritual ground. Those who do not concern themselves with spiritual values will, of course, ignore people who do; but I assure you that when "God and one make a majority," marvelous things begin to happen.

As you trace the lives of the world's religious figures, you realize that those who had an invincible faith in the power of love were the triumphant ones. *"Teach me to know that every hour, Thou art here with me. Thy gentle presence silences all fear."* It is within the temple of our being that we find the presence of the Eternal One, and that's where Christ said to look for it. Yet, too often that's the last place most of us look. We look here and there and everywhere else, even though we are told that the invincible presence of love is within our own hearts. If you will make meditating upon that presence the most important part of your day, you will see that indeed all fear is silenced.

The song continues, *"Help me to know that love healeth every ill."* Now, the reason many people are not healed is that they don't believe it will happen. The power we lend to this statement, *"Help me to know that Love heals every ill,"* and the degree to which we believe and operate in it, determines the outcome. Within your being lives a miracle-working force, and it is activated by your connection with it. I'm not saying that we don't need doctors, but take a look at the power in these statements: *"Love heals every ill. Love has power. All hate and fear be stilled."*

Hate is a cancer of the soul. You simply cannot harbor it if you want a well body and a happy frame of mind. Hate is the most destructive of all emotions, and anyone who gives any energy to hate will soon see the incredible stupidity of taking that force upon themselves.

Fear is another powerful emotion. If we give too much emotional emphasis to fear, we totally defeat ourselves. Some people let themselves become so filled with fear that they can't go on anymore. They get so tired of it all that they finally leave the body.

I had a friend in San Francisco, where I used to live. She was a wonderful lady: a very positive thinker and a good Christian. She worked with me in my church for twenty-two years. She had always enjoyed very good health and vitality, and everything was going great for her—until she reached the age of ninety-five, when she began to get hooked into feeling frightened and anxious by all the dreadful reports in the news. At the same time, unfortunately, she was mugged—not once, but three times—in the place where she was living. Well, all this did something to her. There had been nothing wrong with her, but she simply gave up her desire to live. She decided that she didn't want to stay on this earth plane anymore, and it didn't take very long before she left the body. You see, she could have stayed longer if she had wanted to, but she had such a powerful mind that when fear began to take hold of it, that fear was augmented. It overtook her so completely that she no longer wanted to live, so she left the body. She had enjoyed a good, long life, with perfect health all the way through her ninety-five years, and she knew she could stay. But apparently this very kind and loving soul was ready to leave. So there you are. When people decide they don't want to live anymore, they don't.

On the other hand, people who *want* to live often overcome the most extreme cases of debilitation and illness. Those are the people who have an unflinching faith in the power of love and an indomitable desire to carry on. Even after all the wise physicians have prognosticated death, these people live on for decades. Even when they are told they can't stay, they *do* stay, and often outlive their physicians.

A wonderful man named Browne lived in Florida some years ago. Before he was fifteen, he was told by erudite medical doctors that he would not live to be twenty-one because his body was in such bad shape. (Imagine planting such a thought in the mind of this young man.), Yet, for some good reason, he didn't take those dire predictions to heart.

This young man went on to become a medical doctor with a very successful practice. Later on, he decided to give up his medical practice and devote his life to spiritual healing, lecturing, and writing. By the time he was ninety he had become a keynote speaker, and was invited to conventions and conferences all over the country. Even though he was ninety, he had the dynamism and sharp-mindedness of a young man.

Years after, the doctors who had sounded the knell of doom had passed into the next expression of life, yet Browne was still going strong. He was busy "about his Father's business" right up to the moment he left the body at the age of ninety-eight.

Soon before he left, he called his secretary into his office and said, "George, we have to work a little extra today; I want to clear the desk." So, they worked vigorously right through the day, catching up on his vast worldwide correspondence. When he had signed the last letter and cleared the desk of all remaining paperwork, Dr. Browne stood up and shook the hand of his secretary, saying, "George, you have been a wonderful help. I couldn't have done without you all these years. Thank you very much. I asked you to come in early today, and help me clear up all these odds and ends, because I'm going to leave the body today."

Then, after they chatted a bit, Dr. Browne went over and stretched out on the couch. He folded his arms, closed his eyes, and quietly left his body. He had no fear of death because he knew who he was, and where he was going, and none of it bothered him. He was ready to go. He left at his own bidding, and in his own time. Isn't that wonderful?

Now, I'm not in a hurry to leave this planet. There have been some dim prophecies that I might not be around for very long, but I'm not going to worry about it. I'm going to go on every day as though I will live forever, and I'm going to make the best of every day. You know, every day doesn't have to be fireworks and a big explosion of experience. Take the little things and be grateful for them, and always realize that God is infinitely merciful. *"Oh teach me how to keep my heart with care, that naught but love shall be reflected there."*

The great souls whom we occasionally encounter—the saints and sages, rishis and prophets—are men and women who have learned that God resides within their heart. They have kept that heart with care, for they know that *"naught but love can be reflected there."* I've met a few saints in my life, and I'm very grateful for that. I don't know how I managed it, but God was merciful to me, and it was my good fortune to meet these great souls. Two of them were Catholic saints living in a monastery. Both had an inner consciousness of God's presence of good, and because of that awareness, they simply radiated qualities of the soul that were exquisite and otherworldly. They had *"kept their hearts with care"* so that *"naught but love could be reflected there."* Whenever a troubling thought tempted them, they would take a step inward and silently remind themselves, *"Help to hold when fear would whisper."*

Every one of us has known moments when fear whispers strongly. We wouldn't be living on the human plane if we didn't. We would have graduated into another plateau of life. But we're still in the classroom of the earth experience, where fear sometimes does whisper strongly. Remember, there is no power in fear, except what you give it.

As we become a little more sophisticated in our understanding of the nature of man and his subconscious responses to things, we realize that we ourselves are the mischief-makers; we are the authors of our own troubles, by giving an inordinate amount of energy to fear. We must learn to set our priorities firmly within our consciousness, and decide whether we will keep our hearts with love or with the demons of fear. *"Help me to hold when fear would whisper strong, for no power doth to fear or sin belong"*—except the power we give it. You are the one who has to open the door and let the negative in. Don't think God has copped out on you, or that some gremlin has come in the side door to make life difficult for you.

"Oh love divine, abiding constantly, I need not plead, Thou dost abide with me." Now, some churches teach people to go around in sackcloth and ashes, howling and rolling on the floor, making strange noises, pleading and begging God to save them. Of course there are different types of religions, and I'm very ecumenical. I always say, "To each his own." But when we make begging and pleading our main form of prayer, all we are doing is fastening our consciousness on the fact that what we need or desire isn't there.

Don't plead for what you don't have, because if you do, you will only procrastinate the divine confrontation with your true self. Instead of that, affirm, *"I need not plead. Thou dost abide with me."* This is a statement from Proverbs 23:7: *"As a man thinketh in his heart, so is he."* Jesus repeatedly said that the divine consciousness—that is, the kingdom of expanded awareness—dwells in **you**. Are you going to believe him? Or are you going to latch onto every fear-provoking news you hear, giving it the power that belongs to God?

Just think of how many people have actually died of fear. I remember a story about the countless people who died of yellow fever during the time the Panama Canal was being built. Scores of people contracted the dreaded disease and died from it; but many more people, when they were tested, did not actually have the disease, even though they had all the symptoms of the frightful fever. If the disease didn't killed them, what did they die of? They died from *fear* of the disease.

The mind is so powerful that it can kill or heal us. Our fearful and pessimistic thoughts are the creators of our health, as well as every other aspect of our lives. Cynicism, condemnation, criticism, and fear actually cause the cells of our bodies to contract and shut down. Is it any wonder that people by the thousands are creating disease and killing themselves with their thoughts?

We must remember that we have infinite resources. We can never exhaust the inner supply of energy, love, mercy, hope, wisdom, courage, or compassion. So let us reach in and tap that infinite supply, and use it to create improved health, better relationships, greater financial flow, and more intimate communication with Divine life.

Why is it that we seem unable to grasp the simple truth of our real nature, and thus take hold of the unlimited potential contained within it? Jesus proclaimed and reiterated the divinity of man, again and again. Didn't he say, *"If I do not the works of my Father, believe me not. But if I do, though ye believe not me, believe the works: that ye may know, and believe, that the Father is in me, and I in Him."* (John 10:37-38.)

We love to read those words, but we can't quite grasp the idea that Jesus was talking not only about himself, but all of us too. We can't quite claim his truth as a conscious reality for ourselves. Perhaps it is because we're all so human, and we have so many failings. We think we are so far away from ever measuring up to Jesus, or to any other highly evolved being.

It's very natural for us to feel our shortcomings and think, "Gee, if I accept the idea that God is actually dwelling within me, then I'll have to give up everything and start living like a monk or a nun. I don't know if I want to do that because then I'll have to walk a very narrow path, and I won't be able to have my martini before dinner." We think we'll have to give up too much and be too good.

Well, whether you know it or not, God *is* within you. And whether you want to acknowledge it or not, He will always be there. Your ability to manage the circumstances and opportunities of your life depends entirely on the depth of your realization of the truth of your being.

Now, realization doesn't happen overnight. It is a process that begins by reading (and perhaps attending lectures), by spending time in the company of people who have a good degree of self-realization, and finally, by steady meditation on the divine aspects within the self such as love, wisdom, and joy. As you expand your awareness of who you really are, so will you awaken and flex the muscles of your higher creative faculties. Then, little by little, as the architect of your life, you will become better and better at manifesting your dreams and desires. The more you meditate on the qualities of the soul, the more you will be able to embody them.

You can always spot the people who have made a pact to encourage the consciousness of love and joy within themselves; they are the ones who reflect contentment with their lives. They walk with joyful ease, and create harmony all around them. Those are the people who have realized the divine presence within themselves, and that means they have truly come to know God as light, joy, wisdom, healing, and love.

Love is just another name for God, you know. So let us always remember that, especially during those times when fear may whisper strongly. When the storms of fear come, still them by your invincible conviction that all is well because God is *here*. He lives within the self as spirit, light, and love.

And so, dear friends, throughout this coming week, let us be mindful never to be moved off-center when fear whispers strongly, or even faintly. If you pick up the daily paper and read something negative, know that you can handle it. Put it in its proper place within your spiritual frame of reference, so that you do not become overwhelmed by it. We must be informed, but we must not allow fear to whisper so strongly that we begin to tremble. The closer we come to realizing the truth that God is in everything, and that next to Him there is nothing, the quicker we will liberate ourselves from all sorts of terrifying and foreboding shadows of unreality.

Why not make a little pact with yourself that from now on, you are going to live by love rather than fear? Life's journey is so much more beautiful when you live with the *certainty* that God dwells within you at all times. Life is more rewarding when you *know* that He is all the power you will ever need; and life is so peaceful when you really *feel* Him as the gentle presence which silences all fear. Know that He heals every ill, and realize that His mercy endures forever. Living with this consciousness will not only help you; it will help all those around you. It will make the whole of your existence a thing of beauty and a joy forever.

Thank you, dear friends, and God bless you. *Amen.*

All Things Work Together For Good

Heritage House Presbyterian Chapel, San Francisco, CA
May 16, 1982

Good morning, dear friends. In Romans, we are told that, *"All things work together for good to [those who] love God."* (Rom. 8:28.) This is a very interesting statement, and it is a particularly appropriate selection of scripture, at a time when many disconcerting things are going on in the world around us. If we're not careful, we might get the blues as we think about world events. We don't want to lend our attention and our energies to negative feelings, but instead, remember that we cannot go where God is not. When we do that, we can more easily maintain a consciousness of the presence of good within the center of our being, no matter what is going on around us.

You know, in this wonderful city of San Francisco, buildings are often being constructed and reconstructed. Yesterday I drove past the beautiful old St. Mary's Cathedral in Chinatown, and I noticed that they have replaced the old capstone, or cornerstone of the church with a new one. When I saw that magnificent structure, it reminded me of our own divine capstone. Within the temple of the human heart, within our own individuality, there is always and forever a magnetic keystone. Remembering this: we are eternally filled with the consciousness of God, the goodness of God; and this gives us the certainty that no matter what the storms and buffets of the world around us (and they are indeed considerable), *we know where we are.* Now, I'm not asking anybody to pretend that problems aren't there, because we read of them every day, but we must know that no matter what events may shake the world, we are anchored in God.

As I am well into my seventies now, I chuckled as I read in the paper the other day that if there were a nuclear bombing here in the Bay Area, we "oldsters" would be left behind. Isn't that amusing? I really have to laugh at this, because if anyone ever does such a thing, not only will the oldsters not be left behind—*nothing* will be left!! It will be total obliteration.

Although we certainly have the capability to destroy ourselves, I don't think it's going to happen, because if it did, nobody would win. Even the most misguided people in the world have enough sense left in their mental household not to want to destroy the whole planet. In any case, I don't worry that the "youngsters" will go marching over the Golden Gate Bridge and leave us "oldsters" behind. It is absurd to worry that we seniors are "expendable," as it said in the paper. I'm not worried about that at all! [John Laurence chuckles.] No matter what the politicians decide to do with us "lesser old ones," we needn't worry.

Sometimes our spiritual consciousness is put to the test. At times, we are challenged to make a discrimination concerning those things which stand before all of us, those matters of life and death and eternity. I, for one, am not going to waste five seconds worrying about any of it. If I should ever be so unfortunate as to be in the relative area of a nuclear bomb, I would ask the Lord to please place me right under it—because I wouldn't want to stick around to see all the devastation and horrendous suffering, and *then* die. I'd rather go in an instant—"pufff!" I am not afraid, because I know where I am. I also know *who* I am. We need to know who we are, how valuable we are, and how constructive our lives can be, whether young or old. You know, some of the greatest works of music and art were created by people who were quite advanced in age. Giuseppe Verdi wrote the opera *Falstaff* when he was a very old man. I think he was in his nineties. Countless others created magnificent works of art when they were well along in their lives.

Let us always keep in mind the fact that everything works together for good for those who love God, for those who have a contact with God through prayer and meditation, and for those who listen in the silence— and therein realize the eternal, indestructible nature of their being.

Now, nobody is in a hurry to leave this planet—*I'm not!*—but if we are called to leave, we know the next life is better. The sages, saints, prophets, apostles, and Christ himself, have all spoken to us with profound meaningfulness and eloquence concerning that area into which we ultimately graduate. Whether death comes through some act of foolishness on the part of humanity—playing with nuclear toys—or whether we simply pass quietly from the body into the heaven world, the part of you that stands inside your body instrument and says I AM is the part of you that is indestructible. Men and women of international eminence in the scientific community have come to a deep agreement that nothing in the universe is ever lost; it merely changes form. Why wouldn't it be the same for us, whom the Christ came down to earth to bless? Why wouldn't it be that we, too, continue to live, merely changing form?

You know, there are some people who think that the world, and all the creative workings within it, have come together merely by happenstance. Wouldn't it be silly if, after listening to a magnificent work of art such as the opera *Tristan und Isolde*, you firmly declared, "Nobody actually wrote that piece of music. All those little notes were just floating around somewhere. They just flew onto the page and assembled themselves randomly, accidentally." *Tristan und Isolde* is a magnificent work of transcendental beauty that lifts the spirit and the soul right out of the consciousness of this world. Wouldn't you laugh if I said that somehow Wagner simply found the score, opened it, and *voila!*—there was the entire opera, just thrown together by chance! Everyone would laugh at that because, to us, it is absurd even to think that such a great work was created just by happenstance.

Now, certainly it begs description and baffles the intellect even to try to think in terms of infinity. We live on a little ball of mud and water, on the periphery of a fifth-rate galaxy. There are things out there so vast that we find it literally impossible to comprehend them. This whole whirling mass of immensity out in space, rotating in its orderly fashion, could not have come about, nor be sustained, by mere happenstance. Out of all this precision, there must be a lawgiver. You cannot have law without a lawgiver. So the Lord, the eternal one, has projected into manifestation, by His creative will, all that we see around us, and all that our great scientific minds are looking at. Through the advance and sophistication of sciences such as astronomy and quantum physics, we are now able to see and hear into the cosmos, using remarkable instruments of technology. Today, we are peering into areas never before glimpsed by mortal man. It is all very wonderful and beautiful, and we know that none of this has come about by happenstance.

We know that as man unfolds his own spiritual nature and understanding, he grows continuously, coming closer to knowing the cosmos and God. So, if God has made all these things (including *you*), and He has given you the power to think about the all-pervading Lord of the universe, then *who* is He? *What* is He? Well, the two most frequent symbols used to describe the almighty Creator are light and love. Some people say, "It's very hard to love the Lord because I've never seen Him." All right—you've never seen the wind, either, have you? You've never tasted the wind, and yet you know it is there. We know God by the marvels of nature observed by man in his understanding of the universe around him. We know God by the marvels extant in this cosmos. It is truly wonderful that God has given us an intellect, and with it the possibility of lifting our minds above the ordinary material world toward the immaterial spiritual world of the soul.

In the writings of Saint Paul, he tells us that when we leave this mortal body, we take on a body made of lighter stuff. It is a spiritual body not unlike this one, but much freer, lighter, more wondrous, very youthful, and more ongoing. In time, the physical body dies and is gone, but the spirit never dies, because God has given us eternal, immortal life. The whole of the New Testament tells us that. If all we had to look forward to was the dark pit of the grave, it would be awful! Think of the saints, martyrs, and heroes of the early Christian movement, who willingly gave their lives so that the story and liberating teachings of the Christ might reach all people. Do you think such holy and virtuous ones would fall into the same dark pit of nothingness as the criminal and the murderer? What kind of justice would that be? We humans are not infinite in our present understanding by any means, but even limited human sense would not tolerate such inequity. It simply could not be that whether you lived your life here on earth as a saint or an evildoer, you would still end up in the same pit of darkness, devoid of life. Like Saint Paul, let us know that we have another body made of lighter stuff, and that in due season we will put on garments of light. This should encourage us and release us from all fear.

And so, dear friends, let us not be troubled, for all things work together for good to those who are mindful of the Lord, to those who love the Lord. Instead of worrying, we should apply ourselves to the knowledge and exercise of devotion, or love of God, through prayer. It really helps to give a little time every morning to sitting quietly and meditating on the profound and liberating teachings of the Bible and other immortal scriptures. Take, for example, the Golden Rule: "Do unto others as you would have them do unto you." This is a timeless, eternal statement of truth and great beauty, yet even this immortal truth would mean nothing if the spirit of humankind were not also, as Christ said, immortal.

So when you pick up your morning paper and read that we oldsters are dispensable and not worth worrying about if an atom bomb falls, don't be disturbed. People who write such things are fooling nobody as much as themselves, because in a nuclear explosion there won't be anybody left. It always annoys me a little when I hear someone who is supposed to be a scientist, who should not fall into that kind of trap, say something so absurd as to make us think we can escape the ravages of nuclear war. Last week on television I heard a distinguished man say that America has great resilience, and that America can transcend anything that might happen to it. He said, "America has always survived." Well, that's true in a sense, but none of us has been tested by total atomic annihilation. What is the bottom line in all this? Simply that we *cannot have* a nuclear war, period. Russia knows it, China knows it, we know it, and the rest of the world knows it. We hope no one will ever be foolish enough to take the gigantic step towards the dissolution of planet earth. And as a friend of mine said to me so many years ago, after World War II, "Even if this planet did fall into a thousand billion pieces, we know, by the word of the infinite Christ, that we are eternal, now and always."

So let us not waste time feeling bad and saying, "Oh, I'm scared that there's going to be a nuclear war, and maybe the bomb will fall in my own backyard." I don't think it is going to happen, so I'm not going to worry about it. If it does happen, I have deep confidence in the words that you find here in this scripture, *"All things work together for good to [those who] love God."* I have an unshakable faith in the words of the Christ and his followers, who have given us an abiding sense of the ongoing nature of our being. And that's why we are always urged by the great teachers of religion to purify ourselves, and to bring ourselves into harmony with God. The most powerful thing we have within us is love, and that love resides within the temple of our being as part of the Lord Himself, for God is love.

My dear mother was raised in a convent in Ireland, and she learned her trade there as a seamstress. She could do all the fancy needlework and embroidery that was the fashion in that day, and so much more. She really had an eye for style, and an amazing talent for design. She could look at a piece of lace or a pretty dress in a downtown store, and come right home and make it. I don't know how she did it, but she had a real talent. Mother had a lot of interesting little stories to tell us about her girlhood, and how she was encouraged to have increasing faith.

One day she was standing out in the schoolyard at recess when one of the strict nuns was walking around, supervising, as she always did. The girls were not allowed to touch the apple tree, or any apple on it, but my mother loved apples. She spied a big shiny red apple, so she stood under it and said, "Oh, rosy red apple, please come down to me." With that, the apple fell right down into her hands. It was, of course, a coincidence, but the nun didn't know what to make of it. Mother used to tell us about another nun, a very dear old teacher, who was, in the girls' eyes, quite "ancient." This dear old nun was retired. She used to spend her days in a rocker, gently rocking to and fro, back and forth. Very often the girls would go over and talk to her for a little while. All she would ever say to them was, "Vanity, ah vanity, all is vanity except the love of the Lord." That's what religious life meant to her; and it's beautiful, isn't it? We could all learn something from that teaching.

Now, you don't have to be Catholic, or any other particular denomination, in order to get into the consciousness and love of the all-pervading Christ. Many people ask, "Where can I find that spirit of the Christ? How can I feel the consciousness of the Christ?" Well, you can find it anywhere and everywhere, and you can feel it especially within the temple of the Self. You must nurture that consciousness of truth so that no matter what storms may burst round about you, you will know that the eternal, changeless, and immutable fact of being is that you are *already* eternal. You are already spirit, and you will never be more spirit or more eternal than you are right now. Knowing this, you will not be disturbed. You will know, with the author of Romans, that *"all things work together for good to [those who] love God."* Thank you. *Amen.*

On This Day

Unity Temple, San Francisco, CA
June 27, 1982

Good morning, dear friends. Today my topic is *"On This Day."* In America we celebrate Mother's Day and Father's Day, Secretary's Day,

Independence Day, Memorial Day, Thanksgiving Day, Christmas Day, and so on. In this way, we remember the particular facets of life that hold great value for us, and which, indeed, deserve our remembering. It's lovely to celebrate these special days during the year, but what about *this* very day? I believe, as the Greek philosopher said many years ago, that living life one day at a time is the secret of happiness. All of us are much too anxious: running around, hurrying to do this or that, and rushing to get here or there. We're so excited that we get all tangled up and trip over our own feet—sometimes landing them in our own mouths! We have to learn to be patient.

Many years ago—in 1928, when I was in the seminary—I used to write a little article every day before breakfast. That was a way of sharpening my abilities to write and speak, and it certainly helped me. I remember one little thing I wrote on the back of a laundry slip (we had very long laundry slips, and that was the only paper I had to write on at the time.) I wrote about living day by day, and making this day the most important day, because today is never coming back. Today is the most important day in our lives. No matter how long we live, even if we live to be a thousand, this particular day will never return. So we must make the most of it.

Now, we all know that not every day is going to be perfect. We're not going to be jumping up and down, dancing and tossing rose petals all over the place. That would get boring, wouldn't it? We need variety, and it's the contrasts that make life interesting. Like a beautiful mosaic picture of the Lord Christ, day by day you can make of your life something lovely. Each day you may set one small stone into your mosaic picture, which ultimately will reflect the presence and countenance of the Christ spirit.

Now, not every stone in the mosaic of your life is going to be bright. Surely, there will be beautiful light blues of serenity, and the dark blues of deep religious feeling. There will be the red of vitality, the orange and yellow of autumn leaves, and nature's green that blankets the earth. But in your mosaic there will also be gray stones. You might think of those as representing a rather dismal day; but if you didn't have that gray, you would never know the contrast that must exist if you are to build some sort of intelligent approach to daily living. See, what you do today is the most important thing of all, because tomorrow is never yours until it becomes today. So do the very best you possibly can with this day, and then you will have a perfect reflection of that quality in the days ahead.

We sometimes think that things are not as good as they ought to be, and we feel a little down because of that. But we learn to lift ourselves up through the light of consciousness within the temple of the human heart, where Heaven resides, and where all the answers are to be found. Now, we can do this successfully by not worrying inordinately about what is coming tomorrow because, as I said, tomorrow is never yours until it is today.

So many things that we worry and stew about, and get all pushed out of shape about, never even happen—or if they do, they're not nearly as bad as we thought they would be. Lending ourselves to chronic anxiety does us no good whatever, so we might as well take our poise and work out each day in a quiet way. You know, linear time as we know it on planet earth doesn't actually exist. There is no big clock up in heaven. Time is something we need on the earth plane so that we might bring order to our lives. If we didn't have the organization of time, people would come to church at 10:30 or 12:30, and nobody would be here for the 11:00 service. So we need time to order our lives. But we know from the teachings of the mystics, saints, and sages that time does not exist in the heaven worlds; there is only the eternal now.

It's very important for us to take this into our hearts and not be too anxious for tomorrow. Jesus said, *"Take no thought for tomorrow, what you shall put on, or what you shall eat."* (Matt. 6:31.) He wanted to impress on us the importance of trusting God to provide for us. And he wanted to remind us not to worry so much about the details of our lives that we forget the most important factor: namely that by trusting Him we may make of our lives something beautiful. The most important thing we can do is align ourselves with the divine spirit within and bring about as much perfection, maturity, and understanding as we can *now*, on this day.

I've seen some magnificent mosaics in various churches and cathedrals. Some of them were small; and some were very large and glorious, weighing tons. Some of them replicate images far bigger than life size of the Christ and other saintly figures. These mosaic images are so real that you almost expect the figures to step forward and speak. Every little stone is essential to the composite and total out-picturing of the Christ, and sometimes it takes as long as a year just to polish the stones in a single image. My dear friends, the same life and power that are depicted in these magnificent mosaics of the Christ are also present within the heart of each and every one of us. It may take thousands of stones to complete a beautiful mosaic picture of one's life, and each stone represents a single day in that life. Each and every day of your life is very important, so don't take any day for granted, or put down any one day.

We are living in the eternal now, both today and tomorrow. As we greet each day (hopefully with meditation), that day becomes the most important day in our lives. If we want to get anything done in our lives, even on the level of our ordinary occupations, it's very important for us to start the day by first plugging our extension cord of consciousness into the Infinite. You wouldn't get up and go to work in the morning without having breakfast, would you? Well, I suppose some people do, but they are the minority. Most people like their eggs, cereal, smoothies, or toast and coffee or tea, or whatever they like. Generally, we wouldn't think about starting our day without having breakfast, and yet we think nothing of scampering out into the hustle and bustle of the work-a-day world without first nourishing the self through meditation on the divine essence and source of our being.

Without this daily contact, we get all jumbled up, confused, and "discombooberated." When the world claims us, we don't know if we are on foot or on horseback; and by the time we get to the office, we are in tatters. Why? Because we didn't start the day right. We didn't give even ten or fifteen minutes to silent meditation. We didn't gather in the divine power, wisdom insights, and poise necessary to have a happy, lovely day. What you do with *this* day, in aggregate, becomes a beautiful mosaic of the many days and years of your life. Ultimately, when all these tiny little stones are at last fixed into place, you will see reflected in the mosaic of your life a fine representation of the omnipresent power of the Christ light.

Nowadays, we have a lot of religious programs on TV. I like to peek in every now and then to see what they're up to. Sometimes these preachers are pounding the pulpit into splinters and sending everybody off to be roasted on the divine rotisserie. Very often you find them howling, thumping, and jumping up and down—tearing up everything in sight. I suppose some people need that kind of excitement; and if they do, jolly well. That's their way of expressing their religion. It is each person's privilege to express as they wish, so we mustn't say anything about that. But it is generally conceded by most of the mystics who have brought light to us down through the centuries, that it is in moments of stillness when the voice of the indwelling One may be heard.

So it is very important that we give time to these precious moments, and to absolute serenity, even if it is only for ten or fifteen minutes. This way, you get ready to meet whatever situations—good, bad, or indifferent—that you might encounter during the course of your daily work. The people around you notice and respond to your mood, especially if you're the boss.

If you're the person in charge and you come in on Monday morning all shook up, *everybody* gets shook up. They say, "Oh, Mr. Smith is in terrible shape today. You'd better not ask for a raise or you'll be thrown right through the window—and he won't even bother to open it for you! So don't go near him today; wait till things simmer down." See, Mr. Smith obviously forgot that God comes first. He forgot that it is important to his efficiency, as the manager of any kind of business that might come under his direction, to prepare himself for the work day. He forgot that he is much more effective when he prepares for his day by tuning in and coming into accord with himself and with his Creator. By simply lending himself to a few minutes of quiet meditation, Mr. Smith is ready to head out into the world. By first attuning himself to Divine consciousness, not only will Mr. Smith be successful in his day, the people around him will begin to sense a certain confidence in him. Now, if Mr. Smith has had a nice quiet weekend that includes going to a religious service at a wonderful church like this one, when he goes to work on Monday morning (after having done a brief meditation), then of course, he will be ready to meet the day and whatever comes with it. He will have a certain inner voice that has been established through quietude, silence, and a reverential drawing in of the divine electricity so essential to every one of us.

And so, dear friends, please remember that every day is necessary for our ongoing growth, and every day is important. Scientists tell us that we are constantly renewing this physical body. No matter how old you are—whether twenty-seven, or a hundred and seven—you are never really more than seven years old. Did you know that? Yes, every seven years we are renewing and repairing cells in the body. And, as we age, we want to remain as youthful as we can.

The thoughts you think have a great deal to do with how your body functions, and how you feel. If you concentrate on every little pain, murmuring and complaining, *"Oh, it's a dreadful day. I have this awful pain and I know it's going to get worse. I think I'm getting old. Nobody comes to see me anymore. I'm all alone, and it's just terrible,"* then your days are going to be bummers. If you think you are old, then of course you *are* old, for you have set something afoot within the subconscious mechanism of your mind, which controls the atomic and cellular configuration and function within your whole body. You see, every cell, every tissue, every organ and system of your physical body is enormously plastic to the quality of your thinking. Thoughts are *things*, and if you sit down and meditate upon the source of your being—the infinite divine energy that sustains you in every way—you can consciously draw in rejuvenation right down to the cellular level. It is your right to access this health-giving power, and in a way, it is also your duty. You are responsible for taking good care of yourself so that you can be a light in your world, however big or small.

"It is your Father's good pleasure to give you the kingdom [of heaven]." (Luke 12:32.) Now, this scriptural passage doesn't imply tomorrow or next year, or ten years from now. It means right now, on this very day. We are always growing and becoming more of who we really are. By taking even a few minutes every day to go within and silence the mind and body, you are attuning and expanding your awareness. That awareness is ongoing and ever increasing, and it is very important to "woo" that state of expanded awareness if you are going to make any progress along the line of spiritual maturity.

So, as always, I urge you to put aside a little time every day for meditation; because if you start the day right by tuning-in to the Infinite, the rest of the day will jolly well go right. If you start the day with a negative attitude, you are setting the mode and pace for the rest of the day to be unhappy and troublesome. You see, you bring into your consciousness, and into the expression of your own private little universe, either negative or positive qualities. Now, you can be negative if you want to. You can be miserable if you want to. It's unhealthy and unlovely, but you can be like that if you choose.

Remember the biblical story of Job, when he was sitting on the dunghill covered with sores? Everything was going just about as badly as it possibly could, and what did he say? He uttered one of the most interesting metaphysical truths in the whole of literature. He said, *"Everything that I have feared has come upon me."* (Job 3:25.) Now, that is a great example of *faith in reverse*. What he spent so much energy fearing and pushing away actually came to him and became true for him. Never forget that no matter how bad your headache—even if it is a really big Tylenol headache—you *can* affect it by changing your mind about it. Saint Paul said, *"I am renewed by the changing of my mind."* (Rom. 12:2.) You *can* change your attitude, your approach to life in general, and the way you are living it. And you can change your mind on *this* day.

You know, I recently moved (and when you move you can never find anything for six or eight weeks). But one day, while I was sloughing around in the closet, I came upon a little greeting card I had received some time back from a dear little lady who is a minister in San Lorenzo, California. I don't know where she got it, but I think it is very nice and appropriate for today's topic. It says (in part, paraphrased):

On this day, mend a quarrel.
Search out a forgotten friend.
Dismiss a suspicion and replace it with trust.
Write a letter to someone who misses you.
Encourage a young person who has lost his faith.
Keep a promise.
Forget an old grudge.
Examine your demands on others, and vow to reduce them.
Fight for a principle.
Overcome an old fear.
Take two minutes to appreciate the beauty of nature.
Tell someone you love him or her. (Author unknown.)

"Write a letter to someone who misses you." Sometimes we get so busy that we forget to do even the simplest things, like writing a letter to Aunt Minnie. If you don't have an Aunt Minnie, get one, and write her a letter. It will make her feel good, and it will make you feel good, too. Just by doing these small and simple things, you see, you bring light and blessings to so many.

"Encourage a young person who has lost his faith." How many times do we bump into youngsters whose lives, through drugs or alcohol, have gotten all topsy-turvy, and the whole direction of their existence has become distorted and shattered? They need somebody to say to them, "Look, what you are doing is going to end in total disaster. You have to change now, while you're young. Faith is not just for old people who are going to die soon anyhow. Faith is something we need from the moment we're born until we graduate to the realms of higher consciousness."

"Keep a promise." How many times have we failed to keep promises? Your friend might say, "Oh, Bill promised to come over and help me clean out the garage. That was three and a half months ago, and he still hasn't come." We all get busy and forget to do the things we said we were going to do. We really don't mean to be forgetful and overlook people; we just do. In fact, I see a man in this congregation today whom I promised to get together with some time ago. He's a very good man who is deeply interested in the spiritual life, and I am just as sincere as anybody can be. But as I see this man today in church, I realize that it's been a month since I last saw him, and I never arranged to get together with him. So I'm going to do that today.

"Forget an old grudge." Oh, that's a good one. Forget the grudge, because if you don't, it won't forget *you*. It will move right in and make you awfully miserable. Forget a grudge, because if you don't, it is like carrying a hundred and fifty pounds of steel on your back. Grudges weigh you down. Never nurse a grudge or wish trouble on anyone. Never wish to see another person suffer. If you do that, you insult the divinity in that person. And, after all, God is the real judge. So, dear friends, forget that old grudge.

"Examine your demands on others, and vow to reduce them." Isn't that good? I like that one. We all have demands, and we all have things we want people to do for us. I'm sure God seldom hears a prayer that isn't, "Gimme this. Gimme that. May I have this? May I have that?" Tell me, how often have you said, "Lord, is there anything I can do for You today? Is there anyone whose life I can touch? Into whose world I can bring a little candle—a little glimmer of light?" Try that. You might be surprised what the Lord asks of you, and you may be amazed by what you receive in return. Don't be too demanding of others, because, you see, they too have their problems. Be compassionate and reasonable, and let lots of things pass. There is no use getting angry or upset about things, because the minute you do, your whole emotional domicile becomes a tumbling house of cards and everything falls apart. That doesn't make for maturity or any kind of ongoing happiness.

"Fight for a principle." Be willing to stand up and be counted, and know that you stand for principles. We all need to do that every now and then. Sometimes we meet people who have peculiar attitudes of mind, who hold stereotypical prejudices. They don't like Jewish or Catholic people, or they don't like anyone who isn't white. Can any of you tell me the color of the human soul? We are all divine, whether we're wearing a body garment in brown, black, white, or yellow. So stand up and fight for the principles of tolerance, justice, and goodwill in all forms.

"Overcome an old fear." You know, a lot of people go around looking for boogiemen: those little gremlins that hide in closets and under the bed. We have to wipe that fear out of our consciousness, because most of the things we fear never happen anyhow; and if we're going to go around with them as a big weight upon us, then it is all destructive and quite unlovely.

"Take two minutes to appreciate the beauty of Nature." Now, today is a gorgeous day in San Francisco. The flowers and trees around this beautiful church are filled with smiling blossoms. We who live in the Bay Area are fortunate that we can go to the ocean and gaze upon the ever-changing skies—or walk in nearby Golden Gate Park, where we can luxuriate in the extraordinary color and charm of the endless varieties of plants and flowers. We are blessed with many opportunities to appreciate the beauty of Nature.

"Tell someone you love him or her." Very often you hear someone say, "Oh, my mother just passed away. If only I had expressed how much I love her." Sometimes people will say, "I'm just not the emotional type, but now I wish I had put my arms around mom and said, 'Oh, mother, I think you are the most wonderful mom anybody could ever have in this whole world.'" But they never said it. Mothers always know—in that special intuitive way by which they know everything—that we love them. But when they are gone, how nice it would have been if we had expressed our love to them more often. So think about that, and tell the special people in your life that you love them, again and again. You know, love is just another name for God. As Jesus said, *"By this shall all men know that you are my disciples, that you love one another."* (John 13:35.)

A mosaic of Christ is a nice symbol for the kind of life we are leading, and for the kind of service we are giving. So on this day let us imagine that we have our beautiful mosaic picture of Christ, made up of thousands of tiny stones, polished to a high shine. Day by day, with every thought we think and every action we take, we are adding one little stone after another to build a mosaic of our love and service in the world. In this way, we make of our life something beautiful for God. Wouldn't it be nice, at the end of life, when we have graduated into the higher planes, to look upon the mosaic of our life and see a shining reflection of how well we understood and practiced the simple directions taught to us by the eternal Christ? We can do that by making *this* day, and each day, the most important day, and by greeting each morning with meditation upon the indwelling presence and supreme power of the omnipresent Christ Spirit. Thank you, dear friends. *Amen.*

Share Your Love, Your Smiles, and Your Blessings

Heritage House Presbyterian Chapel, San Francisco, CA
June 27, 1982

Good morning, dear friends. Today I'd like to read from Psalm 130. We all know that these beautiful lyric poems called the Psalms are ascribed to King David. From the fires of his devotional approach to God, and in his deep understanding of the mercies of the Heavenly Father, David gave us these inspired and most encouraging utterances. In Psalm 130, verse 1, David sings, *"Out of the depths have I cried unto thee, O LORD."*

How many times have you cried out to the Lord from the depths of your soul? The only way you can really get your prayers off the ground is to invest them with deep feeling, and not a superficial and pale sentiment. Otherwise, you are just parroting words you've learned from someone else. When you begin to invest the words of your heart with a sense of urgency and conviction, and when you really come into attunement with the presence and power of the omniscient and all-pervading Lord of the universe, then you are really cooking. *"Lord, hear my voice: let thine ears be attentive to the voice of my supplications."* (Ps. 130:2.)

David was a wise man, and he wanted to teach us how important it is to incline the inner ear of knowledge and understanding to the supplications we send out. Sometimes we thoughtlessly make supplications and prayers for this, that, or the other thing, and our prayers never quite get off the ground. Often we pray for things without the spiritual wisdom and discrimination necessary to manage what comes about when our prayers are answered. And very often we implore God for things that are not important to the ultimate development of the inner self. Saint Teresa of Avila, the great mystic who lived some four hundred years ago in Spain, said that more tears are shed over answered prayers, simply because we know so little what is best for us.

With the limitations of our nature, we often fly in the face of both knowledge and wisdom, craving and pleading for things that perhaps are not really good for us, things that we aren't ready to handle. It is always good to pray for spiritual attunement and advancement, and we should always ask for the healing presence of the Christ Spirit. It is right to ask for all good things, for as Jesus said, *"It is your Father's good pleasure to give you the kingdom."* (Luke 12:32.) You don't have to die, you know, in order to get to the kingdom. Jesus said that the kingdom of heaven— that sacred spark of the Infinite—is already within you. It takes some of us a long time to see that.

Our wonderful teacher David says, *"Hear my voice: let thine ears be attentive to the voice of my supplications."* Now, not only is it important to pray for ourselves, but it is very good to pray for one another. The essence of the Christian teachings, and those of Master Jesus himself, is that we spend a good deal of time praying for other people. Now, that doesn't mean we may invade their lives and spiritually "push" for anything. It means that when people ask help of us—or when we know they are ill and we want to help—we send a little prayer that they might receive the energy and healing that is good for them.

Don't be afraid that if you pray for too many people, you'll be left out in the corridor somewhere and won't get a full blessing yourself. The divine essence is mercy, love, and brotherhood; and it is augmented and extended as we pray for one another. Therefore, every time you pray for other people, you are also helping yourself. Prayer for others is an act of Christian charity and love that we leave with the Heavenly Father, in full trust that He knows what is right for each one of us. If someone is ill, the Father already knows his need. Jesus clearly emphasized that it is God's wish to give us the fulfillment of all good things, because that is what the kingdom of heaven is all about. We must remember that; and realize that it is only when we go within and become very quiet that we are apt to hear the still small voice, the inner voice of God, telling us what is good and right for us. Those inner promptings and whispers are the intuitional insights God gives us when we need them most.

"Let my voice be heard by Thee, oh Lord. If the Lord should mark iniquities, then who shall stand?" (Ps. 130:2-3.) What does that mean? It means that sometimes everybody, in one way or another, falls short of the mark. Well, this man David had a lot of wisdom, and here he is saying, "Don't judge anybody." That's what this excerpt means, in just three words: don't judge anyone. I think that is very important.

Down through the centuries, the word "sin" has taken on a very detrimental definition, and it has made people feel awful about themselves. What the word literally means is to "miss the mark"—like an archer does when he draws back the bow, shoots toward the bulls-eye, and misses. That's where we got our word "sin." Too often there is an over-emphasis on sin. We all know how imperfect we are, and we don't need to be reminded of it three times a day. We need to be told that divinity is already present within the temple of our being; and that the purpose of this life is not to count our sins, and the sins of others, for that is the work of the Lord. We have to realize, dear friends, that everyone on this planet needs the merciful blessing of the omnipotent One, because we have all made mistakes. When we see other people who have made errors, we must not sit in a high seat of judgment and say, "Well, you know, she's a big sinner!"

You can go to some fundamentalist churches today and watch preachers splinter the pulpits to bits, shouting at everybody in the room that they are wretched sinners who are going to roast in hell for eternity. That is not love. That is not God. Nor is it Christ. That is not what religion is all about. Such condemnation is an enormous misunderstanding of the infinitely compassionate and merciful Lord. God's forgiveness is so much bigger than any of our failings. Of course, that doesn't mean we should tempt fate. It means we must never become despondent because of the sins we may have committed in the past.

Some people, when they get religious, become despondent. They think they're great sinners who are going to be lost, or at least get into big trouble when they leave the body and head for the pearly gates. Well, God is much more merciful than we imagine, and we should give Him more credit than that. *"If Thou should mark iniquities, O Lord, who shall stand?"* The simple answer to this inquiry is "nobody," because we are all sinners. Very few of us have succeeded in always meeting our highest potentials. So let us accentuate our best and most noble selves by sending prayerful, healing thoughts to others who may be ill, and by giving out a loving vibration to everybody we meet, whether we actually speak to them or not. In this way, we truly show ourselves to be children of God and heirs of the kingdom. Being merciful and loving is to live in a true state of Christ consciousness.

We must know that there is forgiveness with God. *"But there is forgiveness with thee, that thou mayest be feared."* (Ps. 130:4.) Now, when you think of fearing God, does that mean you run around frightened and trembling, hiding under the table? Of course not. "Fear of God" doesn't mean that negative kind of fear. It means having such a reverence toward the Divinity that reigns within the temple of the human heart, that we would not intentionally do anything that would cause Him to leave our presence.

And so, if we mark the presence of God as a spiritual discipline every day, we will quickly discover that every day becomes considerably brighter and more beautiful. Each day becomes more fruitful and blessed, with a sense of good will, love, and joy. We can contribute to the good of the whole human family by our friendship with everyone, by our prayerful good wishes, and by a simple smile. There is a lot in that. You know, just the consciousness of someone who understands the infinite mercy and love of God can change one's whole day. To be near someone who is filled with that awesome love and wonder of the Eternal can change not only a whole day, but also a whole life. "Fearing the Lord" means having such an attitude of reverence and wonder that you could not consciously do anything that would go against the highest divine law.

David continues, *"My soul waits for the Lord more than they that watch for the morning . . . for with the LORD there is mercy, and with him is plenteous redemption. And he shall redeem [thee from all thy mistakes]."* (Ps. 130:6-8.) These very beautiful and encouraging words were written thousands of years ago by David: that man of God, that prophet. David happened to play a stringed instrument of the day, which was something like a harp; and in the outpourings of his beautiful inspiration, he gave forth these timeless teachings. So often we find in the Psalms the mercy of God we are deeply longing for. As we read these psalms (or songs) again and again, we are encouraged to really believe their message, and let them become part of us. *"I say, more than they that watch for the morning."* (Ps. 130:6.) See, by watching the new morning, looking for the new day, we are watching for the growth of our own spiritual nature. We are watching ourselves mature spiritually. And as we watch for that inner awareness, we find that we have hope of a better tomorrow; because we know that He redeems us from all our mistakes. God's mercy is infinite.

The message I would like to bring to you today is that you must never make the mistake of becoming depressed or despondent. You must never think, as some people do, that you are a terrible sinner—convinced that God is going to punish you for something wrong you did ten years ago. God has forgiven you. Stop punishing yourself by calling yourself a sinner; and stop going around in "sackcloth and ashes," so to speak, avoiding the joy and love that God wants you to have. Christ said to change your heart and forgive those who have injured you—and that means you have to forgive yourself too. You have to stop injuring yourself for your own foolishness and lack of understanding. Forgive yourself for your spiritual ignorance. Simply stated, you could not have done the sinful things you did if you had really known better. We all suffer from spiritual ignorance from time to time, and we must learn never to get to the point where we are so bowed down with misinterpretation of what God and Christ meant, that religion becomes a boring, heavy, and lugubrious burden.

Religion is joy. It is health, vitality, and gladness. True religion is the presence of God within, without, and all about. In Latin, the very root word *religio* means "to bind back to the first cause." Well, what is the first cause? God. God projected this whole universe into being by an act of His will and His love. In order for us to have any idea of how that was done, we would have to have a far greater intellectual capacity than our species presently has. But we don't have to know how the Infinite created the cosmos. Humankind is able to perceive only dimly the mystery and marvel of the extraordinary machinery of this universe: galaxy upon galaxy. It is inconceivable for us simple little ones here at this level to comprehend the immensity of the Source and Giver of all life. We are His children; and God is a merciful and loving parent, considerate of our needs. So let us rest in that knowledge and truth, and lean confidently upon the Infinite, who sustains us now and always.

It is such a wondrous and exciting thing to realize that God is mindful of us. Knowing this, we should never underrate ourselves. We must always remember that a spark of the spirit of God, which created all things, resides in the very midst of us. We don't have to go anywhere to find it. The only place we need go is within the temple of the self.

So, dear friends, this coming week share your love, your smiles, and your blessings with everyone you meet. Give of yourself and pray for others' health, joy, peace, and well being. If you see somebody walking down the corridor looking terribly depressed and gloomy, go within yourself and mentally say, "Lord Christ, you are the author of all happiness. Bless this person, and bring light into this soul." That's a beautiful way to do a marvelous work of charity. Thoughts are things, and prayers are real; they are powerful. It is given to us by the teachings of Jesus the Christ to love one another. Remember what he said: *"By this shall all men [and women] know that you are my disciples"*—not by wearing a robe, or a cross on your chest; not by wearing a magic hat, or a gown with long-fringed sleeves; but— *"that you love one another."* (John 13:35.) Now, that doesn't mean you have to have a big emotional love and get all entwined. We can't be emotionally attracted to every living being. But we know that every living being has, at the very center of its existence, a spark of the Infinite; and it is that to which we turn and address ourselves. Overlook everything else, and send a silent uplifting and prayerful thought to those who seem a little unhappy or weary on their path. By sharing your love, your smiles, and your blessings, you are singing the praises of Him who is Lord of us, and of all the universes. Thank you. *Amen.*

How Excellent Is Thy Name

Heritage House Presbyterian Chapel, San Francisco, CA
July 25, 1982

Good morning dear friends. Today I am going to read a little from Psalm Eight: *"Lord, how excellent is thy name in all the earth! who hast set thy glory above the heavens. . . . When I consider thy heavens, the work of thy fingers, the moon and the stars, which thou hast ordained; what is man that thou art mindful of him? . . . thou hast made him a little lower than the angels, and hast crowned him with glory and honour. Thou madest him to have dominion over the works of thy hands; thou hast put all things under his feet."* (Ps. 8:1,3-6.)

I have a special affection for the Psalms, and I particularly like number eight because it reminds us that God has a pretty high regard for us. He made us "a little less than the angels." When I say that, I can almost hear some of you thinking, "Well, I don't know about that. I have some neighbors who haven't always been angels!" Yes, and maybe *you* haven't always been an angel, either! But remember, God made all things, and He called them good. Since God created you, it means you are good; not always perfect, but *good*. We are human, and that means we all make mistakes. We're here in the classroom of the earth experience in order to learn and grow, to become all that we are really capable of being as sons and daughters of God, and true heirs of heaven. Making mistakes only means we are unawakened and ignorant, but we are not *bad*.

As in any class, some students in the classroom of the earth experience are a little brighter than others. Some of them apply themselves and make great progress, while others make little or no progress. What a tragedy it is to see so many people giving up on themselves and on life, feeling no sense of hope or courage even to try. But there are some people whose life circumstances once seemed so totally bleak, desperate, and impossible, that they literally felt they had no strength left to carry on. Then, suddenly, they were touched by the presence and power of the Holy Spirit, and these same people began to feel new courage, dynamism, and strength. Restored by a sense of hope, they began to recover and bounce back to life. With new vitality and purpose, these people began to grow in consciousness. They came to accept the goodness in themselves, which they could not see when they were blinded by the enormity of their mistakes and faults. Accepting their inherent goodness, these once forlorn and hopeless people were renewed and rejuvenated by the power of forgiveness, both for others and for the self, and their lives were completely healed and transformed.

When you break the law and cause harm to others, you have to pay the piper, but God is infinitely merciful and forgiving. Don't ever say, "Oh, what I did was so terrible, God can never forgive me." Don't even say, "I *hope* God will forgive me," because God is bigger than any mistake you've ever made. He can, and *does*, forgive you. But besides God's forgiveness, it is vitally important that you learn to forgive yourself. That doesn't mean it's okay to go around committing crimes and doing all sorts of unscrupulous and hurtful things to people, and then letting yourself off the hook by saying, "Oh, that's okay. I forgive myself." That isn't what I mean. You must be accountable for yourself, for your thoughts and actions, as well as your *in*actions. You are responsible both for what you do, and for what you *don't* do. Yes, you must be accountable, but that doesn't mean that if you make a mistake, you have to punish yourself for the next thirty-seven lifetimes.

There are some people who insist on dragging around a sack of regrets and reproaches, in spite of the reiterated promises the Christ made to forgive us and heal us with his abundant mercy. I'm sure you know some of these people. They're the ones who did something wrong twenty-seven years ago, and they're still carrying the guilt of it around on their shoulders every day. They are very sorry for what they did, and they have even made restitution for it, but they are still burdened by the weight of self-condemnation. Look, if God has forgiven you, for heaven's sake forgive yourself. Let the guilt go, and do not permit yourself to wallow in self-pity and self-condemnation, because if you do, you are just sitting on the sidelines of life, turning your back on God's love, and refusing to participate in the glorious gift of life.

Refusing to forgive yourself is a way of holding yourself back, and it is a deliberate choosing to sit out this incarnation. You are certainly not contributing anything positive or worthwhile to yourself or anyone else when you allow guilt and shame to overshadow and dominate your life. Let go of the guilt, the shame, the sorrow, and the blame. Just let it all go, as though it never was; and determine deep within yourself that you will never repeat the mistake that has caused you, or anyone else, this kind of unnecessary anguish. Accept that you are worthy of God's understanding love, His mercy, and His gift of a new beginning. You don't have to walk around with a broken heart because of something somebody did to you thirty-seven years ago. Pick yourself up, and realize that there is healing for you. Understand that you *can* change, that there are unlimited opportunities for you, and that, with a fresh start and a commitment to prayer and meditation, you *will* begin to live in a whole new way.

Some people are very busy being sinners and feeling bad about themselves and their nature. They walk around in "sack cloth and ashes," with their heads hanging down and their eyes staring at the floor. They sit on the sidelines of life, never getting involved with people or activities that require anything of them. This kind of absence and separation from life is not true detachment, nor is it true humility. And mentally, it does nothing for you except keep you down. You'll never get off the ground with that kind of stance. Instead, why don't you accept the image God has of you as inscribed by David here in this wonderful Psalm Eight? Read it again and again this week. Rejoice and be exceedingly glad that the Heavenly Father, in His creation of the universe, has made you just "a little less than the angels." That's not too bad, is it?

Now, if we don't always behave like angels, it is only because we are ignorant. We don't know any better. Some of the greatest philosophers, theologians, and mystics have said that those who err, particularly by doing harm to their brothers or sisters, do so out of spiritual ignorance. If they had known better, they literally could not have done what they did. This is a wonderful truth to take into your meditation. It is very important to realize that when you make a mistake, most generally you do it out of spiritual ignorance, not because you are a no-good sinner or a bad person. Meditate on this until you *can* forgive yourself. You know you are truly repentant of your errors, so let God bless you.

The Bible tells us, *"Though your sins be as scarlet [and as numerous as the sands of the sea, yet God in His infinite mercy will wash them away till they become] white as snow."* (Isa. 1:18.) We must take hold of this promise of forgiveness. Continuing to berate yourself, even after the Lord has given you His benediction, does not honor Him. We have to realize that within each and every one of us, from the birth of our being until forever, there resides a spark of the Infinite, a spark of God Himself. We must become aware of this Christ spirit within us, and begin to *live* the Christ just as the saints do. The holy ones are profoundly aware that, with the help of God, they are able to make a real contact with the consciousness that Christ had, and so they do. With this consciousness, these people are spiritualizing their daily lives and changing the world in many ways. Now, you don't have to be a monk or a nun in order to do that. And it doesn't make any difference whether you are a Catholic, a Buddhist, a Hindu, or a Baptist. The important question is whether you have really accepted what all the great teachers have told you about the divine nature of your being.

In many cases, we find that we are forever procrastinating the divine confrontation, because we are timid about going too deep into the waters of mysticism and living a truly spiritualized life. Spiritualizing your life simply means filling the ordinary aspects of it with spiritual consciousness. That's all we have to do, and that is what it means to *"pray without ceasing."* (1 Thess. 5:17.) See, when St. Paul wrote about praying without ceasing, he didn't mean you have to be down on your knees all day. He meant that you should go through your day-to-day activities with an attitude of mind and heart that recognizes the supremacy of good. When you recognize and accept the supremacy of good, it becomes your sure reality, and then nothing can come nigh unto you that is anything other than good. It is up to you to "choose whom you shall serve": the light or the dark. When you turn your mind toward a more positive attitude and approach, you will see out-pictured in the circumstances of your life a more positive reflection of the inherent light and beauty that dwells within the temple of your being.

Jesus was an eminently practical psychologist, so when he gave us his marvelous Lord's Prayer, he put a condition on it, *"Forgive us our trespasses, as we forgive those who trespass against us."* (Matt. 6:12.) When you pray the "Our Father" you are really nailing yourself down to that promise to be forgiving. Just as we expect God to be merciful with us, *we* must be merciful, *we* must be compassionate, and *we* must forgive. Jesus said, *"By this shall all men know that you are my disciples, namely that you love one another."* (John 13:35.) So be kind and compassionate to others, and to yourself.

When I say that, people get a little nervous and whisper, "But I can't love *that* person." In fact, there *are* people in the world that you really don't care for, but you would never raise a finger to do them any harm. Certainly if they needed something, you would be the first person to help them. Spiritual love doesn't mean you have to be involved with them emotionally. So, dear friends, let us try to develop a more positive and loving approach to life. Let us enlarge the compassion of our hearts, and bow to the divinity that resides within every person we meet. When you do that, life's journey becomes much easier, much more pleasant, and much more beautiful.

There was a dear blind lady that I knew for a good many years, who went around with a guide dog. Today I found a little notice posted outside the chapel announcing that she has passed on. I think she was eighty-six. This lovely lady had a beautiful singing voice, and although she had been sightless since she was eight years old, she loved to take part in musicals and all sorts of other music projects. She was one of the happiest, most loving and delightful souls I ever met. One day I asked her, "What would you do if you could get your sight back?" She answered, "Oh, that would be wonderful. But if the return of my physical eyesight meant that I would lose my inner sight, the claim that I have on my spiritual nature, I would not accept it. I would rather remain as I am."

She was a truly beautiful soul, and a true Christian. She was always forgetting her own problems and thinking about others instead; always offering her love and asking, "What can I do for you today?" She expressed her great joy with the beauty of her voice. It was a gorgeous voice, and in her own way, she made an offering of herself through her singing. She was preaching the Christ by the marvelous example of her spirituality, which was so genuine and real because it came from deep within her. These are the kinds of Christians we like to think about, because they inspire us to be better Christians too.

Over the years, she and I sang a lot together, and I've always had a great affection and reverence for her. I was honored to dedicate a song to her at the start of our service this morning. She was indeed a very special person, because she was somebody who took God at His word, and lived a life that fully expressed the wealth of spiritual qualities He placed within her. She was fully aware of the inherent and triumphant divinity of her own nature. And she understood that despite her physical limitations, she could control most anything that came nigh unto her, by leaning upon the sustaining Infinite, and knowing eternally and forever that God intends good things for her.

Ultimately, we all have to come to know the nature of our own spiritual being as coordinated with the all-pervading One. We're not just little ants crawling around down here, separated from God by millions of light years. God is always and forever, and He intends good things for us. "It is His pleasure to give you the kingdom." Get out of your own way, and let Him give it to you!

So today, dear friends, let us think on these wholesome things. Let us practice thinking happy, healing thoughts. If you get up in the morning with a little headache, and your mind says, "Oh, this is going to be a rotten day. Look, it's windy outside. Oh, I hope they don't have fried rice for lunch today, because I hate fried rice," then you've begun your day feeling bad, and it will surely snowball throughout your entire day. Instead, just remind yourself that you have a choice about the kinds of thoughts you think, and about how you make yourself feel. When nasty little thoughts creep into your mind, just stop and mentally say to yourself, "Now wait a minute. I have a choice here: I'm not going to let myself be put down by these pesky, pessimistic thoughts first thing in the morning." Then ask God to help you turn your thoughts around, to lift you, and help you to be more optimistic and cheerful.

After you've had a cup of coffee or tea and a little breakfast, you'll feel very good again, and you'll realize it is because you made the choice of turning your mind around. See, God doesn't do it all for you. You have to ask for what you need. When you ask, He does come with the help you need in order to bring about that marvelous transformation of mind and heart. It begins with the magic and marvel of the teachings within the holy scriptures. So give a little time to reading this beautiful Psalm Eight again during the coming week. And remember, dear friends, you are "a little less than the angels." God has crowned you with glory. Meditate on that, take it into your heart, and try to live as closely as you possibly can to the picture God has of you. Thank you. *Amen.*

Be Not Anxious

Unity Temple, San Francisco, CA
August 15, 1982

Before I begin my talk today, I want to read from Matthew, Chapter 6, verses 28-30: *"And why take ye thought for raiment? Consider the lilies of the field, how they grow: they toil not, neither do they spin: and yet I say unto you, That even Solomon in all his glory was not arrayed like one of these. Wherefore, if God so clothe[d] the grass of the field . . . shall he not much more clothe you, O ye of little faith?"*

Father, fill our minds and hearts with the meaning of this text, so that we might lean constantly upon the sustaining Infinite and realize the truth, the power, and the drama of these words, so anciently spoken by the Lord Christ. Amen.

This scripture is very appropriate and timely, because many people seem to be disturbed over economic changes and all sorts of other problems occurring within the boundaries of our beloved country today. In these times, we must arm ourselves with a kind of living faith, and lean deeply and confidently upon the shoulder of God. The many parables and teachings of the Lord Christ are there to inspire us to an ever-increasing faith—and an ever-increasing positive dependence upon the way, the truth, and the light, which He set before us. It is the dominion of prayer, and the elevation of human consciousness, that transcend those things round about us which seem like dark clouds. It is important for us these days to have an attitude of mind that will keep us in a positive state, so that despite what is going on around us we should not (as my topic for today says) be anxious.

It is natural that sometimes we begin to be over-anxious, but let us not join the parade of "doomsdayers." The Lord Christ has taught us to rise above our humanness, and apply the principles of undying and invincible faith with a dedicated and positive attitude. He asks us to enter into a consciousness that will liberate us from being over-anxious. He asks us to light a candle within our consciousness, knowing that nobody can light that little part of the universe but *you*. When you see that you are becoming anxious, it is important for you to change how you are thinking and feeling.

Now, many people let themselves slip into a little rut of uncertainty and doubt. That's very natural, very human. But the Christ taught us that we possess a unique power of the mind, and that is the power of prayer, which transcends all these mortal effects. If we follow what Christ taught us, we will have no doubt at all in our hearts or minds that no matter what comes we are at one with Him, for He is all-pervading. Statistically, the newspapers may be right about there being ten million unemployed people. But if you're looking for a job, you don't want ten million jobs; you only want one. All you have to do, as an individual incarnation of the living truth, is know that the power of prayer, plus your divinely expressed gift of awakened imagination, can lead you into the green pastures of total solvency and all good. Then, you see, you are acting in cooperation with the law of the spirit of the Cosmic Christ, and the Holy Spirit.

I've been around a long while, and I've learned that things take time. The world goes through problems of various sorts, and from time to time we all respond to them with anxiety. It seems that this is a time of testing. When you become a little over-concerned about our present situation, or the future, or things in general, instead of letting anxiety overtake you, why don't you ask the Christ for an increased faith and confidence in His love?

Down through the ages there have been many wonderful teachings that have come to us through the great masters in the Orient, the Greek and Roman philosophers, and the Christian mystics and saints. All of them have reminded us of the transcending power of a living faith. Sometimes we have to fan the flames of that living faith because we get so careless that we begin to find ourselves slipping into fear and doubt. I find myself doing that from time to time, and I'm sure I'm not terribly different from everybody else. So when I notice I am slipping into doubt, I remember the old saying, "The brave man, the man of courage, dies but once. The fearful one dies a thousand times." So let us make these years our best years, even as we find ourselves in a world that is in some confusion. This is a time of transition, a time of great and small changes.

Instead of being anxious, let us steadfastly fan the flames of faith so that we can stand forth as beacons of light, representatives of what can be done by those who lean upon God. There are always trials and tribulations upon planet earth, and these remind men and women everywhere that this is not the only world; this is not the end. We grow through a certain amount of friction. If there were no friction, there would be no growth. Remember when you were a child at summer camp, and the camp master taught you to rub two sticks together and start a nice bonfire? Well, if there were no friction, there would be no energy; and if there were no energy, there would be no flame; and if there were no flame, there would be no fire. Think of how an oyster produces a beautiful pearl. A little sand gets in the oyster and causes irritation. It irritates and irritates, and what does the oyster do? It produces a beautiful pearl! So the next time a very bad irritation comes, just say to yourself, "I am going to use this little irritant, this grain of negativity, to quicken my consciousness and produce a pearl of absolute faith, a pearl of unimaginable beauty, a pearl of great price." In that way, you see, you begin to flow rather easily with the problems and challenges that come into your experience. In this way, with the help of God, we are certain to triumph. If it were not so, then all of philosophy and religion and the whole search and journey would be a mockery, wouldn't it? God didn't set us down here to play games with us. He brought us here so that we might know Him and grow ever closer to Him as truth, light, and love operating in our lives as a living reality. When trials and tribulations come, make them a useful factor in your life. Fan the flames of faith in order to transform anxiety and doubt—just as the little grain of sand causes irritation and thus creates a beautiful, priceless pearl.

In another part of the scripture we read that, *"Are not two sparrows sold for a farthing? And one of them shall not fall on the ground without your Father [knowing]."* (Matt. 10:29.) And: *"Your Father knoweth what things ye have need of, before ye ask him."* (Matt. 6:8.) Now, in that last scriptural line it is assumed that we will ask; but if we do not ask, we must not be surprised when things get all tangled up and our world turns upside down. All success, spiritual force, health, vitality, and liberation are a result of a living faith. In so many places in the Bible it is taken for granted that we ask for what we need—but so often we forget to ask. We get busy with the immediacy of our problems, and we lose consciousness of the fact that there is an invincible power that can be contacted through prayer. So do not fail, dear friends, to pray to the all-loving Father and to ask for even simple things. Don't say, "Well, the Father is very busy, and I'm sure He hasn't got time to worry about one of my little problems." As I read earlier in Matthew, *"Consider the lilies of the field, how they grow: they toil not, neither do they spin: and yet I say unto you, That even Solomon in all his glory was not arrayed like one of these."* When we read this beautiful story, we realize how faint our faith really is sometimes, and how dim our prayers. So let us ask for what we need, and let us not be anxious.

Affirm right now that you're not going to jump on the bandwagon of fear. Anxiety and fear can become an epidemic like the measles. Pretty soon everybody catches it, and all you hear is a chorus of, "Oh, isn't it awful. Isn't it terrible." You know, if we would only stop for five minutes, we could really turn things around. We could begin to invest in ourselves by creating a better concept of tomorrow. And so, dear friends, let us remember to meditate and pray every day. It's so easy to let time pass, and then before you know it a whole year has gone by and your problems remain unchanged. Don't let that happen to you.

We hear so many sermons about prayer and about faith, and yet sometimes in the clinches, we forget to operate this wonderful aspect of our divine nature. From time to time, we all fail in being firm in our daily practice, but we must gather our forces together and come to an increasing realization of the importance of making that daily contact, that daily communion with God. Don't wait till dire things are happening. The Lord is so compassionate that He *will* answer, so make it a rule of life that you will touch daily into that supreme and transforming power of truth. In practicing contact with the all-loving God *every* day, you see, you begin to build an invincible spiritual strength, and that is *very* important. So don't neglect it.

A generally accepted truth, transcending even religious considerations, is that we get out of life what we put into it. What we put into something returns to us in kind. That which you cast into the ether, or into the realm of faith, will come back to you multiplied. Again and again, we are urged to emphasize positive prayer; to elevate our minds and create a contact between us and the great unseen force: the great liberating power that humankind calls God. It's wonderful to do that every day, not just once in a while or when we are in great need. We have to practice every day.

Christ said, *"Whatsoever ye shall ask in my name, that will I do."* (John 14:13.) If you find that you occasionally feel a lack of living faith, a faith of great power, ask the Father for your faith to be quickened. When faith awakens in the life of anyone, miracles begin to happen. So, during your meditation, ask for a clear insight that will unwrap and rouse your faith. When you open your faith to its fullest, those things which humankind has called miraculous really do begin to take place. The only reason they don't happen more often is simply that we lack the kind of simple faith that Christ and other miracle workers throughout time have possessed. God is so merciful, and He works through simple clay pots like you and me. His flowers of healing, love, and faith blossom in those who live in and express a conscious realization of His immanent presence and power.

Throughout the scriptures, we are alerted to the fact that God is mindful of us, that He is not far off. "The Holy Spirit is ever nigh." You may have read this twenty-seven hundred times before, but now, suddenly, a light is turned on. When that which you have read and heard so many times takes on a new quality of vibrant faith, your whole life cannot but change.

Throughout the Bible you find encouraging words like these: *"Ask in My name,"* (John 14:13.) and *"ask believing."* (Matt. 21:22.) Don't be afraid to ask, and don't be a piker when you are asking for a miracle. God is bigger than anything you could ever imagine in a thousand billion years, and His compassion is infinite. *"It is the Father's good pleasure to give you the kingdom [of heaven],"* (Luke 12:32.) so ask for what you really want, and let your desire for more life be as large and as broad as it can be, until it encompasses all things.

Why don't we take the Master at His word and become the miracle-workers of today? We put stumbling blocks in our way when we think, "If I have too much faith, if I meditate and pray too much, if a miracle happens through me, people will think I'm a crank or a fanatic." Well, never mind those people. You don't have to trumpet your faith all over the place. Faith is a living quality within the temple of your own marvelous being, wherein the Christ dwells. And so again, I urge you to read this scripture of Matthew. Take God at His word, and you will find that as you lean upon the sustaining Infinite, those things which the uninitiated call marvels *will* happen in your life.

So let us make up our minds today to be so filled with a sense of the same immanent power, light, and bliss that filled the Christ ministry, that we may begin to see it work in our own lives, too, in small and in large ways. A very wise teacher, Paramhansa Yogananda, used to say, "A saint is a sinner who never stopped trying." We never know at what moment Spirit will touch us with a light so enchanting, so incredibly marvelous, and so revealing, that the whole of our lives will be transformed. Even our bodies become transformed and healed as we are lifted up in consciousness. Let us cooperate with Spirit in bringing about these wonderful transformations, by using the remarkable God-given aspects of our wonderful minds.

You know, yesterday morning when I got up, I was only able to speak in a hoarse whisper. I must have sounded like a man coming down to earth on a flying saucer from some other planet. I thought, "Gee, I'll never be able to give the two talks I'm scheduled for tomorrow." Then I looked at the church bulletin and saw the title of my talk, right there in living print: "Be Not Anxious." "Wow," I thought, "I'm giving a marvelous example of being anxious, so I have to change my mind." So I got to work and determined that I AM well, and that I AM going to be able to give both of my talks this morning. The first one was at the Presbyterian Chapel at the Heritage House, and it went very well. And now here I am, talking to you, and my voice is holding up just fine.

We have to have the kind of confidence that gives us an imperishable, invincible faith in the reality of the marvelous faculties of mind. Using these higher faculties, we can bring about our healing and the fulfillment of our dreams. We must wake up that faculty and use it. We have to practice picturing, feeling, smelling, tasting, and touching, but most importantly we must walk, talk, and think as if the new reality is already here, right now.

And so dear friends, I want to urge you to *"be not anxious."* (Matt. 6:25.) Remember the lilies of the field, and realize that the Lord Christ said, *"Solomon in all his glory was not arrayed like one of these."* (Matt. 6:29.) Know that within your expanded awareness you are infinitely more; you are indeed the sons and daughters of God, and heirs of the eternal heavens. When those things which beset and disturb you come, and you think, "My word, this is terrible. This is awful," (and it is sometimes), don't give them any energy. Why? Because we have been taught by the Christ that God is mindful of His own, and that we are much more valuable than the lilies of the field. Remembering that bolsters our faith when things get a little rough.

Christ taught in so many marvelous parables, and through so many extraordinary examples of healing. We must realize that his miracle-working power is as real today as when he walked the earth. His presence and power are as vital, ongoing, marvelous, and thrillingly within us as they were two thousand years ago. Jesus said that we must *"store up our treasure."* (Matt. 6:20.) What does that mean? It means we must store up our sense of ongoing values within the self, within our expanding consciousness, and then we will be triumphant. Nothing can take that treasure away from you. So make a little pact between yourself and your God that you will never let a day go by without practicing the presence and releasing all anxiety and worry. Then you will be wonderfully happy and delightfully rewarded. You will have a more beautiful understanding of what life is all about.

We should never be anxious or worry unduly, for *behold*—take hold of this—the Lord Christ, who could move mountains, stands by your side. To the degree that you will consciously and vitally accept this challenge to anchor your trust in the promises of Christ, to that degree will you find that your whole mind and heart will become more tranquil and sure.

Jesus the Christ taught with simple lessons and stories in order to remind us of the importance and power of prayer. He promised us that when we call upon the Father in his name, we *will* be heard. So when the winds blow, and storms billow, begin to give thanks to the Father that the protective and healing grace of the infinite Light has been implanted in you, and *know* that it resides in the very midst of you. That power is unspeakably wonderful. It lifts us up physically, mentally, morally, spiritually, emotionally, and in every other way—so that life's journey becomes truly beautiful, truly wonderful. Then, even the biggest challenges of life can give us a kind of excitement. Once we are attuned to this power, we discover a resilience and strength we didn't know we had. So, dear friends, be not dismayed, be not disturbed, for God is always in the very midst of you. You cannot go where he is not.

"*If God so clothe[d] the grass of the field . . . shall he not much more clothe you, O ye of little faith?*" See, if God cares so much about those little flowers and grasses of the field, imagine how much more He cares about you. God has created you in His own image, in spirit, and He has given you dominion. Claim your dominion. If you don't claim it, you won't have it. Claim that dominion, accept it, give thanks for it, work with it, and you will find that the days of your life will be joyous. We want our days to be light and joyous. Who wants to be miserable?

So, dear friends, practice every day. Use the power of your awakened imagination and the power of your enlivened faith. Do those things that will bring this whole wondrous game of life to a triumphant winning point. Don't worry that you don't have what it takes, or that you can't do it by yourself. You don't have to do this work alone. You do it with the power and grace of the Christ within, for with Him all things are possible. Thank you. *Amen.*

Your Awakened Imagination

Unity Temple, San Francisco, CA
August 15, 1982

Good morning, dear friends. Today I am going to talk about one of the greatest gifts God has given us, our creative imagination.

Now, just what is awakened imagination? All of us have known this imaginary quality at some time in our lives. When you were a child and you used to sit and daydream, your mother might have said, "Oh, don't mind little Mary. She's got her head in the clouds again," or "Johnny's in a brown study." At those times you were lost in a kind of reverie; you were somewhere far away, in a trance-like state, believing that you could fly like a bird or live underwater like a mermaid. When you were a little kid, you had all kinds of thoughts like that.

All children have very active imaginations, and it is a great pity that as we grow up, many of us are discouraged from using our natural gift of creative imagination. Let's say that little Bobby comes in with some tall and colorful story, and his mother or father says something like, "Oh come on now, Bobby, you know that's all fantasy. It's just your imagination." Well, eventually Bobby gets the idea that using his imagination is not a good thing.

Like Bobby, many children are talked out of using this wonderful creative faculty, and pretty soon they regard imagination as "the land of make believe"—a pretend world, reserved only for fantasy. Sadly, as youngsters grow up, many of them put away their wonderful dream-fulfilling imagination, along with the other playthings of childhood. But imagination is not just for children. Those who have delved deeply into the science of metaphysical thinking will tell you that the creative faculty of imagination is one of the most marvelous of all the divine attributes of humankind. But it must be awakened, and it must be concentrated; it must be projected into your universe as a positive, dynamic fact of the present. It must be quickened and exercised in the NOW. How do we do that? We do it through the dynamic soul quality of *enthusiasm*.

I urge you always to remember that imagination is a wonderful, divinely natural gift. Using it properly is the first step in creating anything. You are always using your subconscious mind power anyway, whether positively or negatively, consciously or not. When you focus the power of this marvelous and ingenious tool, you can intentionally call forth your good creations by directing the beam of your concentration toward that which you would like to see materialized in your life.

In the vast and boundless dimensions of Spirit, there is no time, so always remember to make the future NOW. Then, truly, you will be a living confirmation of the scripture, *"Therefore I say unto you, what things soever ye desire, when ye pray, believe that ye receive them, and ye shall have them."* (Mark 11:24.)

Last week I went for my annual physical, and I'm happy to report that I'm in very good shape. While I was sitting in the waiting room, I overheard four people discussing a television show they had seen last week. One of them anxiously said, "Did you hear that two million people are now out of work in this country?" Now, it's very hard not to be anxious about the thought that you might join the ranks of the jobless. Statistically, they may be right about the number of unemployed; but if *you're* looking for a job, you don't need two million jobs, you only need one! As an individual incarnation of the living truth, all you have to do is cooperate with the cosmic law of the Holy Spirit, and know that you and your divinely given gift of awakened imagination can lead you into the green pastures of total solvency and all good.

I've been around a long while, and I've learned that things take time. The world has gone through problems of various sorts in every period of history. In my time I've been through a few biggies myself: two world wars and the Great Depression. But we mustn't jump on the bandwagon of fear, broadcasting it all over the place, because then it becomes an epidemic like the measles and pretty soon everybody catches it. "Oh, did you hear about *this* . . . did you hear about *that* . . . isn't this awful . . . isn't that terrible."

Don't join that crowd of doomsday-ers. Instead, make up your mind that you are not going to give in to fear and anxiety, and then get busy using the divine tools that you have been given to make life's journey beautiful. Remember, we have been given authority over our lives, but it is up to us to exercise that power of dominion by activating the wondrous faculty of awakened imagination.

In the second book of Timothy 1:7 we read, *"For God hath not given us the spirit of fear; but of power, and of love, and of a sound mind."* If the fear mongers would only stop for five minutes and devote a little time to concentrating their mind power, they could project their consciousness into a wholly better concept of tomorrow.

When you talk to these people, they say, "Oh, sure, I'd *like* to work with my consciousness, I really would. But I just don't have time to meditate and work with my inner self." They'll tell you about all the books they've read, the lectures they've attended, and the seminars they've taken. But reading and listening are not enough to build your mind power. If you want to evolve and become all that you are meant to be, you must exercise your consciousness and use the awakened faculties of your inner self.

We may be lifted by lofty thoughts found on the written page, and occasionally we are stirred by an inspired speaker. Our mental vibrations may even be raised for a time. But while reading may inspire us, it does not strengthen the mind; it only provides material for thought. You may read a great deal, but your mental growth depends on how you *use* what you read. If you overload your mind with a lot of information but never assimilate it, that material, instead of nourishing and strengthening your mind, may actually become a burden that causes you to suffer mental indigestion.

We have to learn to quiet the mind and keep it focused on one thought, and that takes practice. Why don't you make a little pact with yourself that after you read for five minutes, you will think for ten minutes. You may be very surprised to discover that your ability to still the mind and focus it in one direction is not as strong as you thought.

At first you might become annoyed with yourself, when you see that you are unable to hold a single thought in your mind without the interruption of a thousand other thoughts. And you may be tempted to abandon this little exercise because you find it too painstaking and boring. But you mustn't procrastinate and drag your feet in this area if you want to develop the higher faculties of your mind. The only way you can direct your thoughts with any success is to develop and control your mind power.

With practice, your thoughts will become the clay with which you mold the dreams of your life. But you must work at it; you must exercise the mind and awaken your imagination. Always remember that when you are working with the creative faculty of your mind, you must use the *present tense*, not the future tense. That's very important, because if you say something is *going to* come about in the future, you are declaring that you are *separate* from it. Everything is *already* a part of infinite consciousness, and therefore available to you *now*.

Let us say that you are having a problem of some sort, and you want to resolve it. You've read all kinds of spiritual and metaphysical books—you've heard a thousand and one lectures on positive thinking, and now you're ready to implement this knowledge. What do you do? First, sit quietly and begin attuning yourself to the ocean of divine consciousness within you, this mighty Kingdom of Heaven that is your Father's good pleasure to give you. Now, focus on your heart's desire as if it were *already* materialized, already accomplished; and become involved with it totally, giving it all the qualities and tones of reality. Rehearse your awareness of the wish fulfilled, enlarge it, and then project it into expression by your awakened imagination.

For several years I have taught a five-week class designed to help people develop their sensitivities and awaken the dormant faculties of the higher mind. One of those classes is devoted almost exclusively to contacting the infinite power of the subconscious mind. We all have a subconscious, you know, and whether you are aware of it or not, you brought it with you today.

Now, most people don't know that the subconscious mind does not reason. It is *in*ductive, not *de*ductive. Therefore, you can kill yourself with your subconscious mind power—or you can literally resurrect your body, your emotions, and your whole life by turning it into a dynamic, positive force for good. Whether you want to improve your health, get that new job, or meet the love of your life—the subconscious will do it for you if you invest it with the power of enthusiasm, plus awakened imagination. That is the formula that energizes and gets things off the ground.

If you say you want to change your life, but all you do is sit at home and moan, *"Oh, isn't it awful . . . two million people are unemployed . . . I guess in three months, twenty million more will be unemployed and then we'll all starve together . . ."* you will never get anywhere. That kind of thinking only leaves you stuck in the mud of your own mental lethargy, and it might even dig a deeper hole of negativity for you to fall into. As you work with your thoughts, keep them positive, hopeful, and expectant. In Mark 11:24 we read, *"Therefore I say unto you, what things soever ye desire, when ye pray, believe that ye receive them, and ye shall have them."*

Maybe some of you remember the Depression, the big one back in the 1930s. Franklin Delano Roosevelt was famous for his "fireside addresses to the nation." He would draw up his imaginary fireside; and his voice would be broadcast over the radio from Washington, all across the country. He had a rather robust voice, and he used it well to announce to the people, "We have nothing to fear but fear itself." He broadcast that phrase again and again, and eventually people began to feel hopeful. They began to bring together the artillery of concentrated emotional energy, and they began to expect better days. In time, that which had been the deepest depression in the whole of our nation's experience was resolved, and we went on to greater and greater prosperity.

As we read the Four Gospels of the New Testament, we are amazed at the number of appeals that are made, not only to our faith, but also to the specific act of asking. Remember what the Christ said, *"Ask what ye will [in my name], and it shall be done unto you."* (John 15:7.) In another chapter he says, *"Ask believing, and it shall be so."* (This is a paraphrasing of Matt. 21:22: *"And all things, whatsoever ye shall ask in prayer, believing, ye shall receive.*") We have to ask, and we have to ask believing. With a kind of meditative stance, we have to make contact with that marvelous aspect of the subconscious mechanism that arouses the human imagination.

There are two times in daily life when you can make contact with this marvelous aspect of yourself: one is upon going to sleep, and the other is upon waking. During those times you are floating in a nice little cloud of consciousness in which you are neither awake nor asleep. Scientists love big names, so they call this the *hypnagogic state.* (Sounds impressive, doesn't it?) As I said, it happens twice every twenty-four hours.

So, let's say it's a Saturday or Sunday morning and you don't have to run off to work, so you can give a little time to this. There you are; you just woke up, and you're floating peacefully. It's so nice and restful. Now, maybe you have a physical illness of some kind, an emotional problem, or even a spiritual dilemma. During the hypnagogic state you can make contact with that area of your consciousness that is, shall we say, the "vestibule" of the heaven worlds, where miracles are born.

Now, the secret of bringing about the fulfillment of your need or desire is to declare it as being so right NOW. Don't say, "I'm *going* to be better." *Going to be* is a long way off. It keeps you in exile and separation from your good.

I can almost hear some of you saying, "But I only have thirty dollars in my bank account," or "I can see the bruise right here on my knee; I can't just wish it away." Of course, your present conditions appear quite different from what you would like to see. You have to focus your mind power, awaken your capacity to imagine vividly, call forth your faith, and declare your healing as already accomplished. Many mystical people tell us that both disease and healing come about on the inner plane before being reflected in the outer plane of the physical body. We don't care how it happens; all we really have to know is that inherent within our very nature is a marvelous tool of creative consciousness. It is a most reliable wonder-working aspect of the self, and it works outside the confines of our definitions of time and place.

You know, there really is no such thing as time. Time is a noise the clock makes. There isn't any time in the heaven worlds; it's all an eternal NOW. Time is a convenience for us down here on *terra firma*, on this solid earth plane. For example, we say our Church service begins at 11:00 A.M. That's fine; we all agree to come together at a specific point in time so that we can talk about spiritual principles and learn to live in harmony with them. But time is not a fixed reality or a linear event, determined by the kitchen clock.

It is difficult for us earth creatures to comprehend the multidimensional reality of Spirit with our limited three-dimensional perception. Light is all-pervading and not confined to one place; it vibrates more rapidly than solid objects, captured as they are in this dense physical world. When things move more slowly, it is easier to measure them.

Of course, this is a very simplistic explanation of time. All you really have to be concerned with is the consciousness of the ever-present NOW. Then you will bring about the manifestation and fulfillment of your heart's desires. So always remember to say, "I am healthy NOW in body and mind."

Through the marvelous faculty of your own creative imagination, you can develop the conscious power to direct your tomorrows. The degree to which you are able to do that will depend on your willingness to sow the seeds of positivity. There is no better time than now to begin using these tools and faculties of the higher self. If you will only take hold of that positivity, laying aside all worry and anxiety, you will make for yourself the life that you really wish for.

Scripture says, *"Be not anxious."* (Matt. 6:34.) Anxiety is a form of fear, and fear is *faith in reverse. "Be not anxious."* I can almost hear someone say, "Yeah, well, that's easy for *him* to say, standing up there in his ivory tower. He doesn't have the troubles *I* have." Well, every one of us has some sort of difficulty to deal with. There is an old saying (and I believe it deeply) that God never gives us so much to bear that we are totally crushed and cannot transcend it. There is no problem of yours so great that God cannot fix it. Aren't you denigrating God when you say nothing can be done? "God can do this for him over here, and He can do that for her over there, but He can't take care of my problem right here. It's too big." Well, then, your faith is too little! God can fix anything!

I have a dear old friend who grew up in the South. She is very fond of saying in her thick drawl, *"Honey, when God fix it, iss fixed!"* God is bigger than all of our problems. He gives us the help we need; He shows us the way, and He provides the power to transcend all our trials. We grow into divine partnership, and we become co-creators with God as we bring into activity that marvelous aspect of our being, namely: awakened imagination. Then our whole life changes.

Do you really want to see a change in your life? How much do you want it? How badly do you want that new car, that new job, that physical or emotional healing, that life partner, or your dream home? Are you willing to spend a little time every day, sitting in front of the screen of your inner mind, vividly imagining your shiny new car sitting proudly in your driveway? Or your beautiful new home, filled with lovely furniture and the smiling faces of a reconciled family? You must visualize your dream as true NOW, with all the sensory awareness of which you are capable, in finest detail. It doesn't matter whether it is a physical healing or some material thing that you want. Ask, and ask abundantly. Now, we don't ask for the truly impossible, like sprouting wings so we can fly off tall buildings; not at all. But we *can* bring about any reasonable and right desire if we become very still and consciously visualize it on the screen of the inner mind, remembering to give thanks for it, even before it appears.

Many years ago I had polio in my right foot. The doctors couldn't even diagnose my condition, that's how long ago this was. They thought it was something else, and they said, "You'll never walk without crutches." Well, I didn't believe them. I saw myself jumping around like a flea on a hot tin roof, and by George, it didn't take long before I threw those crutches away.

The doctor, not to be outdone by my display of bravado, came up with a solemn announcement that seemed to say, "How dare you contradict medical science!" He told me I would never walk without a cane. I responded, "Bull feathers (or something stronger)! NO WAY!" I hurled the cane over the fence—and, you know, I was so enthusiastic when I did it that, I forgot that I had borrowed that cane from a friend. So then, I had to go and buy a new one for him! But it only goes to show that what we accept in the household of our consciousness today becomes the reality of our tomorrows. It is as simple as that. We have to lean upon the sustaining Infinite with the kind of confidence that gives us an imperishable and invincible faith in the reality of our awakened imagination. We must arouse that sleeping faculty, and use it.

We have to practice and practice seeing, feeling, smelling, hearing, and touching our mental picture. But most importantly, we must walk and talk and think *as if* our dream is already here. How would you *feel* if your dream were realized? How would you walk, talk, and sleep at night?

Stir up your enthusiasm; wake it up. Wake *yourself* up. Most of the time, you know, people are just sort of floating around, half asleep, having a pleasant time, saying, "Oh yeah, someday I'll do something about this stuff that John Laurence talks about all the time, but right now I have to take a nap." That pale energy will never work if you want to get the ball rolling.

You need much more enthusiasm and conviction, if you are ever to overcome the obstacles in your life. You need the power of enthusiasm, plus action, if you really want to rid yourself of a bad habit or addiction, or to call forth the fulfillment of your dreams. Don't work with feeble energy. If you want to change a negative or toxic aspect of your life, go home and pound the pillow and declare, "I am NOT going to have this in my life!" You must use enough energy to activate your entire nervous system. That will really get the ball rolling. Then, meditate daily, and give thanks to the Father that you are liberated from whatever it is that seems to hinder you.

So dear friends, I want to urge you to remember that imagination is one of the greatest gifts God has given us. As I said in the beginning of this talk, it is the first step in creating anything. Always use your subconscious mind power positively and consciously, and call forth your good and worthy creations by directing the beam of your concentration toward that which you would like to see materialized in your life. In the vast and boundless dimensions of Spirit there is no time, so remember to make the future NOW. Then, truly, you will be a living confirmation of the scripture, *"Therefore I say unto you, whatsoever things ye desire, when ye pray, believe that ye have received them, and ye shall have them."* Thank you. *Amen.*

If Thine Eye Be Single

Heritage Presbyterian Chapel, San Francisco, CA
September 26, 1982

Dear friends, this morning I am going to talk about light. In every religion, light is a symbol for God. Let us read a line from the Gospel of Luke, the great physician: *"No man, when he hath lighted a candle, putteth it in a secret place, [or] under a bushel."* (Luke 11:33.) When we light a candle, we don't stick it under the coffee table or hide it behind the refrigerator. We always put it in a place where it can bring light to the whole room. When we say to someone, "Don't hide your light under a bushel," we usually say it to encourage them. We are fond of telling children not to hide their talent under a bushel, but to step forward and let it shine.

This scripture can also be quoted as a way to keep the egotistical pride of a youngster in check. My dear, wonderful mother was deeply religious, an Irish Catholic, and once in a while she was not above bringing in the scriptures to let me have it if she thought I was getting a little too proud of myself for something I had done. One time, with playfulness and the sweet lilt of her Irish brogue, she said, "Ah, John, be careful now. Why hide your light under a bushel, when a half pint will do!?" That was the way she reminded me not to become too proud.

Now, I love what Luke says here because, you see, light is a symbol for the presence of God, for the cosmic essence and power of divinity within ourselves. It's fine to speak of the light as a poetic expression, but how do we really experience it? How do we make it real? It is by your dedicated practice of meditation and prayer that your consciousness ripens into a profound identification with the Source of life and light. When light enters the sanctuary of your inner self, all that was enshrouded by darkness is uncovered and swallowed up. Where does the darkness go? It vanishes like a vapor, and all darkness is erased from your mind. Only light remains to illumine your thoughts.

It is very important that you anchor your thoughts to the positive, spiritual side of life, because that is the best way to heal yourself, and to be of service in the healing of others. Whether you are a minister, a priest, a student, a worker, or a mom or dad, try to be an example of what it really means to live in the light, to be sustained by the light, and eventually to *become* the light. Then you cannot but radiate and impart that light to the world. Dedicate your life and your spiritual practice toward ultimate unification with the luminosity and life-giving essence of God. And when all the darkness and smallness of the individual self will have vanished into the infinite cosmic Self, you will stand hand in hand with Jesus, together declaring, *"I am the light of the world."* (John 8:12.)

"The light of the body is the eye." (Matt. 6:22.) Isn't that an interesting statement? We must be careful to train our minds to look for that which is truly beautiful and constructive. Do we really look for the good in life? Do we really try to see the lovely and noble qualities in people? Or

do we sometimes lean toward a pessimistic view of life, and dwell on the shortcomings of others? Well, you know, throughout the Bible we find passages that are devoted to teaching us to lean toward the positive side, and think upon those things that are lovely, uplifting, and beautiful. When we train our minds to do that habitually, we become aligned and identified with that which is lovely and ongoing, and we are less likely to err and fall into negativity.

Now, I know that everything isn't going to be jolly and perfect all the time, but we do have some control over it. The great physician Luke was more of a psychologist than he knew. Of course, in those days they didn't have psychologists; but he certainly was one, because he knew how to tell people that they must identify with the light, and hang onto it (light being the symbol for God). He knew that when people took hold of the life raft of light within themselves, it would cast out every sense of sin and sorrow, every failure and regret, every guilt and shame; and it would forever banish bad moods, discouragement, depression, lack of faith, and every other disease of the spirit. We have to let these demons go, and instead, cling to the light.

Before you sit down for your meditation (and I'm sure you all take a little time to meditate everyday), open your Bible or some other inspiring book, and read a verse or two. I have a very nice Bible with big print that I like to bring with me to church. These inspired texts carry within them the energy to awaken and lift us into a clearer perception of divine reality. Even the single verse we read today can light a candle in the darkness of your understanding, if you take it into the silence of your heart and meditate deeply upon its meaning.

If we want to have a good life, feel good about ourselves, and be of service to others, we must meditate upon the light. *"If . . . thine eye be single, thy whole body shall be full of light."* (Luke 6:22.) See, when we turn our eyes away from mortal affliction, and begin to fix our gaze upon the glories of spirit, then indeed our body temple is filled with light. Then, just as the dimness of night retreats before the oncoming sun, all that is unlike good begins to fade away. *"But if thine eye be evil, thy whole body shall be full of darkness."* (Luke 6:23.) In other words, we have a choice. We can think of light, or we can choose darkness.

Some people, to their great peril, choose darkness. It's very sad, but it is not an accident. It is they who are driving their destiny, by their own creative faculty of imagination and by the power of the words they speak.

Thoughts of failure and poverty, self-condemnation and unforgiveness, become the threads that weave the tapestry of their lives. Sadly, the stories of such people are the stories we see on the nightly news. If we could only realize that our world reflects back to us our moods and thoughts, we would change them. By changing our minds, and moving into a bright acceptance of the healing presence of God, we are moved out of the darkness of ignorance, unforgiveness, and a thousand other woes that hasten ill health and death. When we change our view of the world from fearful to friendly, and begin to see ourselves not as forgotten and unloved, but as purposeful and cherished, we increase the light of our lives. Then, through the grace of God and the power of the living Christ, our lives cannot but be altered for the good.

Who wouldn't want to live in a lighted room, feeling joy and a sense of well-being, rather than in a dark room, feeling bad? Who wants the latter? Who needs that? Nobody. So remember, you do have a choice, and you can make that choice right here and now. You can choose to be unhappy, unforgiving, wounded, and broken-hearted; or you can choose to let all the hurts go, and embrace the light of a happy heart.

Now, we have all been offended by certain people at various times in our lives, and sometimes those people didn't even know that they hurt us. In any case, it is up to us to forgive them. How is the light going to fill your temple of being if you have reserved a special little corner of darkness, where you store all the ashes of resentments, hurts, and unforgiveness? How can the light pervade the holy shrine of your consciousness and overflow into your day, when all morning you are rehearsing offenses, criticism, judgment, and dislike for somebody— just because when you passed them in the hallway and greeted them with a cheerful "Good morning," they walked right past you without saying a word? That person might have been thinking very deeply about something, and didn't hear you. But you didn't think about that. You just concluded, "Mr. So-and-So doesn't like me anymore."

Don't let that sort of thing grow on you. Just say, "Well, I guess he didn't hear me." Let it pass, because you don't need to crowd the temple of your mind with a lot of extraneous mental static. Better still, why don't you mentally say, "God bless Mr. Snodgrass. May the light shine in him." This example is a simple illustration of how easily we can get our feelings hurt, but the same principle is at work with larger hurts and betrayals.

The saints, mystics, and holy ones are people who have dedicated their lives to seeking truth and a higher reality with such intensity that, like Christ, their whole consciousness became filled with blazing inner light. When you look at such a person, you see radiating from them a beautiful aura of happiness, simplicity, and sanctity; for in the infinite wellspring of light, they have realized the foundation of life. Follow them, and model yourself after them, until all your affairs are made smooth and harmonious, your health is restored, and your heart overflows with joy and newness of life. Then, silently declare, "I am full of thanksgiving, for I am restored, and my whole body is full of light."

And so, dear friends, I urge you to spend a little quiet time every day in meditation upon the all-pervading light of God. Breathe that light into your temple, identify with the living presence and ongoing life of that light, and then truly you will know that Christ dwells in you, and you in Him. When you make that a habit, your journey through life will be much more joyous and healthy, and you will be a beacon of light for everyone you meet. Thank you. *Amen.*

Seek and You Shall Find

Heritage House Presbyterian Chapel, San Francisco, CA
October 16, 1982

In Matthew we read, *"Ask, and you shall receive; seek, and you shall find; knock, and it shall be opened unto you: for every one that asketh receiveth; and he that seeketh findeth, and to him that knocketh it shall be opened. For what man is there among you, if his son asked for bread would he give him a stone? . . . If you then, being lesser, know how to give good gifts unto your children, how much more shall your Father which is in heaven give good things to them that ask him?"* (Matt. 7:6-9,11.)

You know, when you knock on someone's door, your purpose is generally to make him aware of your presence and your desire to speak to him. It alerts him to come and open the door to you. It's as simple as that. Now, Christ wants to encourage us to ask for what we need, and he tells us that all we have to do is knock and the door will be opened to us. He wouldn't have made such a point of this, if he didn't want us to elevate our consciousness to the level where we are able to commune with the omnipresent light of God in the silent temple of our soul. Here we have a direction and a promise from the Lord Christ. He tells us, in wonderfully simple language, just to knock. But we don't often do that, do we?

When you enter into quiet meditation, even if it is only for fifteen minutes a day, you can bring with you any need or desire you may have. Knock on the door of consciousness, and ask the omnipresent Christ for whatever you need. If you ask for bread, He will certainly not give you a stone. You have that assurance and promise, because *"for you that knocketh, it shall be opened; and for you that seeketh, you shall find."* We have to knock. We have to seek. This passage in Matthew assures us that if we, who are so much less than God, would never give our son or daughter a stone if they asked for bread, then surely our heavenly Father, who is infinitely more compassionate and loving, will give us what we need.

Now, let us look at the word "heaven." We are told that heaven lies within—but what is heaven? You probably know that many of our English words originate from ancient Latin and Greek roots. The Greek word for heaven is *Oranos*, which means "expanded awareness." Isn't that interesting? It means simply expanding your consciousness to embrace and incorporate into the very depths of your soul all that is in the Christ spirit. There, in the very core of your being, is a temple of silence where you can go to seek communion with God, who has always been there. Jesus said, *"I and my Father are one,"* (John 10:30.) because he knew that the eternal, divine flame and the action of Spirit are not up in the sky somewhere, but right in the very midst of you.

The great mystics, saints, and healers we read about in the early Christian movement, as well as some of those in more recent times, are all people who have taken Christ at his word. They actually believe that when they knock, God will, in His infinite compassion, give them what they need. Now, you may not get exactly what you ask for, simply because it might not be right and good for you; but you will get what you need. Sometimes we do get exactly what we ask for, even if it isn't good for us; and then we have to learn from that. Other times, in a silent and mysterious way, God will bring into our lives those great and joyous experiences that let us know undeniably that our prayers have been answered. Perhaps it looks like a simple coincidence, or serendipity, and you just nod to it with a smile. Often, it comes like a huge "ah-ha" in your consciousness, and it brings about a total shift in your way of living and thinking. Once in a while, it comes as an immediate and direct improvement in your physical, emotional, or financial well being. Sometimes, like a flash, you receive the answer to a problem you may have been struggling with for years. And all you can do is stand in awe of it.

"Seek, and you shall find." You know, sometimes we read these words over and over, and we wonder, "Okay, just how do I seek?" Well, what is the deepest desire of your heart? It's probably far more than a Mercedes or a pair of Gucci shoes—although those are fine, too, as long as your happiness is not pinned on owning them. What is it that you *really* want? You might want something that makes life a little easier in your ordinary work-a-day world: more harmony with a co-worker, or a better rapport with your boss. You may desire improved health, more money, a slimmer figure, gladness of heart, or a loving partner to share your life with. You may seek more patience, deeper devotion, a more disciplined spiritual practice, or any number of other things. If you look deeper, you may realize that what you are truly yearning for is a more meaningful understanding of your purpose and place in the world, or a more vivid sense of being loved by God.

How do you seek? First, by entering the temple of silence deep within the self. See, it's like mining for gold. Gold miners seek their fortune in the hills. So they pack up their picks and shovels and head for the very best spot they can find. There they dig ever deeper into the earth, with a great hopefulness that they will find the gold they are seeking. Like the miner who digs deeper and deeper into the earth, searching for gold, you must dive deeper and deeper into the silence of the self. That is the mine you're working in when you ask for spiritual gold, or material benefits, from the hand of the infinite One who lives inside of you. There, in the temple of the Self, you pray with absolute childlike confidence to your Creator, asking for that which you need. With infinite compassion, God *does* answer, because the very nature of the Divine is boundless love and mercy. Let us always remember that.

In the early Christian days, there were many great souls like Saint Augustine and Saint Jerome, who dedicated their lives to teaching. They understood clearly that, when they asked for something, they had to ask *believing*. Nobody goes down into a gold mine if they think there is no gold there. So, when you go into the depths of your consciousness, silently and persistently ask for the insights that will lead you in a positive direction. Ask *believing* and *expecting* that you will receive the guidance you need.

In the process of asking and seeking, you may discover that what you thought you wanted most was not really your heart's truest desire; it may actually be something else. God is ever present with wisdom insights, and He often awakens in us a vision or prospect that we had never thought of before. So, when you ask, realize that God has full knowledge of your need before you ask. I once knew a very dear spiritual lady whose daily prayer was very simple: *"Dear God, please give me what I need most today, and teach me what I need to learn."* Isn't that a nice little practice?

"To him that knocketh, it shall be opened." All the way through the gospels, Jesus is trying to bring about in us an increased confidence and expectancy. *Expect* your answer. *Expect* your miracle. You honor God when you do that. Don't let yourself become entrenched with the idea that you don't have what you need. Sometimes people belabor prayer so much that it actually becomes an obstacle to fulfillment. Even as they are asking, they have a negative expectation. That's attracting what you *don't* want. And as long as you do that, you will probably never get what you are seeking. So toss aside all that doubting and old negative thinking, and leave everything in the hands of the omniscient One. Ask believing, and expect a positive and fulfilling answer.

I've mentioned many times that, on the front of the pulpit in the church I had for twenty-two years, I put up a nice little sign that was given to me by a wonderful Christian mystic. In great big gold letters it said, "EXPECT A MIRACLE." Newcomers to my church might not have remembered anything else that went on during the service, but they would always remember that little phrase. They would come back weeks later and tell me, "You know, that sign really struck me." For many, that thought is a key to fulfillment of a positive act of faith.

Psychologists tell us that no matter what we are striving to do or become—whether in the field of science, art, business, or education—expecting that we will succeed stimulates our inner resources and brings about positive results. Doctors in the field of psychosomatic medicine can attest to the fact that emotional blockages are often reflected in the body as illness and disorder. The source may be some sort of repressed trauma, or perhaps unburdened guilt and a lack of self-forgiveness. Most of you know that I was raised a Catholic. We all had to go to confession and tell the priest what sinful things we did during the week, and what impure thoughts we had. Now, I think that sometimes people use going to confession as a kind of cop-out, in place of taking responsibility for their actions and changing their behavior; but I can attest to the fact that confession is very good for the soul. You see, the very act of confessing cleanses the self. It lightens and lifts the soul. Then, instead of dwelling too much on your mistakes and being burdened by unexpressed guilt and shame, you begin to open up to God's absolute and total forgiveness.

The redemptive power of the Christ spirit is absolute. It is eternal in the heavens, and it conquers everything you might feel bad about having done. When you humbly and sincerely ask for forgiveness, the spirit of forgiveness, which is the Christ, does indeed redeem or cancel out your sin. Scripture says that even if your sins are scarlet and as numerous as the sands of the sea, God's love and compassion are infinitely above all of them. So open your heart and accept God's forgiveness. Expect your miracles from the hand of Providence, and forgive yourself.

In reality, many of our difficulties come to us simply because we haven't forgiven ourselves for our blunders and sinful errors of the past. If God has forgiven you, and if Jesus has forgiven you, then for heaven's sake follow their example and forgive yourself! Stop carrying around all this blame and shame, guilt and regret, sorrow and discouragement. It isn't good for your emotional or physical health. In a way, carrying the burdens of life ourselves, refusing to *cast our cares,* is an insult to the Lord of the universe, whose sole activity is to love, sustain, and encourage us to grow and become. When we deny the healing and transforming power of God, we are rejecting the very power that can give us the life we say we want. Instead, let us accept and embrace that healing power. In full trust, let us offer our sorrows and suffering to that compassionate spirit of love—that infinitely merciful One who beckons us ever onward, like a divine magnet, toward full realization and total fulfillment in God.

Modern doctors are working very hard to get people to meditate two or three times a day, and visualize on the screen of the inner mind those things they would like to see realized on the outer plane of expression. It doesn't hurt, you know, to take a little time during your prayer work for others, to visualize yourself as going about your Father's business with vitality and joy, physical and emotional wellness, and efficiency and purpose. Don't say, "Well, I'm getting a little older now, and I don't think it will work for me." Don't think that way. Just imagine yourself "in living color" doing all the things you wish to do, and having all the things you want in your life.

The other day, there was a picture of a man in the paper along with a nice little article about him. At the ripe age of one hundred eleven years young, this man was running around like a kid, doing all sorts of things. That's pretty good, and he said he isn't about to stop. He isn't looking over his shoulder to see if some terminal illness is coming around the corner. He hasn't got time for that. He is a man of very simple habits; and I'm sure if you talked to him, you would be inspired by his direct and uncomplicated faith. This is a man who takes the wondrously uplifting message of the Christ as a reality, not some sort of rhetoric.

You know, we hear an awful lot of rhetoric in politics, and sometimes this barrage of verbiage gets so superbly mixed up that we don't know what any of the pundits are actually talking about. By contrast, the great teacher of this planet, Jesus the Christ, was eminently simple and direct, encouraging, and always forgiving. Thank God the apostles were not politicians! Not that there aren't any good and honest politicians; of course there are. But the apostles "told it like it is." In a dynamic and positive way, they expressed their confidence and faith in the living presence and power of Christ—and when they did that, all things began to change. They were transformed by a kind of divine alchemy, in which the baser metals of unknowing and lack of faith became the gift of gold in the expectancy of all good things.

Jesus said, *"For it is your Father's good pleasure to give you the kingdom."* (Luke 12:32.) We read these pleasing and pretty words over and over, but we forget to really get in there—to ask, and really seek. People sometimes feel undeserving and afraid to seek, or even to ask at all. They doubt that God would ever give them anything lovely or satisfying. God will never give you anything that is hurtful, punishing, or ugly; that's not His nature. He will only give you that which is uplifting, beautiful, and right for your highest possible state. So never be afraid to ask, no matter how far away you *think* you are from the perfection that God sees in your true self.

And so, dear friends, let us take the message of Matthew to heart, and let us give thanks for the power of these simple words. Let us recognize that not only were these gospels appropriate and applicable in ancient times, but they are totally in concert with the best and most modern findings of psychology today. Yet even now the mind of man remains something of a mystery. And despite the research being undertaken today, the ramifications of consciousness remain a marvel, vast and unfathomable, even by the most astute scientific investigators. Let us accept that the mind of man, when it is attuned to the Christ Spirit, is part of the infinite cosmic consciousness that hears your knocking and wants to answer the door. So knock, and know that the door will be opened to you; seek, and trust that you will find; ask, expecting that your answer will be given. When you ask of Him anything at all, the limitless Giver of life and love *will* give you that which will best help to awaken and transform you into the saint you are destined to become. So accept that with humility, reverence, and great love.

In your daily meditation, remember to say a prayer for your neighbor as well as for yourself. Maybe there is someone you know who is not feeling well. Send them a silent blessing, for that is the light and consciousness of the Christ Spirit. Sending your neighbor a simple and silent blessing is like sending them a smile from God. Like a fragrant bouquet, it touches and lifts them into a more positive and happy feeling. Anybody who has ever felt the presence of God within *has to* be uplifted; they *must* live with a certain sense of joyousness, because that is God. God is bliss. He is light, love, and supreme good. And God is freedom from all that is unlike Him. Now, God doesn't always come to us in a burst of blinding brightness, wherein everything changes in the twinkling of an eye. That isn't the way it usually works—and thank heavens! That would be too much for us to take, all at once. The input God gives us through inspiration comes gradually and surely, increasingly lifting and illuminating our consciousness.

So, dear friends, spend a little time during the coming week re-reading and meditating on the beautiful truths found in the gospel of Matthew: *"Seek, and you shall find. Knock and it shall be opened to you. Ask, and it shall be given unto you."* The secret is to ask *believing*. Then, be of good cheer, and *expect your miracle*. Thank you. *Amen.*

Your Faith Is Your Fortune

Heritage House Presbyterian Chapel, San Francisco, CA
February 27, 1983

Good morning, dear friends. I am glad to be with you again. Now that I am sort of retired from twenty-two years at my own church, I have time to visit other churches and temples as a guest speaker. I always enjoy speaking and singing in this lovely chapel at the Heritage House. Today I am going to talk about developing a deeper faith—a dependable, tangible faith. So let us pray:

Heavenly Father, You have created for us a world that is wholly divine, entirely permeated with life and brimming over with love. Help us to become sensitive enough to perceive this wonderful truth, and to know that we cannot go where God is not. Therefore, may we walk with confidence along the avenues and byways of our lives, knowing that anywhere and everywhere there is a man or woman of faith, there is the Christ. Thank you. Amen.

First of all, what *is* faith? Faith is a profound conviction in our ability to accomplish something, to be healed, to triumph over obstacles, or to make a success of some kind. Nobody ever succeeded or achieved anything important in the world without faith that it would come about. Some people's faith is so powerful that it is absolutely astonishing. There are hundreds of amazing and inspiring stories of athletes, artists, musicians, scientists, politicians, entrepreneurs, and parents who, at one time or another, lived under extremely difficult and dire circumstances. But in spite of what seemed like colossal and supernormal obstacles, they triumphed in some area of their lives. Faith, to them, truly became their fortune. When you read these stories, you realize that for almost every one of these people, there were times when, despite their best efforts and determination to overcome, they fell into a deep depression over their sense of impotence and failure. They all report experiencing moments of despair, when their hearts sank into feeling, "Oh, I will never be able to make it." And yet, they tell us that when they sat down and meditated in the silence, making contact with the all-pervading power of the liberating Christ spirit, they emerged with the energy of hope and renewed enthusiasm. They found a force to transcend all the inequities, limitations, challenges, losses, and failures that had burdened them, sometimes for decades; and they succeeded in making a whole new, triumphant, and fulfilling life for themselves. Without that faith, and daily contact with the healing power of the Christ spirit, their triumph could never have come about.

Now, to many religious people, Christ is the surname of Jesus, the only Son of God. For others the term Christ is interpreted a little more broadly, but it remains a mysterious spiritual entity: something rarely, if ever, experienced by them. For still other spiritual aspirants Christ is understood not as a person, but as a state of consciousness reflecting beautiful soul qualities. For many people, God is understood in the heart intuitively as a loving and powerful presence, but it is felt only in those rare moments of inspiration. Often this presence eludes us and we end up frantically running through our repertoire of techniques and prayers, trying to recapture the sense of divine communion which we have occasionally glimpsed but struggle to hold onto. However we define the Christ spirit, we all want a sense of being anchored in a truth that governs, protects, and guides us through the ups and downs of our busy lives.

We all seek companionship and a sense of belonging, and many of us seek answers to the deeper questions of our origin and existence. Where do we go to find the answers to these deep and abiding questions? We may get glimpses of God by reading books and attending lectures and seminars, but we cannot grasp spiritual reality with our human intellect. Spiritual truth cannot be reasoned out; it must be received within. So our biggest job is to develop our spiritual receptivity so that we can experience the divine as a real and very practical aspect of our daily lives. It is up to us to cultivate and continue a spiritual practice of daily quieting and attuning ourselves to this indwelling presence and inspiration. Only through quiet meditation and deep communion do we become participant in the same divine life and love that was revealed to us by Christ Jesus, the saints, and many other mystics. As you expand your awareness and understanding of the Christ presence within you as an intimate and vivid reality, you will find that not only does it sustain you and bring peace to your heart, it begins naturally to radiate outward to bless others round about you.

As we read the various gospels of the Bible, we find that the teachings of Christ are always substantiated by marvelous acts of healings. There are accounts of all manner of physical, emotional, and spiritual healing, and even stories of raising the dead. When we place our meditational attention on the healing spirit of the Christ, we naturally refer again and again to these stories. And as we meditate deeply upon these accounts of divine healing, a positive and dynamic feeling arises within us concerning the reality of the omnipresence of good. We are inspirationally lifted by the realization that our universe is filled with a healing power that can affect positive change anywhere and everywhere, but especially within the temple of the self.

Now, let us read from Matthew, Chapter 9, verses 20-22: *"And behold, a woman . . . came behind him and touched the hem of his garment: for she said within herself, 'If I may but touch His garment I shall be whole.' Jesus [turned towards her], and when he saw her he said, 'Daughter, be of good comfort; thy faith has made thee whole.' And the woman was made whole from that hour."* Another time, *"Jesus came into the ruler's house, and saw the minstrels and the people making noise, he said unto them, 'Give place: for the maid is not dead, but sleeping.' And they laughed him to scorn. But when the people were put forth, he went in, and took her by the hand, and the maid arose. And the fame thereof went abroad into all that land."* (Matt. 9:23-26.)

In the time of Jesus, there was no way to transmit his powerful teachings except by working miracles, and his "publicity" was by the villagers' word of mouth. Stories of his teachings and miracles were spread not only by the enthusiasm of those who were healed, but also by those who observed such marvelous events. We must realize that the therapeutic and healing factors of the Christ consciousness demonstrated by Jesus two thousand years ago are still available to us today. Throughout the corridors of time, stories of this miraculous healing power have been brought to us continuously so that we might live in faith, harmony, dominion, and true liberation in body, mind, and spirit.

I think it is especially interesting to note that in this scripture, Jesus asked for all the people inside the house where the girl lay dead to be taken out and moved aside. Why do you suppose he did that? Well, quite obviously he was a great teacher, and he recognized the importance of putting aside those who were filled with negativity and doubt, those who were not in accord with the probability that healing would take place. The musicians and neighbors were already making a big clamor—well, of course, that was their custom. In fact, the villagers had so much doubt that they laughed him to scorn. So Jesus said, "Take these people out of the room." Why do you suppose he did that? Why did he insist that all these doubters and squawkers get out of the house and away? Jesus didn't want his pure faith to be interrupted in any sense whatever.

It is also very interesting to note that he, who was filled with the abiding consciousness, gave thanks before he did marvelous things. Why? Because he knew that the Father always heard him. He had a faith in the presence and power of God. They laughed him to scorn, but he went inside anyway. Now, having first moved aside those who had no faith at all, Jesus took the dead girl by the hand, and with the authority of his dynamic faith, he said, "Arise." And the maiden awoke and walked out among the people. Of course this became noised abroad, because it was not the sort of thing that happened every day.

This healing is truly one of the greatest miracles in all the gospels, and the thing I find particularly worthy of remembering is that the Master thought it best to get the doubters out of the way before he worked his miracle. He wanted them away from him in order to let the free, pure mind of the Christ presence operate through him, unobstructed by any noises made by the mortal mind of ordinary man. This is a lesson to us all.

We give thanks to the Heavenly Father for the lesson in today's scripture, which reminds us again and again of the importance of having that fullness of faith, so that the healings and other marvels which were wrought in the life of the Christ might be manifest today unto all and everyone.

Everything Jesus did was to teach us. Now, if you want to achieve the kind of faith that will inevitably become your fortune, then you must first begin to find yourself in the company of those who already have a blazing faith. If you're going to hang out with people who are very negative and don't believe in anything, you're not going to get too far. You have to stop running around with people who scoff at anything spiritual, saying, "All that stuff about healing is a lot of nonsense. I don't believe in miracles, and I don't think there is a power anywhere that hears or answers prayers." Those doubters will deride and try to shake your faith by saying things like, "Those healing services are fake. The people supposedly healed are really just actors paid to say they've been healed. It's all a big scam." Sometimes, unfortunately, there *are* charlatans, and scams *do* happen, but we also know that there is no doubt about the healing factor of the ministry of the Christ spirit, the Holy Spirit. So if we want to acknowledge the fact that indeed our faith is our fortune, then we must accept it, practice it, and live it totally, now. If you want to cultivate a mighty faith, you must begin by placing yourself in the company of those who already have that kind of faith. If religion is ever to have a personal meaning for you, you must develop a glowing and invincible faith and *live* it with all your heart and soul and mind. You must work to develop the dynamics of a positive attitude of mind and heart: those are the true faces of faith.

Now, as I said, if you want to develop a very deep and unshakable faith, it is very helpful to be around other people who have such a firm, strong sense of it that it kindles your own faith. In this way, you see, you augment that which is already inside you. When you light a little fire under your own faith, it gradually begins to blaze brighter and brighter, until it sheds its spiritual light to all those around you. When that happens, you begin to see the truth about your very nature, your truly divine nature. Know you not that you are sons and daughters of God, and heirs of the kingdom of heaven?

So dear friends, I pray that you will know, undeniably and joyfully, that whatever need you may have today, great or small, it is your faith that will bring about its fulfillment. Cultivate that faith, and meditate on that kind of faith. Read Matthew 9, verses 20-22 sometime during this coming week. Sit with the text in the quietness of your room, for it is in the quiet where things really happen. When you are alone, sit very still, watch your breath and quiet your mind, and completely drop the cares of your life. Gradually, with daily repetition and practice, you will enter that secret place of the most high: the divine silence, wherein you will find the answer to any question you may pose. Whatever need you have today, take it into the silence of prayer, and ask faithfully for the indwelling Christ spirit to bring about its fulfillment. Then listen deeply for what emerges from your consciousness.

Even in the most mundane matters of our daily lives, faith plays a part. For example, you trust that when you put your dollar into the vending machine and push the button for coffee, you will receive a cup of hot coffee. You have a certain faith in the fact that if you go to work every day, you will receive a check on the first of the month. We are very trusting of these aspects of our everyday world. In fact, we take many of them for granted. We have faith that things will work for us. Before we get into an elevator, we don't demand that the engineer who designed it get inside the shaft and inspect it to see if there is anything wrong. If we did, we would be waiting a long time to go up, especially in a structure like the Bank of America Building in San Francisco, which has fifty-two stories! We have faith that elevators and other things around us in our work-a-day world are in fine working order, and, thank God, they generally are. Now, those are examples of the most ordinary and mundane aspects of faith. If we rely on the working order of elevators and coffee machines, how much more then should we trust and depend on the workings of Spirit?

"Your faith is your fortune" is never so truly understood as when you are in need of healing. Now, in today's text we have a marvelous example of a living faith. Here is this village woman who comes to Jesus and touches the hem of his garment, saying to herself, "If I but touch the hem of his garment, I shall be healed." She really believed that. And later on Christ says, "Your faith hath made you whole." In other words, this simple woman had a faith so dynamic, so wondrously filled with enthusiasm, and so deep and abiding, that her life was changed by what the uninitiated called a miracle. We must develop that kind of living faith, and when we do, we too shall experience the wonders and marvels of Spirit.

The faith of some people is so powerful that it is absolutely astonishing. These are the people who inspire us and spur us on to surmount the challenges that confront us in our own lives. Faith, to them, is truly their fortune. It is helpful to remember, in our own moments of doubt and discouragement, that though these people accomplished their goals in the end, their road to success was not without struggle. We must also remember that these stories are about ordinary people with an extraordinary faith. They understood the importance of sitting down and entering a state of quiet, wherein they could make contact with the all-pervading power of the liberating Christ Spirit. When faced with their enormous hardships and ordeals, they took hold of that power, and they finally succeeded. Without faith in their ability to tap their inner resources of perseverance, vigor, courage, and determination, their triumph could never have come about.

I believe that miracles of healing take place when we have a living faith which creates within us a condition, or quality, that *naturally* makes healing possible. All of these extraordinary things are in divine order; and all of them are actually divinely natural, not *super*natural. We are awestruck by such occurrences, and we simply don't understand them because they are often instantaneous and seemingly without cause. But there is within us that natural, though sometimes unawakened quality of enduring faith in the continuity of good. Now, that doesn't mean we will never catch a cold or get the flu; we all do. Those are just little challenges. But people who have faith fall ill more rarely and rise more quickly, quite simply because they are anchored in a profound consciousness of the miracle-working quality in the divine order of being. It is very important to remember that. Sometimes we forget, and we deny the gifts of the Holy Spirit. We say. "Oh, I'm not good enough. I'm not worthy." Well, we don't want to wait too long to become good or worthy enough. Accept God's gifts *now*, accept His promises *now*, and accept the beautiful confirmation of His works on earth.

Now, there are a number of prominent doctors today who understand the importance of faith, and they realize that people are sometimes spontaneously healed. However, the great majority of allopathic physicians will say, "Well, now, your lab tests are in, and according to the medical books, there is no cure for you. You might as well forget about getting well, and pack your bags for the trip to the other side." But some people don't believe the medical books, and they don't accept the good doctors' prognostications. When we reach into the deepest aspects of the self and draw upon that divine Christ spirit with total faith, then things happen which are *not* in the medical book.

Though many of our medical people will not come out and say they believe in miracles, more and more of them are permitting, and even suggesting, the participation and assistance of the minister, priest, or rabbi. This is a positive step forward for medicine, because there is no doubt that with the addition of spiritual support and the presence of faith, healing is more likely to occur. Many hospitals are now conducting research and have compiled impressive statistics that compare the rate of recovery and degree of healing in patients who receive spiritual support and prayer with those who do not. These statistics clearly indicate that patients who receive spiritual assistance obtain results which far exceed scientific probability. So what do we prove here? We prove that by awakening and expanding faith in an individual, we are lighting a candle, as it were, in the room of his consciousness, wherein he may begin to perceive the timeless and all-pervading truth of the healing power of Spirit.

Down through the centuries we have had examples of marvelous healings, and right here in this little chapel people have experienced healing and transformation. I have seen dramatic changes in people (and I know you have too), when they are touched by Spirit and awakened in consciousness.

Some years ago, I observed the incredible healing work of Kathryn Kuhlman. I'm sure many of you remember her. There is no question that hers was a ministry blessed by the Holy Spirit. People from all over the country came to her services, many arriving in ambulances and wheelchairs. She brought people together and really made the occasion by her warmth and enthusiasm. She stirred up people by her irrepressible joy and keenness to serve God; but it was the Holy Spirit that smiled upon the group, and brought about the many marvels that took place during the course of her meetings.

She always said, "I am the most ordinary person in the world. If you believe that I, as an individual, have any power to heal, you are dead wrong. I have had nothing to do with any miracle or healing that has taken place in any physical body. I have no healing power whatsoever. It is the power of God that enters this room and touches us with His mercy." Whenever anyone praised her tremendous works of faith, she was the first to say, "I am not a woman with great faith. I am a woman with a little faith in a great God!"

One of the things that bothered Kathryn a great deal was that not everybody was healed at her services. She said that when she got to the heaven world, one of the first questions she was going to ask was, "Why wasn't everyone healed?" She really wanted to know why some people were healed, while others were not. Some of these people came with a critical, cynical, and disbelieving spirit. Perhaps they held such grave doubts and resistance that they obstructed the flow of the divine healing energy. Certainly, the events that took place in the presence of Kathryn Kuhlman were genuine healings. This modern healer proclaimed the same truth that Jesus repeatedly emphasized in his ministry: that it is not *her* energy that heals. It is the light of God coming *through* her that permeates the physical body and eliminates all manner of ills.

Curiously, some of the people who came to Miss Kuhlman's healing services had no faith at all. But, just as curiously, they had no resistance. As we always say, God doesn't care if you're a Christian or not—if He wants to heal you, you'll be healed. If you have an open heart that accepts and allows this incredible strength and light to permeate the cells and atoms of your physical body temple, or the emotional, mental, or spiritual self, there can be nothing other than renewal.

Jesus himself encouraged us to lean upon the power of this living force and allow it to bring about changes within our body chemistry, our emotions, finances, relationships, careers, and all the affairs of our lives, in a way that is nothing less than miraculous. We should take hold of what the Master said with such vigor and enthusiasm that not only will we allow that divine force to heal us, we will also bring that healing light to others.

Throughout history there have been wonderful servants of God: those great healers, saints, and sages, who lived and worked for God. We find that through them, in all times and climes, and in all the varied theologies, there have been miracles. All of these wonders were accomplished with the same all-pervading divine light. Some of these great souls exhibited at death what is called "incorruptibility." That is, after death, their bodies remained in a state without decomposition or odor of decay. These mystics were permeated with the power of the Holy Spirit. They were people who *knew* that their faith was indeed their fortune.

Let us light a candle in our hearts, and kindle its flame until it becomes a blazing faith. Let us open our consciousness to the unobstructed flow of divine light, and let it pour through as a living presence. For it is only when we have a living faith that extraordinary things begin to occur in our lives, and we realize that indeed our faith has become our fortune. The more you feel that flow of divine love and power, the more you will recognize that everyone is potentially a healer. It is wonderful to impart healing to others, but we're not supposed to invade anybody's consciousness by moving in and trying to heal them unless they ask us to. It's a kind of special law required of any healer that they must be asked to heal. When you are asked, get yourself out of the way and let God do the work, because He knows how to do it so much better than you do.

And so, dear friends, I urge you to pick up your Bible this week and turn to Matthew, Chapter 9, and read verses 20-22. *"And behold, a woman . . . came behind him and touched the hem of his garment: for she said within herself, 'If I may but touch His garment I shall be whole.' Jesus [turned towards her], and when he saw her he said, 'Daughter, be of good comfort; thy faith has made thee whole.'"*

Spend a little quiet time with yourself this week, and let these inspiring words fill your mind and heart. This is the way to follow the example of Jesus the Christ in your consciousness—and don't say, "Oh, I couldn't do that. I'm not good enough. I'm not spiritual enough for that," because if you wait till you're good enough, you might have to wait an awfully long time. You will never be more spiritual than you are right now. God is infinitely merciful, thank heavens! Otherwise, who knows what would happen to us. So don't wait. Do it now. Know that you don't have to do anything but express love. Be still and feel your kinship with the Christ. Then get out of the way and let God express His healing love through you. There is an added benefit to you when you do that, because as this wondrous power flows through you to touch and bless others, it cannot but touch and bless you in a very wonderful way. Then, you will walk with the holy ones, the blessed ones, the ones who have realized within the depths of their being that God has created for us a world that is wholly divine, entirely permeated with life, and brimming over with love and power. Having faith in that loving power will give you the consciousness that your faith is truly your fortune. Thank you, my dear friends. *Amen.*

PART FOUR

What Comes After Life?

Reverend John Laurence at age 94 in San Diego

Life After Death

Redwood Spiritualist Church, CA
March 21, 1981

Good morning, dear friends. Today I am going to talk about the change called death. The question of whether life continues after physical death has troubled people down through the ages. The cardinal principle of all religions is that the individual personality—the self, entity, or soul—continues a conscious existence after this mortal coil is long dissolved. We are told in the scriptures (and reminded often by holy men and women, and by writers of various philosophical and theological texts) that we are indeed immortal—right now. You don't have to die to be immortal. The only thing you are going to lose when you die is the old body form, the overcoat that you have been wearing for so many years.

When you leave the body, you leave this vehicle behind, and what do you find? Well, Saint Paul tells us that after the change called death, we are clothed in a finer body, not unlike this very body we inhabit now. He speaks of the spiritual (or astral) body, made of light. Down through the centuries saints and sages have constantly reminded us of the eternal, ongoing, and immortal quality of our being. If indeed God has planted in you a spark of the infinite, then that part of the infinite is part of you. It is indestructible, ongoing, and continuous, and it can never be defiled by anything you have done or experienced on this earth plane. So we must expect the continuity of life.

What is religion but to "bind back to the first cause," which, of course, is God. Now, some orthodox religions were quite horrified when they found out people were actually trying to *prove* the principle upon which their religions were founded: namely that life continues after the change called death. If you ask any Jesuit, "Do people survive after death?" he will recite a whole series of theological statements that say we do. And so it goes with most denominations of Christianity. I have addressed Catholics, Presbyterians, Methodists, and many others who speak of their belief in life after death; but few, it seems, are determined to give proof of ongoing life.

It's rather sad when you find religious people who don't seem to have much faith in the continuity of life. Now, the Church tells us to believe, but a lot of people are weak, and they find that difficult to do. So when a loved one passes away, they grieve endlessly and cry, "Shall I ever behold that dear one again?" Well, the answer is certainly a resounding YES, and that affirmation comes to us from the articles of faith, the holy scriptures, the teachings of religious bodies all over the world, and through all of Christian history.

Many orthodox religionists have said, "We mustn't have mediums or messages from the dead." Well, if you took all the mediums and prophets out of the Old Testament you wouldn't have anything left but the cover. Some orthodox people tell us we must not deliver messages from spirit because such communications are from the devil. But I tell you, when messages from spirit reform the sinner, reclaim the drunkard or the drug addict, and give people a sense of hope and vindication through an absolute conviction of the ongoing nature of life, such things are truly from God and nobody can doubt it. Now, if by chance your faith is so weak that this kind of demonstration of divine power isn't quite enough, then you can look to scientific research.

Throughout all time, but particularly in the last hundred years, there has been a very careful investigation along scientific lines into what is called the "probability" of life after death. In the annals of psychical research in London and New York are vast files of carefully screened stories—not ghost stories, but verifiable information that proves beyond a shadow of a doubt that when man leaves this mortal coil he retains his individual self-identity; and he carries it into the next world, where he is very much alive, aware, and totally conscious. These are very striking investigations, and the research material is vast. I don't suppose that anybody could read all of it, but those who have had the privilege of reading even part of it have seen ample evidence and strong scientific proof for the continuity of life after death.

These investigators are intelligent and modern, thinking people. They do not see and hear spooks at every turn of the corner. Researchers and people who possess the "gifts of the Spirit" are a distinguished flock, to be sure, and their list is long. The beauty and power of Spirit at work is not just in phenomena and communication but also in divine healing and the total transformation of lives.

I remember the great Rev. Florence Becker. I watched her for over thirty years, and occasionally I attended services at her Golden Gate Church in San Francisco. I have never, ever, anywhere, seen her equal. Her gift was truly a light from the spirit world. A talent like hers is so rare. Such a gifted soul comes along perhaps only once in three or four hundred years, to offer positive proof of self-identification and the continuity of life at the change called death.

The democracy of the spiritual trip is that you go into the next expression of life clad in the garments you have woven for yourself by your actions, reactions, and inactions, for both good and evil. There is no old gentleman with a long gray beard and a bad temper beating you over the head with a stick. You can't buy your way into heaven, and nobody can pray you in or out, either. The democracy of the spiritual trip is that *YOU do it*. You are totally responsible for yourself, for what you do right, and for what you do wrong. You are responsible for *not* doing what you should have done, and for doing much more than anyone asked of you.

You may remember Dr. John Rhine from Duke University, the internationally famous researcher in parapsychology. His wife, Louisa, worked with him for over thirty years. Papa did all the lecturing, but when it was all over and they were both retired, it was his wife, Louisa, who wrote the book *Hidden Channels of the Mind*. In each instance where there was striking evidence for survival, Louisa Rhine did everything she possibly could scientifically to disprove it. However, she had to admit that there were four or five stories that came to her attention during her research that simply could not be brushed aside.

One of the most remarkable stories in that book concerns a young couple in the Midwest who ran a small rooming house. At a very young age the man fell ill and died. Naturally, his wife was deeply upset by the sudden loss of her husband, but she did her best to carry on the family business. She knew there was a metal box in which her husband kept receipts for bills that had been paid, along with the deed to the house and other important papers, but she was unable to find it. She searched high and low, but still could not find the box. She was becoming quite disturbed by the fact that merchants began bringing bills to her which she knew had been paid, but she could not produce the receipts. She was very distressed by all this, and it was becoming too difficult to work and take care of her young son. So she asked the people at the school if they would be kind enough to take her little boy. After some time, the school finally agreed to accept her son, and so little Johnny went to kindergarten.

One day, after he had been in school for about six weeks, Johnny's teacher walked into the room and noticed this little fellow sitting at his tiny desk with a pad and a pencil. He was scribbling away with such intensity and concentration that she chuckled. She thought, "I've never seen such concentration on a youngster's face." Here was a little boy who didn't even know the alphabet, and certainly could not read or write, but he was totally absorbed in his scrawling. The teacher went over to him and picked up the pad, expecting to see scribbles. Instead, what did she find? She found a message written to Johnny's mother from her dead husband, telling her exactly where to find the box that contained the deed to the house, receipts, and other important papers. The message was signed off with a loving and endearing term that they used only between themselves. More striking, the message was not written in ordinary English, but in an archaic form of shorthand, which fortunately this teacher had learned in her student days. The teacher read the message, understood it, and immediately took it home to the grieving wife. By following the instructions in this message, Johnny's mother was able to find the box containing all the important papers and materials.

Now, there was no possibility of chicanery, fraud, or collusion in this case. The FBI couldn't have done a better job than the researchers did in trying to disprove the authenticity of this story. When a small child, who doesn't even know how to write an ordinary letter in English, writes a complete and coherent message in an archaic form of shorthand, and such a message provides verifiable information as to the whereabouts of a hidden box, it is rather impressive. And there are thousands of such stories.

Scientists in the great universities of the world are profoundly interested in studying paranormal phenomena. They call it "*para-psychology*" because it transcends the ordinary. Whether the religious authorities of any denomination accept such phenomena or not, it happens anyhow—which reminds me of another story.

There was a dear Irish lady, a good Catholic, who was very mediumistic. Father Flanagan heard about her spiritual activities, because in those days Father Flanagan knew everything about everything; he ran the show, and you'd better believe it! So he says, "Maggie, you've got to stop all this nonsense with spirits and things. If you don't, ya won't have the sacraments anymore." Well, Maggie promises humbly that she will have no more table tipping or spirits or lights or messages, or any other shenanigans. So about two months later Father Flanagan meets her and asks, "Maggie, have ya been a good girl? Now, you're not foolin' around with any more of this spirit business, are ya?" Maggie says, "Father, I've been very good. I haven't done a t'ing with the spirits at all—but it makes no difference—they're there just the same!" So you see, no matter what church you attend—whether you are Episcopalian, Catholic, Presbyterian, Baptist, or whatever—you are going to have spiritual experiences.

Most of us have read the book called *Life After Life* by psychiatrist Raymond Moody. Dr. Moody was a professor of Greek. He had a doctorate and taught at one of the universities, but after a while he decided that he wanted to expand his expertise by studying medicine, so he went back to school and got his MD. Then he had further direction. He wanted to get a PhD and practice psychiatry, so he studied even further in his field. This is a man with a lot of courage.

Now, while he was studying, he had a professor who liked him and treated him like an equal. After all, here was a man who had already completed his doctorate. So, as equals, they became buddies. One day Dr. Moody said, "Look, there is something very different about you. Will you tell me what it is? I can't put my finger on it, but there is a certain peacefulness and tranquility about you that is undeniable. Why is this so?" The professor said, "Well, I hope you will understand me; and I think you will, because you are open-minded and mature enough. I have been clinically dead twice in this life. For several minutes I had no respiration, no heartbeat, no blood circulation, and no signs of life; but I was resuscitated. What I saw and experienced while out of this physical body was life-altering. I was in another realm of existence, and it was enchanting."

Dr. Moody became very interested in this subject, so he began keeping records wherever he could find them of people who had similarly "died" and had been resuscitated. Once Dr. Moody had found records of these cases he conducted research to find out how long those people had been "dead" before they were revived. One man had been dead for two hours and fifteen minutes. Why there wasn't total brain damage, one can only wonder, but the man came back fully intact and very much alive.

People who have had these near-death experiences tell pretty much the same story. They go through a dark tunnel and come out into a place of light. They greet their father, mother, or other relatives and friends who have preceded them into the spiritual world. Of course, none of us is in a big hurry to get over to the other side of life; but on the other hand, it's reassuring to know where we are going.

As I said a little while ago, when we leave this body we will go clad in the garments that our actions and reactions have woven for us, for we have absolute and total responsibility as the incarnating ego. We are indeed the architects of our own destinies, for good and evil. The information that has been gathered from various sources is very reassuring. People report that when you find yourself in the spiritual realm, in your new body made of light, you are totally conscious and totally alive. You understand the absolute rightness of where you are. You comprehend all that has happened to you, and why. You go to that area in the spiritual realm that you have earned. *"In my Father's house are many mansions."* (John 14:2.)

Apparently some areas of the astral worlds are dreary and depressing, but as far as these researchers have determined, there is no *eternal* hell. We are taught that sooner or later, through our own efforts, and with the spiritual help of others, we can lift our consciousness. That's very nice to know. Catholics speak of a place called *purgatory*. This is an interim place where people go after death in order to atone for the sins they have committed. It's a place of purification before going to heaven. We must believe in the great mercy and redeeming love of God rather than thinking of Divinity as a mean old man with a long white beard and a terrible temper. God is infinitely loving. He does not cast us onto the eternal rotisserie just for making a few human mistakes here on earth. I really believe you have to be terribly evil to get thrust down into the astral hells—and in any case, it is not for all eternity, for there is no place you can go where God is not. But there are many mansions, many regions in the spiritual realm, and we go to the appropriate place wearing the garments we have woven by our own thoughts and actions.

I am the chaplain at the Heritage House in San Francisco, which is a wonderful home for well-to-do senior citizens, run by the Presbyterian Church. I've been conducting services there for eight years, and I am absolutely amazed that after almost every service people will come up to me and say, "Oh, Reverend Laurence, thank you for talking about the evidence of survival and about all the wonderful things in Dr. Raymond Moody's book, *Life After Life*." I like that title, life after *life*, not life after death, because, you see, life after life is the symbol of absolute ongoing. The end is never. You often hear people say, "He died and went to

Spirit." Now, maybe they don't quite mean it like that, but I hear people say that. I've got news for you: you are as much spirit now as you will ever be. And you will be spirit for as long as eternity lasts. The only thing you will shed when you "die" is the old overcoat of your physical body.

When Moses heard a voice speaking from the burning bush, he asked, "Who is it that speaks?" and the answer came, *"I AM THAT I AM."* (Exod. 3:13-14.) Jesus said, *"Before Abraham was, I AM."* (John 8:58.) Now, it is the real you that stands within and declares, "I AM." This is simply another way of saying, "God is present." I AM is a very powerful phrase. In a certain sense, it is the name of God within each and every one of us, and the only difference between the saint, the sage, the philosopher, the illumined one, and us, is a matter of degree. The person who does not seek illumination or advancement remains sort of static. Those who do seek, very quickly begin to realize the essential divinity within themselves. But this is very hard for many people to accept, because for hundreds of years we have been listening to preachers who pound the pulpits and tell us we're very bad and that we are going to be roasted on the divine rotisserie in hell—for all eternity! We have to overlook that kind of ignorance and realize that essentially within us is a divine factor that is immortal.

All cultures have stories about evil and how to punish the wrongdoings of man. In the Christian Bible we have the story of Adam and Eve and the talking serpent, which warns against evil. In India they have a story about how evil comes into the world and what we should do about it.

It seems there are three gods who came down to ground level, most likely from over the Himalayas somewhere. These wonderful old gentlemen have, of course, very long white beards. They have come down to determine how we humans should be punished for our sins. The first god says, "Brothers, let us punish humankind by hiding their divinity from them." The second god strokes his beard and says, "Very good, brother. Let us hide it under the highest mountain; it will take eons for them to dig it out." The third god strokes his beard and says, "Ah, brothers, I have a better idea. Let us hide their divinity under the deepest sea." "Very good, very good," they nodded. So, they go off to the Himalayas to meditate for ten years. When they all come back again to ground level, the oldest and wisest god stokes his beard (which is, of course, the longest), and says, "Brothers, I think I have the best solution. Let us hide man's divinity *within* him; he will never look for it there." Now, because we are supposed to be sinners, we are not often encouraged to look for our divinity at all. As long as a sinner remains in sin, he lingers in the darkness of separation from his Divinity.

Now, many of you know that I was a Franciscan friar and spent quite some time in the seminary. I went all the way up to solemn vows and left just before taking them, so I was never ordained as a Catholic priest. But out of a kind of friendliness, people sometimes call me Father John, or Papa John, and that's fine with me. I help people as much as I can and in every way that I can, and I enjoy speaking in many churches and temples. I am totally ecumenical. So let us come together in this unity of spirit, and let us realize that all religions are there because of the need of people who are operating at that level of consciousness. All of them are doing good work, and we must never condemn or criticize any religion.

I like to make jokes and have a little fun with my Irish background, so I'll tell you a little story about the good ole Irishman who used to go to church very regularly but fell by the wayside. He, like many Irishmen, had a strong weakness for the bottle, and so Father Flanagan said to him, "Look, Paddy, if ya don't stop coming in here on Sunday all scarred up from yur battlin' and trouble in the pub, I'm not gunna let you come to the sacraments." Of course, you can't say anything worse than that to a good Catholic, so Paddy promised to be good. But a little while later he slipped again, and Father Flanagan met him on the street one day and he said, "Paddy, I see you've slipped again. Haven't I told ya time and again to stop this drinkin' and fightin'? You must *love* humanity." "Oh, Father," said Paddy, "I *do* love humanity—it's *people* I hate!"

Now, one doesn't want to be converted to narrow-mindedness. One wants to be converted to ever more broad-mindedness—ever more inclusive in the understanding of man's efforts to reach Self-realization through going within, meditation, and divine prayer. Then we will liberate ourselves from so many of the limiting things to which we are heir. There is a wonderful spiritual tenet: that the door of reformation is never closed to anyone here or hereafter. Now, that doesn't mean you should waste time in this life. Remember that when you get over to the other side you will be dressed in the garments you have woven by your actions here; and if they were not good actions you are going to be in a rather unhappy place for awhile, until you learn better. On the other hand, don't make the mistake of thinking that the minute you die you will sprout wings and go flying off to play a harp somewhere. I would be bored to tears if there were an eternity of harp music—I couldn't bear it! If you were an SOB *here*, you will be an SOB *there*, and nothing changes until *you* change. Always remember that.

I believe in praying for the dead. That's one of the wonderful things Catholics do. Before she passed from this plane, I went to see the beloved and magnificent lady, Reverend Florence Becker. I had heard her speak so many times, and had observed her work closely over many years. From the day I first met her, I never missed a day sending her light and love, and giving thanks for the noble work she did in the cause of Spirit. We are all called to serve Spirit in some way; and it doesn't matter whether we are called to be lecturers or message bearers, to teach, to parent, or to pray for others like the Carmelites do. Just do the best you can, and give a good account of yourself. Be so loving and serviceful that everyone will want what you have. Be the poise, the power, and the certitude that comes with knowing that life is ongoing and the end is never.

And so, dear friends, do not worry about life after death. When you die, you'll know that you are more alive than ever. Whether you are an atheist, an agnostic, or a true believer, the facts strongly indicate, scientifically and spiritually, that humankind has the answer already deep within. The truth has been given us by the scriptures, by the saints, by the teachings of the Church, and in the answer to good old Job, who cried out, *"If a man die, shall he live?"* (Job 14:14.) The answer is a resounding, "Yes, yes, *yes!*" Thank you. *Amen.*

The Continuity of Life

Redwood City Spiritualist Church, Redwood city, CA
October 11, 1981

Good morning, dear friends. It's very nice to be here with you again. Today I am going to talk a little about Spiritualism. You know, Spiritualism is not new. It goes back long before recorded history, and its rebirth in this wonderful country one hundred and thirty-three years ago was an act of divine providence. Because of the breadth, the power, and the depth of this marvelous liberal and living philosophy, Spiritualism is both a science and a religion.

Spiritualism enunciates the marvelous democratic attitude of mind and heart on the spiritual journey we call life. The beautiful philosophy and belief of Spiritualism emphasizes the cardinal principle of all religions: that life continues after the change called death. If you ask any priest, "Do people survive after death?" he will gladly recite a series of theological statements that say we do. And so it goes with most denominations of Christianity. I have spoken to Baptists, Presbyterians, Methodists, and many others who speak of the belief in life after death, but Spiritualists alone, it seems, are destined to give proof of ongoing life.

Many orthodox religions have said, "We mustn't have messages from the dead, and we mustn't have mediums." Well, if you took all the mediums and prophets out of the Old Testament you wouldn't have anything left but the cover. Some people tell us we must not deliver messages from the Holy Spirit because they are from the devil. I tell you, when the Holy Spirit begins to reform the sinner, reclaim the drunkard or the drug addict, and gives people a sense of hope and vindication through an absolute conviction of the ongoing nature of life, that is truly from God, and nobody can doubt it.

Spiritualism teaches us the democratic principle of existence, of our ongoing life. The democracy of the spiritual trip as exemplified in the philosophy of Spiritualism is that YOU do it. Nobody can do it for you. People who have joined Spiritualism accept that principle totally. You know, some people may think Spiritualists a little strange. Many people do. But as I look around here, I see a group of intelligent, educated, and nicely dressed people. Most people think that Spiritualists see and hear spooks at every turn. Frankly, they think you are a little flaky and touched in the head! Well, some of our finest men in politics, as you know, were Spiritualists. I won't go into that because it is a long and distinguished flock. But the beauty and the power of the Spiritualist movement is not just *phenomena*. (Which of course we love; we all love messages.) There is so much more.

I remember the great Reverend Florence Becker. I watched her for over thirty years, and occasionally attended services at her Golden Gate Spiritualist Church in San Francisco. I have never, anywhere, seen her equal. Her gift was truly a light from the spirit world. It is so rare, given perhaps once in three or four hundred years, that such a gifted soul comes to offer positive proof of the continuity of life and of self-identification at the change called death. The democracy of the spiritual trip is that you go into the next expression of life clad in the garments you have woven for yourself by your actions and reactions, for both good and evil. There is no old gentleman with a long gray beard and a bad temper beating you over the head with a stick. You see the absolute inevitability of the rightness of where you go on the other side. Isn't that democracy? You can't buy your way in, and nobody can pray you in or out. *YOU do it.* You are responsible totally for what you do right and what you do wrong, for not doing what you should have done, and for doing so much more than anyone asked of you.

Now, it seems that Spiritualism hasn't always had a rose petal path anywhere in the world. People seem a little frightened by it. You know, we're supposed to prove eternal truths, but that's not quite respectable in the view of some churchgoers. In short, it seems that when you go to the average church, you're expected to leave your brains at the door and listen to what the man says—and don't think too much or you'll get into big trouble!

When you think about this, you realize that in the Middle Ages eighty thousand people or more were murdered simply because they possessed spiritual vision, or extrasensory perception. A lot of people who possess the gifts of the spirit today would be in big trouble! Some years ago the American Society for Psychical Research sent out questionnaires to various universities asking professors how they felt about ESP. Was it all balderdash, was it worth researching, or was it simply some flaky idea a few nut cases had rolling around in their empty heads? Well, the first time they sent out that questionnaire something like 15% of the professors said they had some conviction that ESP might be worth looking at. However, more recently, within the last few years, another questionnaire indicated that something like 80% (that's quite a jump!) accept ESP and spiritual phenomena, particularly at the mental level, because that is something they deal with most frequently.

Scientists in the great universities of the world are profoundly interested in studying paranormal phenomena. They call it *para*-psychology because it transcends the ordinary. Years ago we were fascinated by "ectoplasm." Today it is called "teleplasm" or something else, and psychical research has blossomed into "parapsychology." It is the same thing. So you see, we have to chuckle a little, because even the scientists get tangled up with words every now and then. For example, remember years ago when we all had measles? That doesn't exist any more; it's called rubella now. That sounds better, doesn't it? It is the same disease. So ESP has existed since man began his journey on planet earth. It shall never be otherwise, and all religions should welcome it, for believe me, whether the religious authorities of any denomination accept such phenomena or not, it happens anyhow.

I am chaplain at the Heritage House in San Francisco, which is a very wonderful home for well-to-do senior citizens, run by the Presbyterian Church. I've been there for eight years. I am absolutely amazed that after church so many people will come up to me and say, "Oh, Rev. Laurence, thank you for talking about the evidence of survival, and about all the wonderful things in the book by Dr. Raymond Moody called *Life After Life*." I like that phrase: life after *life*. Not life after death, because you see, life after life is the symbol of absolute ongoing life.

I'd like to mention another phrase I find very interesting. Now, you are all good Spiritualists and you know better, but I hear even Spiritualists say: "He died and went to spirit." Now, maybe you don't quite mean it like that, but I hear it. I've got news for you: you are as much spirit now as you will ever be, for as long as eternity lasts. The only thing you will shed when you "die" is the old overcoat of your body.

Now, when one of your friends here passes on, you don't go down to the cemetery every day and put a flower on an old overcoat. You know that the real you stands within and declares that I AM, which is another way of saying God is present. Jesus said, "Before Abraham was, I am." (John 8:58.) So I AM becomes a very powerful saying. In a certain sense it is the name of God within each and every one of us, and the only difference between the saint, the sage, the philosopher, the illumined one, and us is a matter of degree. The person who does not seek illumination or advancement remains sort of static. Those who do begin to realize the essential immortal divinity within themselves.

There is a wonderful Spiritualist saying and principle about the door of reformation never being closed to anyone here or hereafter. Now, that doesn't mean you should waste time now, because as I said, when you get to the other side you will be dressed in the garments you have woven by your actions here, and if they are not good garments you are going to be in a rather unhappy place until you learn better. On the other hand, don't make another mistake that some uninformed Spiritualists make and think that the minute you die, you sprout wings and go flying off to play a harp somewhere. (I would be bored to tears if there were an eternity of harp music; I couldn't bear it!) Just remember that if you were an SOB *here*, you will be an SOB *there*, and nothing changes until *you* change. Always remember that.

And don't forget to pray for the dead. I believe in praying for the dead. That's probably one of the few things that Spiritualists and Catholics have in common. I remember that when the beloved and magnificent lady, Reverend Florence Becker, passed from this plane, I went to see her. I had heard her speak so many times and had watched her work over many years. From that day to this I have never missed a day sending her light and love and giving thanks for the noble work she did in the cause of Spirit. We are all Spiritualists, and whether we are called on to be lecturers or to be message bearers, never mind, do the best you can and give a good account of yourself. Be so wonderful that everyone will say that there must be something to it all, because spiritualists have a kind of poise, power, and certitude that people who wander around in the desert of unknowing do not.

So, dear friends, I think that is about what I have to say today, and I am very, very happy to be here in this spiritualist community. Thank you. *Amen.*

O Death, Where Is Thy Sting?

Spiritualist Church, Redwood City, CA
December 1981

Good morning, dear friends. I am very happy to be with you again.

Today I am going to talk about the cardinal principle of all religions: namely the affirmation that there is life after death. We read in 1 Corinthians 15:54-55: *"O death, where is thy sting? O grave, where is thy victory?"* and *"Death is swallowed up in victory."* Now, if you go to any minister, priest, rabbi, or swami and ask, "Do we live on after death?" they will say, "Yes, we do survive the change called death. Each one of us is part of the all-pervading, eternal, and ongoing Power supreme. As individuals, we are a spark of that infinite One, and therefore, we can never die."

Now, scripture references certain "gifts of the Spirit." Among them are the gift of prophecy, the gift of healings, the working of miracles, and the discerning of spirits. It is important to remember that while these abilities are extraordinary, they are not *super*natural; rather, they are divinely natural. In John 14:12, Jesus said, *"Verily, verily, I say unto you, He that believeth on me, the works that I do shall he do also; and greater works than these shall he do; because I go unto my Father."*

God often uses simple clay instruments like us to perform His marvels. He uses people who are born with special talents, or "gifts of the Spirit," to serve in the awakening and healing of His children. There are those who can perceive angels, and others who can communicate with people who have passed on. These "sensitives" are able to give evidence to the belief that man does survive death—for man is one with the eternal divine spirit, not in degree but in essence. Many of these gifted people are born with the ability to make prophecies, to discern spirits, or to heal people and animals. They have a natural sense of heightened perception, and they can enter into deep inner states effortlessly. Those who are not born with these talents, whose higher faculties are dormant, spend years trying to develop them so that they may experience super-normal contacts.

There are countless wonderful books which thoroughly document the evidence of the survival of the human personality after the death of the physical body. If you pick up any of these books you will read stories that have been very carefully screened so that we may have no doubt about their authenticity. In the late 1940s I had the privilege of studying with the great researcher, Dr. Hereward Carrington. During his fifty years of investigative work he wrote a vast number of books, and he tested every great medium known during that time. He was, of course, very scientific, thorough, skeptical, and cautious in his work. After half a century of research, Carrington concluded: "The evidence for survival after death is mountain high." It is truly wonderful to hear a man of his stature in the scientific community make such a statement.

Dr. Carrington was a marvelous clairvoyant and mystic himself, and he wrote in the first person, as a true believer. He lived and worked in California, and passed away in Los Angeles. Among his many books is one of the finest ever written on the development of our latent higher faculties. It's called *Your Psychic Abilities and How to Develop Them.* Hereward Carrington was a man who lived in our time, and he did a marvelous job of bringing this fascinating work to the world.

Now, when you enter into spiritual communion, don't make the mistake of thinking that the spirit you are trying to communicate with is in some far-off galaxy. That idea obstructs and inhibits a lot of people. Spirit is right here. You don't have to go anywhere. There are thousands of intelligences right here in this room, listening to us. Those who are clairvoyant are able to catch a glimpse of them. Some of these souls come to learn what they didn't learn when they were in the body on earth. These spirits will say, "There's a funny little Irishman speaking at the Spiritualist church this morning. Let's go down there and listen to him because he might tell us something we should have learned when we were on this plane." So they come and they listen. That's all part of the reality of the essential spiritual nature of our being.

Last week one of my students came over to visit me. He brought a friend who was full of questions about contacting the spirit world. The first thing I said to this man was, "You have to get rid of any fear about contacting your guardian angel and others in the spirit world." Angels and other incorporeal beings are with us to guide, teach, and inspire us. So let go of the idea that it is a spooky, unnatural, and weird sort of thing. It is divinely natural, and as practical as the ingredients in a batch of biscuits. If you look at it that way, you'll never waste your time being fearful. Like the saints, embrace the smile of the spirit world as it comes toward you, bringing guidance and messages of love from those across the veil. Through your faith, through your love, and through your service to your fellow man, you will build a bridge of light between yourself and the eternal worlds.

Now, you would be surprised how many religious people have a great fear of death. I once knew an eminent Episcopal divine who had no belief in life after death. Here was a supposedly pious and anointed man, and he had all the special regalia to prove his high and holy position, but he had a terrible fear of dying. Some people don't want to think about death; they don't want to think about spiritual dynamics. They are very careful to keep away from all things spiritual. Now, I don't think it's a morbid thing to think about death, and I don't think we should go around worrying about dying all the time. I think we should accept death as a natural part of life, just as we accept birth. Death is inevitable, and the minute you are born you are terminal. There is no question about it. When we meditate on this for a while, we come to realize where we are going, and from where we have come. Then we find ourselves very conveniently abreast of our trip through the classroom of the earth experience, and we have no fear of our "graduation" into the next expression of our ongoing, eternal life. When we graduate from this plane—I like that word *"graduate"*—the only thing we lose is the overcoat of the body. We get a better one when we get over to the other side. It is a body of light, made of the stuff which we have woven by our actions and reactions here.

Now, some people think the word "die" is a terrible word, and they find all kinds of euphemisms to use in its place. But death is not something to fear or become morose about. Do you know anyone who came on the planet who didn't die? As one of our well-known comics was fond of saying, "Not one of us is going to get of here alive." So be of good cheer and raise your heart. As they say in the Latin Rite Catholic Mass, *Sersum corda*: lift up your hearts.

Now, we have just entered the Christmas season. Christmastime is a spiritual celebration, a time for religious observances and practices, and it is a joyous season for children. In working with countless people over a number of decades, I have learned that, curiously enough, people sometimes get a little depressed at Christmastime. Sometimes it's the nostalgia of thinking back twenty-five years, when mother and father, brothers and sisters, our neighbors, and friends were all together. And now, of course, some of them have passed on, and we can't be with them at Christmastime. Realize that ultimately you *will* see those you have loved and lived with on this earth, as truly as I see you and you see me in this room right here. So don't let the sadness of missing your departed loved ones come upon you at Christmas or any other time.

You know, an awful lot of people go around looking terribly sad, like they are going somewhere to bury their best friend, their dog, and everything else they hold dear. Such people have to let go of that negativity and learn to be happy; they have to let gladness take hold. Jesus the Christ reiterated that truth time and again when he said that we should be glad and know that God dwells in the heavens, *and* within the temple of our being. When we realize that truth, we begin to radiate more and more happiness and a sense of ongoing life.

We mustn't allow ourselves to be overcome by the fear of death or the materialistic attitudes of the world. Learn to bring your consciousness into a one-pointedness, and make the temple of your heart a place where the Christ spirit may dwell. The more you do that, the more you come into the marvelous sense of God's unending life and presence everywhere, but especially within you. Then you cannot but reflect a gladsome spirit, which radiates outward and becomes a blessing to everyone you meet. Today even science and modern medicine tell us that if we have a happy attitude we are more apt to be healthy. A state of happiness boosts our immunity so that the little wild animals called viruses and germs don't attack us as easily. So let's not waste any time going around looking unhappy. Let us be "smile millionaires," as a beloved saint, Paramhansa Yogananda, used to say.

Millions of people are getting facelifts these days, but surgery doesn't make them more beautiful if they are not uplifted from within. You can have a hundred plastic surgeons work on you, and still sag with unhappiness. We must realize that our real facelift comes from within, and nothing does it better than a smile. It doesn't cost anything to smile, to radiate joy outward to the world—and it is a very beautiful thing to do. When you smile, the people around you begin to smile, too. When you feel good because you are filled with the joy of the Christ presence within your own heart and mind, other people feel good, too. Pretty soon people will come to you and say, "There is something different about you. What is it? Why are you so happy most of the time?" Then you can tell them.

So let us enter into a joyous sense as we move into the Christmas spirit. Let us take the Christ spirit of joy from deep within ourselves and radiate it outward so that when people look at us they feel uplifted—not as if everything is terrible and we're all going to die any minute.

You know, a man came to me the other day wanting some help because he was totally consumed with frightful, gloomy thoughts. He said, "Oh, I think the world is going to come apart. I think the atom bomb is coming." I said, "Well, if it does come, do you know where I want to be? Right under it! I don't want to stick around to see what's going to happen, if someone gets so stupid that they destroy the whole planet." There are countless things we can fret about, but I'm not going to give myself to any of them. I'm not going to sit at home and wonder, "Is the big earthquake going to come? Is the bomb coming? Are terrible things going to happen?" You know, we have prophets of doom all over the place. Some of them look like undertakers going somewhere to bury an idea! Well, let us not join them. Let us simply take hold of an invincible faith, and lean upon the sustaining Infinite. The best thing we can do is organize ourselves in a spiritual way and set aside a little time every day to meditate on the omnipresence of good. Then we shall be liberated from inordinate fears and all the boogiemen. Drop your fears; don't carry a three-hundred-pound sack of fear on your back. It only obstructs and ruins the joy of life.

And so, dear friends, it is very gladsome to have a spiritual understanding that there is no death. With mountains of evidence for the survival of the human personality, and the promise that truly we will see our departed loved ones, we may rejoice in 1 Corinthians 15:54-55: *"O death, where is thy sting? O grave, where is thy victory? Death is swallowed up in victory."* Thank you. *Amen.*

Is Spiritualism Really Spiritual?

Redwood Spiritualist Church, Redwood City, CA
March 14, 1982

I am very happy to be with you this morning. I enjoy my visits here in Redwood City. There is a beautiful spiritual vibration here. As you know, I serve many churches in many areas, and each one has its own distinct quality. So today, inasmuch as this is a spiritualist church, I thought it would be nice to talk a little bit about Spiritualism.

Now, some people ask, "Are spiritualists really spiritual? Is Spiritualism really spiritual?" Well, of course, anybody who has taken fifteen minutes to peruse the matter will agree in a resounding way that Spiritualism is indeed spiritual; and so are the people who come within its gates. They come seeking contact with the divine reality which men call by a thousand names, God. Whatever you call it, it is the same: the all-pervading One, the Father of lights, the Father of wisdom, the infinite Spirit of love. And so, we indeed know that spiritualists are not just a group of spook hunters wrapped in bed sheets running around here and there seeking thrills in otherworldly phenomena.

Now, of course, there have been some people who called themselves spiritualists who ran around with bed sheets on. We're very sorry for those people, and we're sorry about the bad press their actions have given Spiritualism in general. But suppose you went to the bank and they gave you a bad ten-dollar bill. You might say, "I don't believe in American currency anymore! It's false! It's all worthless because I got a counterfeit note!" Now, wouldn't you be shallow and foolish, to react like that? Would you give up all currency simply because there was one bad bill among billions? No, of course you wouldn't.

Many people who reject the word "Spiritualism" are in fact good spiritualists. Some of them are Catholic priests. So here is a story about just such a priest and a spiritualist medium, whom I knew years ago in Connecticut. One night a medium was having trouble getting to sleep, and while she was lying quietly in her bed, a voice came to her inner mind and said, "You must get up and go to Saint Mary's Hospital, to Room 421. There is a priest there who wants to talk to you. He needs you, so please go." Well, she felt very unsure. How do you go to a Catholic hospital and barge into a priest's room, declaring yourself a spiritualist medium who has come in the middle of the night in response to a voice from the other side?

Well, despite these doubts, the medium was finally fortified with enough courage from Spirit that she got up, got dressed, and went to the hospital. As she walked into the room, she saw a very old gentleman sitting in a wheelchair. She looked at him and said, "I don't know how to explain myself, but here I am." "Oh," the priest said, "I've been expecting you." He said, "I am a priest, and I have worked in the area of Spiritualism for many years. I have written a book about my experiences, about the proof of the survival of spirit and the total identity and recognition of the self which survives beyond the mortal garb. I have put all this into a book, and I feel it must reach people. I know that I'm going to leave the body very shortly, and when I do, in all probability my superiors will take this book and drop it down the garbage chute, and that will be the end of it. So I want you to take the book with you and do everything you can to bring about its publication." Well, this was a good many years ago, around 1949 or '50, and I've lost track of the medium, so I don't know if she ever did get the book published, but it is a wonderful story about a medium who followed an urgent message from Spirit.

You see, it doesn't make any difference if you are a Catholic, a Buddhist, a Hindu, or a Baptist—you are a spiritualist when you know in all truth and certitude that Spirit is; that eternal, ongoing life is a matter of fact; and that it doesn't need to be proven again and again. Although the spiritualists are definitely patient, and have proven it a hundred thousand times, and then even more. Why? Because people need encouragement, and they need to be reassured constantly that there is no death.

Many people look down on Spiritualism, saying that spiritualists are a bunch of fuzzy-brained folks, running around looking for strange phenomena. And yet, some of the finest minds in the world have been profoundly interested in the spiritualist teachings, and not just in phenomena. I love phenomena, who doesn't? Everybody likes phenomena. But in addition to phenomena, there is a supreme philosophy, a foundation, a structure and dimension of absolute positivity in Spiritualism that gives us strength from within, and that is what is important.

So dear friends, never be afraid to acknowledge that you are naturally inclined to want to know about life after death. People in different religions will say different things about it. But it shouldn't be a taboo subject. There are some who think Spiritualism is just spooky, and they dismiss the whole thing. There are others who say, "Spiritualists are playing around with demons! Very bad!" Well, demons do not bring about reformation and healing, and it is a fact that countless people have been reformed and healed through the operation of the many spiritual gifts demonstrated in spiritualist churches.

Christ himself said that a *"house divided against itself shall not stand."* (Matt. 12:25.) Do you suppose demons would work against themselves by healing and reforming people? Through the operation and guidance of spiritual messages, people's faith has been shored up and brought into such brilliant focus that they literally no longer doubt whatsoever. Think of all the people who have been healed here at your ministry. Think of the sick, the alcoholics and drug addicts, the burglars and other criminals, and sinners of all kinds, who have been released from whatever trouble they got themselves into. Countless people have been brought out of their suffering because of the good work done in this ministry.

I remember years ago when I studied the work of a wonderful spiritualist minister at a church in San Francisco. She was an excellent medium who passed on several years ago. One evening she was doing readings for a group of people, and when she came to a certain young man, she said, "Please stay after the service, I must speak with you. Will you promise me you will stay?" The young man reluctantly said yes, and after church she spoke with him. He was literally on his way to commit suicide by jumping off the Golden Gate Bridge. The particular message the minister brought to him provided so much evidence that it could not have been come from anyone but his deceased mother. Through this vehicle of spirit communication, the man not only became totally persuaded that he mustn't jump, but he realized it would be possible to heal and change his whole life. Along with taking drugs, he also had a problem with liquor; and while the medium was talking to him after the service, she picked up a glass of water and said, "Son, your mother says not to drink anything but this." This young man was certain that all this information and guidance was coming from his deceased mother, because the words contained in the message were exactly those his mother would speak, and because there were so many other pieces of evidence.

One of the greatest mediums I ever studied was Reverend Florence Becker. For thirty years I watched her do wondrous things to change people's lives, and bring them back from the brink of despair into total hopefulness. Through her unobstructed and clear contact with the spirit world, Reverend Becker was able to deliver messages that were so powerful and evidential that people were moved beyond believing to knowing without any doubt that God is real, and that we as spirit exist here and hereafter.

Remember when you were a little boy or a little girl and you went to the Episcopal or Catholic Church, or to some other orthodox church, and you were given a little holy card with a picture of a guardian angel? Of course, the angel had wings and, I don't know why, but they all had blonde hair and blue eyes! At any rate, our guardian angels, or spirit guides, don't necessarily have to have wings. They know what this earth experience is all about because they have been here before. Now, in spirit, they are helping us not to make the mistakes they made. They are watching us grow, and they are learning and growing too, on the other side. Knowing there are angels around to help gives us freedom from anxiety, especially the anxiety of death.

I think the most beautiful thing about Spiritualism is that it makes you responsible for your own choices. You learn that in addition to being responsible for your actions and reactions, you meet yourself coming around every corner. When you arrive in the astral world you will see the whole picture of your earth life with immense clarity, both the plusses and the minuses. As you view both the positives and negatives of your actions, you will know the absolute rightness of it all. When people have been touched by the Holy Spirit, they come to know the truth beyond a shadow of a doubt. Think of the marvelous healers that Spiritualism has brought into being. But remember, healing does not come from the healer. The marvels of healing come from the Holy Spirit working through the healer.

We've all read about miracles; and we've all heard about the great healers of the East, as well as the legendary British, American, and Brazilian healers. Many investigators have gone to these healers with grave doubts and have returned as true knowers. One of them was a medical doctor who went to Brazil with cancer, and with more than a healthy dose of skepticism. He returned home with a glass jar which contained a large tumor that was taken from him by a marvelous spiritualist healer. The tumor was removed without the use of standard surgical procedures. The man still has the tumor in a jar of formaldehyde, and he shows it as a kind of testimonial to anyone who is interested. So, you see, when people begin to look into Spiritualism, they lose all fear of it. They come to realize that the "gift of discerning spirits" is in fact a holy, blessed talent that is bestowed on a rare few for the healing and welfare of all.

The Roman Catholic Church has practiced healing for quite a long time and at quite a good level, but for many years spiritual healing was not practiced in most other churches. In the primitive Christian movement healing was one of the most important parts of the service. For many people, spiritual messages were the primary reason they came to church, because everybody had something wrong with them and they all wanted to be healed. So they came. The marvels that happened to them, as a result of the information contained in the messages from the spirit world, would fill volumes.

I am totally ecumenical. There are countless people in various religions and denominations who are consciously or unconsciously receptive to the divine forces of healing. This healing energy is poured out through the man or woman who is attuned to the flow of divine love—this benediction that is given to those who come to them for help. It is very important for us to note that even the greatest healers have never claimed to heal anyone. They know it is God working through them that is the real Healer.

Now, here is a little story about Lourdes. You've all probably read many beautiful stories about this famous holy shrine in France. I think I told you about the miracle of healing that Dr. Alexis Carrell witnessed at Lourdes and how it changed his life. There is another story about a gentleman who lived in a small town in France. He didn't believe in anything, neither God nor man; he was a confirmed atheist. He was the editor of a communist magazine, and all he was interested in was social revolution. Well, because of his cynical and pessimistic approach to life, he ended up creating a revolution within his own body and he was diagnosed with terminal cancer. His wife, a good Catholic, kept badgering him to make a trip to Lourdes. He didn't want to go because, first of all, he did not believe in healing. He thought it was a lot of rubbish. But he finally gave in to his nagging wife, thinking, "Well, if I'm going to have any peace at all with my wife in the months left to me, I'd better go, because she will never leave me alone about it."

So, reluctantly, he went to Lourdes. The first thing he did was to watch them dunk people in the healing, holy water. The priests created an atmosphere that was quite beautiful and wonderful, with candles, incense, and prayerful songs. But the atheist wasn't having any of it. In fact, he was revolted by it. However, he observed that everybody was kneeling down; and so, not out of reverence, but just because he wanted to conform, he knelt down too. While he was kneeling, the atheist noticed a very dear and sweet little girl not far away from him. She was profoundly afflicted and seemed to be near death. As he looked at this child he was deeply touched, and great compassion was awakened within him. He uttered the first prayer he had ever spoken in his entire life. He whispered, "If there is a God, never mind about me. Heal this little girl." Instantly, both of them were healed.

Now, how about that? This man is no longer an atheist, nor the editor of a communist paper. He goes to church regularly and tries to help all those in need who cross his path. That was a marvelous example of spiritual healing, and it demonstrates God's power and great love for us. With the whispered prayer of an atheist, a human soul was totally changed, and two people were healed from terminal illnesses.

And so, dear friends, we have to realize that Spiritualism has a great deal to tell us, and we should be proud of it. Spiritualism is not only a metaphysical design for living here and now, it is a design for living in the next world as well. Spiritualists are the happiest people because, you see, they are not afraid of death at all. Very few people think about their own deaths. Their minds may tell them, "My neighbor is going to die one of these days, but not me. Everything is going to be fine. I'm not going to die." Now, I don't expect you to go around thinking about death all the time, nor to wear a black rag over your head as you sadly trudge through your day, looking around every corner for the Grim Reaper. But you can be like the spiritualists who, because of the phenomena involved in the spiritualistic movement, are sure of the marvelous divine power that reforms criminals, drunkards, and drug addicts, heals all kinds of other maladies, and literally changes people's lives for the better. That's why this cannot be the work of demons. If it were, then it would be a "house divided." When, through the workings of Spirit, you can save people from themselves and from the evil in their lives, and bring them to the feet of truth, that indeed is a thing of immense beauty. It is divine.

So you see, dear friends, Spiritualism is more than phenomena. But we all love phenomena. We love it when we get a wonderful message, especially one that contains so much evidential information that it proves beyond a shadow of a doubt that the person talking to us from the astral plane is exactly who they say they are. Then we know the message is authentic. Now, our guardian angels and spirit guides come and touch all of us, and it doesn't matter what your religion is or what type of work you do. I know some very fine, down-to-earth medical doctors who have phenomenal spiritualistic qualities. Because of the attunement they have with Spirit, they have become marvelous diagnosticians.

Very often while I am counseling people, tuning in to them and reading their auras, their living relatives will pop in on the line of spirit, though they are not in the room at the time of the reading. Not long ago I was counseling a lady at The Seeker's Quest in Campbell, California, and I repeated what I heard on the inner plane from Spirit. I said, "Your mother doesn't live in this city, but the next time you talk to her on the phone, please tell her to go to her doctor and have him check on her thyroid, because there is something that must be taken care of." When the woman got home she called her mother, who did not reject what I had advised. She immediately set up an appointment with her doctor. Last Thursday she had surgery on a hidden tumorous growth on her thyroid. I had never seen the woman in my life, and I probably never will, but on the day I was reading for her daughter I was right on the beam. There was no static on the wire, and the information from my spirit helpers was coming right through, loud and clear. I was very happy to be of service.

I had a call from a Celtic priest two days ago. He was talking to me about a Roman Catholic priest who works with him. He said, "You know, my associate is quite ill, and I'm really disturbed about him. I'm not happy with the medical attention he's getting. I think that maybe

I should take him to my doctor." As I listened to my friend, I inwardly asked the Holy Spirit if there was anything I could do to help. Without pausing to question the information coming through me, I said, "Listen Father, don't wait one more minute. Even as we speak, it may already be too late. Take him to the doctor right away; don't waste any time. It is later than we think." Now, you see, this input from Spirit can come very quickly, and when it does the knowing is immediate and direct. You don't have to sit down and draw a picture; it just happens. As soon as my friend hung up the phone, he took the priest to his doctor. They got him to the hospital and into surgery within an hour. His aorta was bursting.

Now, how about that for receiving spiritual guidance? Who do you suppose gave me that information? Did I get a letter? Did somebody write to me and say, "Oh, the priest has this and that, and you must tell your friend about it, and then he will think you are quite wonderful." No, it all popped out like toast from a toaster. It just pops into my consciousness. And that's the way it should be. We can all touch in to Spirit if we simply relax, allow the spiritual forces of good, and surrender to them. When we do that, we can serve our fellow man in a way that is truly marvelous.

You see, when we experience these marvels of Spirit, it convinces us that this material world is very limited. The spiritual dynamics of reality, of both this world and the ongoing worlds, are amazing and awe-inspiring, and we can touch into them. We have to want to, and we have to work at it. We have to study, sit in a class, meditate, purify ourselves, and develop our sensitivity and receptivity.

Some people acquire the gifts of spirit spontaneously and instantly: "just like that." I'm not always sure this is the best way, but we have to leave that in the hands of Providence. I think the safest way is to grow gradually and to understand what you are doing. However, if Spirit wants you to become instantaneously mediumistic, you will. But for some people it is a very heavy load to carry sometimes. I've known people who did not understand what was happening to them because they had never heard of the gifts of the Spirit. But, you see, the spirits over there don't care whether we have heard of them or not. Contact with spirit is a total commitment to the realities of the eternal, ongoing nature of existence, both here and hereafter.

Some years ago, a good Episcopal minister was conducting a funeral service, and while they were lowering the casket into the ground and saying the usual prayers, "Ashes to ashes, and dust to dust . . ." (I'm not a "dust and ashes" man (congregation roars laughing), I'm an ongoing "eternal life" man.) But anyway, while the minister was saying that prayer over the grave, he saw Mr. McMahan, the deceased person, plain as day, standing right beside his wife, trying very hard to comfort her. But she couldn't see or hear him. Because she believed it was wrong to develop one's spiritual gifts, this woman's natural faculties were shut down, so of course she couldn't see that her husband was very much alive. Never forget that spiritual gifts are the gifts of the Holy Spirit, and don't be afraid to develop and use them. This woman couldn't receive the message from her deceased husband, but the minister both saw and heard him. Later on a good friend heard about this incident, and he asked the minister, "Why didn't you go and tell Mrs. McMahan about what you saw?" "Oh, I wouldn't dare," the minister replied, "I don't know what the bishop would think." Well God, guardian angels, and spirit messengers don't care what others think. They are only interested in truth: that which is eternal, ongoing, and provable.

So if you feel that you have the gift of discerning spirits, meditate more, keep your feet on the ground, and try to develop that gift. Each and every one of you has the gift latent within. You should work with it and try to develop it. Don't be afraid of these divinely natural faculties; and always do your work by first declaring yourself in the blazing light of divine protection: "I welcome all those who come through the divine light, but I do not permit negative spirits from the skid row regions of the astral planes." There are skid rows over there, you know, and they are populated with "tramp souls." So watch out for them and their shenanigans.

Well, dear friends, it has been a delight to be with you today and to talk a little about Spiritualism. We know that Spiritualism is truly spiritual, and we know what spiritualists are doing is truly spiritual. They are making contact with the all-pervading reality and truth of the infinite God of love, compassion, and wisdom.

So, let us remember that the "gifts of the Spirit" are divinely natural. There is nothing spooky about them. Protected by the light of the Christ, we can walk with confidence through the corridors of the spirit worlds with absolute faith and courage. We can be grateful for receiving the gifts of the Holy Spirit, and gladly offer them to those who call to us for help. That is true Spiritualism. Thank you. *Amen.*

To Die Is Not Death

Spiritualist Church, Redwood City, CA
January 24, 1981

Good morning, dear friends. I am glad to see all your happy, shining faces. Today we are going to talk about the continuity of life after death. The Bible is full of marvelous stories of prophecy, the appearances of angels, levitations, and all sorts of other marvels. Indeed, life does go ever onward, and it gets better and better; for as the Christ told us, *"I go to my Father in heaven."* So let us take the Christ at his word. Let us take hold of the true meaning of Easter and celebrate the glorious resurrection of Christ. Then we will be truly liberated by the knowledge and assurance of the continuity of conscious existence.

Now, there are many people who speak about death in a terribly gloomy way. They go around looking very sad because they think death is the end of everything—that you go down into the grave and disintegrate, and that's the end of it all. Even some ministers do not believe in the continuity of life after death.

Horace Westwood was a Unitarian minister who wrote on parapsychology. He was born in 1884, in Wakefield, England. He was first ordained as a minister of the Methodist Episcopal Church in 1906. And then in 1910 he joined the Unitarian Church and was pastor at a number of churches until he became head of the First Unitarian Church (a very liberal Christian church) in Berkeley, California until his death in 1956. Having studied psychic research for a number of years, he became one of the finest writers in the area of parapsychology. He describes his personal observations in his marvelous book, *There Is a Psychic World.*

Now, in the beginning Horace Westwood did not believe in survival after death at all. He thought that religion was a kind of ethical force that helped people not to kill each other and not to steal their neighbors' valuables. He believed that if people behaved properly and treated each other with respect that everything would be quite all right. He believed that you were born, you live a while, and then you die; that was all there was to it.

In time, Horace Westwood's notion of death changed. Rather than viewing it as a sad and gloomy occasion, he saw passing away as a joyful graduation from the earth plane—a birthday, as it were, into a new life in the eternal, ongoing, and unobstructed universe. Westwood's church was very liberal and very *now*. He was very open-minded, and he opened the doors widely to welcome scientific investigation into the question of life after death.

Recently, in one of the little rag papers (those funny little newspapers that come out locally), there was a headline that caught my eye. It was the story of one hundred and six people who had been pronounced clinically dead, but who were resuscitated. These people described their near-death experience as passing into what appeared to be a beautiful, golden atmosphere where they met their so-called *dead* friends; and their so-called dead friends were very much *alive* over there. Each of these cases was carefully scrutinized by medical doctors and researchers. We are hearing more and more of these stories because today our medical technology is much more sophisticated than ever before, and more people are being brought back from the death experience on operating tables and in emergency rooms all over the world. In fact, what we used to call a "near-death experience" is really an incomplete experience of dying.

I remember a dear old lady, a wonderful mystic, who told me that she went over to the other side for a visit. She said it was a beautiful experience to meet her mother over there. And she said, "I threw my arms around her and cried. I didn't want to come back, but they told me I had to because I still had work to do here in the classroom of the earth experience."

Now, the principle of ongoing life is indeed beautiful. No church on earth, and no religion anywhere, could possibly deny it. It's a declaration of absolute faith concerning the continuity of your personality as an individualized part of God in the next expression of life. And that's what death is all about: it's a resurrection, a rebirth into ongoing life. When you die, you're not just some sort of smoky wisp somewhere out there who doesn't know who he or she is. You're a conscious, dynamic, living being. You are your *self*, living in the next expression of life, and you are inhibited only by those obstacles which you have created for yourself by your actions and reactions in life. You have to learn to get rid of those obstacles; and as I say all the time, the great democracy of the spiritual trip is that *you* do it.

The literature concerning that which comes about after the change called death is abundant, and the research is enormously persuasive. In the earlier days of scientific research into life after death people were a little frightened, and of course the major churches were a bit hostile because they didn't think you should try to prove anything spiritual. However, there were a number of scientific men who decided that because God had given them intelligence, He certainly had not forbidden them to use it for researches into the probability, as they called it, of a future life. And so these brave researchers went about their investigations in a most wonderful way.

People like Horace Westwood are very happy because they have already made their peace with death and they are not afraid of it at all. Death is as much a part of life as birth itself, and of course even scientists tell us today that death is generally a very easy process. Sometimes people looking at the body think, "Oh, he is suffering." They interpret the process as some kind of agony, but the body has a curious way of anesthetizing itself as death approaches.

Lottie Von Strahl, born in 1895 in Oldenburg, Germany, became a baroness through marriage. She was internationally known and revered as a truly great spiritual intuitive—a medium and clairvoyant—and she was regularly employed by the German police to trace criminals and to assist in solving crimes of all descriptions. Lottie wrote to me and told me about the passing of her husband, Otto Von Strahl. He was a hard-nosed Lutheran, and although he accepted his wife's marvelous spiritual gifts and mediumship, Otto had a great fear of death. He was filled with uncertainties concerning what would happen after he died. Lottie said that when her husband passed she was sitting by the side of his bed. At that moment a marvelous serene smile came over his face and he began to greet his father, mother, brother and various other members of his family. Lottie said she saw the most beautiful radiance about him. She saw his spirit form leave the physical form and go off into the ether; and of course, all Otto's fear of death was completely absorbed and taken over by the realities of ongoing life.

I studied and worked with Lottie Von Strahl for four years. She used to tell us that when she worked with British intelligence and with the police in London she would look at the auras of the people they were investigating, and she knew when they were lying. She could discern all kinds of things about them from reading their auras. In fact, she interviewed Adolf Hitler three times. She said that the first two times she read his aura it was pretty good, but the last time she saw him his aura had become completely black. On that very night, after reading for him, Lottie fled the country to Norway, and from Norway to England, and from England to South Africa, where she spent the remaining war years. Baroness Von Strahl spoke nine languages, so she was an important figure during World War II. She was a wonderful lady, and I'm very glad to have known and worked with her.

You see, dear friends, you are immortal right *now*. You are spirit now. I wish I could impress that on everybody. We hear people say, "Oh, Mrs. Jones died and went to spirit." She did, but she was already spirit before she left. She just happened to be wearing a cloak we call the human body.

Down through the years a countless assortment of books has been written that delve deeply into the scientific evidence for survival. Some of them have been written by enormously erudite men and women in the academic community. One of those books is *From Séance to Science*. (I like that title.) It is truly a marvelous book written by Doctor George Meek and Bertha Harris at the time when they were working at Stanford University, where Bertha was being tested for her extraordinary sensitivities.

George Meek was a British doctor who came to the United States with Bertha Harris: one of the great spiritual talents and mediums of this century. Imagine a mainstream scientist working at Stanford University, writing a book by that title. When I met and observed Bertha I was enormously impressed by her work. She was a very great lady. In his book, *From Séance to Science*, Doctor Meek devotes the first part to absolute, cold, hard science. He doesn't let anything get by his sharp scrutiny. He outlines the latest scientific findings regarding the spiritual nature of the universe; and he talks about electromagnetic force fields, potential energy, subtle energy fields, and other aspects of the universe that change before our very eyes as we observe them, and yet remain in a certain sense the same. Science tells us that nothing is ever lost; it merely changes form. So while a scientist is watching the K element in the lab in Berkeley, it actually disappears under a certain bombardment of electronic energy. And yet, researchers can prove it is still there. It has simply become invisible.

My word, these scientists are talking like mystics! They really are. Just think, a few years ago they would have been laughed out of the courts of the academic community, but they are becoming always better informed, and more consciously aware of the marvelous spiritual nature of this wondrous space in which we live. Our universe is so inconceivably marvelous and vast—and that is merely the *physical* universe. Behind, under, and around all of this there exists a spiritual universe, much greater than even the far-flung galaxies that humankind is able to glimpse through our most sophisticated technical equipment.

The second half of George Meek's book highlights the work done by the great Bertha Harris. Now, as I said, Bertha was a mystic with a vast sensitivity and extraordinary vision. She was quite famous in Europe, and she was the favorite spiritual advisor of Winston Churchill and Charles De Gaulle. She used to see three auras around people. Most clairvoyants can see only one. Because she was born with a great sensitivity Bertha could see the spirit forms of people just as clearly as we see each other in physical form. This is a gift of the Holy Spirit. You can read about these gifts in Corinthians by Saint Paul: *"Now concerning spiritual gifts, brethren, I would not have you ignorant."* (1 Cor. 12:1.) The gift of clear seeing, or clairvoyance, is divinely natural, and that is what we are talking about today.

Now, I'm going to share a couple of stories from the book *From Séance to Science* because I think they are beautiful. Bertha Harris told us these stories herself at a group meeting in San Francisco. One time she was called to Ireland by a very wealthy man who had a castle there; so she went, all expenses paid, and lived in the castle for a few days. Since nothing unusual was happening, she wondered why she had been called there. Finally one night at dinner the owners of the castle told her that they had brought her there because they wanted to get rid of an entity, who was, shall we say, haunting the premises. They asked, "Can you get rid of this man who is banging doors, making all kinds of rattling noises, and causing all sorts of other confusions?" Bertha said, "I will do my best. I will try."

They were having dinner a few evenings later when they heard strange noises out in the hall. Bertha said, "I'll go and look." She ran down the hall to take a look, and there he was. He looked like a pirate. She said, "You know, sir, these people are very unhappy with you, making all these noises. You're disturbing them. Now, you really should find yourself another home on the spiritual side of life where you belong. You don't need to be here on this physical level. In a certain sense, you are limiting yourself by staying around here. You should move on into the glorious and absolutely unlimited universe that awaits you."

He felt very bad when he heard that his presence was making these lovely people so unhappy. He said, "Oh, I'm so sorry. I don't want to offend them. And I hate to go because I have really become fond of them, even if they aren't fond of me." So he agreed to leave, and he did.

Well, you won't believe the second part of this story. About six or eight months later, Bertha got a call from the people in Ireland, asking her to come back to their castle. She thought, "I wonder what's happened. Perhaps the spirit has come back. What shall we do?" So she went. At dinner she was astonished at the request the people made: "We miss him. Do you think you can bring him back?" Bertha said, "I'll try." She went into the hall and sat very still and became deeply quiet. When she called him back, he came.

She said, "Sir, the people here miss you." "Oh," he said, "I'm so happy because I do want to come back. I tell you what I'll do: I'll give them a nice present." "What is it?" asked Bertha. "Well, there are three big trees just outside the dining room windows. When you go to the north of the third tree, move about two feet and then dig down three feet, and there you will find a small metal box with some gold coins and jewelry in it." "Oh," Bertha said, "that's wonderful. Thank you. I'll tell the people tomorrow morning."

So, at breakfast the next day she told them. They went out and dug just as the spirit had instructed, and they found the box with the gold coins and jewelry precisely where the spirit had said they would be. But by law they had to turn the gold coins in. That was too bad, but that's what happened. So apparently the living "ghost" is still around, enjoying being part of his adopted family.

This dear and wonderful lady, Bertha Harris, has had a thousand marvelous experiences of this sort; so much so that she, like some of us who are less gifted, became a little blasé about it. I am so used to seeing lights and beautiful auras around people that if I didn't see them I would feel that something was wrong. After a while you sort of expect it. We should all realize that each of us comes into this life with a different spiritual gift. We must make the most of our gifts and be very happy with them, honor them, work with them, and develop them. We should regard our clairvoyance and other spiritual talents as the Bible does, as a gift of the Holy Spirit.

Now, I hold a class in spiritual development in San Jose, California. It is a short course: we meet once a week for about five weeks. I always start the class by teaching people how to set their minds upon the divine light. I teach them how to draw in that light, how to clad themselves in that protective light, and how to reach out in consciousness to the positive, never to the negative. We must always keep our attention on the light so that we filter out and protect against any sort of negativity, and attract only the good.

About eighty-three percent of my students have learned to read the aura very well, and many of them use this skill as a diagnostic tool in their medical practices. The best way to develop your sensitivities is to sit in a class with a good teacher with whom you feel comfortable. I like to let the class run for a couple of years, maybe even longer. When I was studying I sat every week for four years with the same teacher. Unfortunately, sometimes the demands of the ministry where I teach are such that we need to streamline everything and make it very compact, so I give this five-week intensive training on how to still the body and quiet the mind in order to become receptive to spirit.

Unless you quiet yourself it is very hard to hear the whisperings of spirit or experience any sort of extraordinary phenomena, except the occasional and spontaneous kind. In order to hear the "still small voice" of spirit you must first quiet the body, and then quiet the mind. If the mind is jumping around like a flea on a hot tin roof you are not very concentrated, and you're not apt to get very many beautiful inspirations coming in on the wings of the divine. So first we learn to quiet the mind.

Quieting the mind is much more difficult than quieting the body. By the way, there are marvelous extra benefits that are accrued by quieting the mind. During our five-week class we often see spontaneous healings. Once people learn to be quiet and get in touch with the deeper aspects of themselves, there is a very good chance that they will be able to touch somebody in the spirit world who wants to communicate; it might be a friend, a relative or a guiding influence.

I teach these skills very carefully. I work with students for five weeks, offering ten hours of very specific information that is carefully designed to help them cultivate a deeper awareness and receptivity to spirit. Some of them have become very fine, prominent public servants in the spiritual vineyard. I have taught many psychiatrists, psychologists, and medical doctors, several of whom have become quite famous because of their highly developed diagnostic skills, by focusing on the aura, or energy fields, of their patients. I have teachers and all sorts of other people in my classes, and they are all doing extraordinarily well in their professional practices by employing their intuition and awakened sensitivities.

In order to awaken the dormant faculties of your higher nature you have to lend your attention to your practice. You have to quiet your body and your mind so you can hear the vibrating strings of the eternal harp. Then you begin to have clairvoyant experiences in a very safe and controlled way because you always ask for them to come through the divine light. Of course, I can never guarantee that each and every person who attends my classes will become a world-class medical intuitive or clairvoyant, but if they take the time to gather the most important factors of spiritual development and put them into a sound and safe structure, it will surely bring about the kind of results they are seeking.

Now, every one of you here is sensitive to some degree. And for every one of you it is possible to see the human aura. Sometimes it is rather amusing when you read the aura of your friends and you catch what's really going on, even though they may try to hide it.

I remember one time when there was a gathering of students in San Francisco. They were serving coffee and cake in a very relaxed and friendly atmosphere. A very charming, middle-aged couple came in late. They were smiling and warm to everyone as they said, "We're so sorry we're late. What's going on?" Someone said, "John is reading auras." The lady of the couple said, "Oh, I want you to read mine next." I said, "Okay, as soon as I get through reading this one, I'll read yours." I did, and in her aura I saw all these flashes of red lightening and I thought, "Oh, anger, anger, anger. My word, what is going on with this woman? She is smiling and couldn't seem nicer, but she's irritated and full of resentment." I also saw that this was quite temporary—a sort of momentary flash, and not her usual state. I could see that both she and her husband were delightful, well-balanced people, but in her aura I saw all these flashes of red lightening.

I asked within, "What happened to this woman tonight?" The inner voice answered, "On the way to this gathering, papa and mama had a little set-to in the car. They left the argument out in the car, but their auras still have the anger imprint in them." So I told the woman what I saw. I said, "You and papa had a little argument in the car on the way over here tonight." She said, "Oh, yes we *did*. How did you know?" I said, "Because I see your aura, and your aura doesn't lie."

Now you see, anybody can learn to be more receptive. Don't think it is something you can accomplish only by living in a dark cave, sitting in a pretzel pose for five years, and eating only three grains of rice every other

Wednesday. Learning to use your higher senses is not something from a foreign and ancient era, nor is it something terribly "woo-woo." It's very practical, very down to earth, and very now. Seeing an aura is just like seeing a colorful new hat on somebody; you enjoy looking at it. It's a kind of out-picturing of one's psychological climate, in living color. When you study you learn how to interpret the colors, and then pretty soon symbols and figures appear in the aura and you learn how to interpret those, too. You become an aura reader with your own unique style.

So here we are in 1982, and we see that psychologists and psychiatrists who thirty years ago wouldn't touch spiritual sensitives with a ten-foot pole are now talking about entities invading their patients. This gift of spiritual phenomena is moving out into all churches. I remember dear Reverend Becker, who had the beautiful Golden Gate Church in San Francisco. She served spirit with such nobility, such sincerity, and such humility and poise. The continuity of her contact with spirit was beautiful. I watched her on and off for thirty years. Her work was truly marvelous. After watching Rev. Becker work, nobody could doubt the reality that there is a future life; but more importantly, that there is communication with spirit *right now*.

You know what they called this communication in early Christianity? The communion of saints. Catholics would recite the Nicene Creed: "I believe in the Holy Ghost, the Holy Catholic (or universal) Church, the *communion of saints*, the forgiveness of sins, the *resurrection of life*," and on and on it goes.

There is nothing about the communion with Spirit that is in any way challenged by clear thinking and scientific observation. Of course, some scientists are so eternally and absolutely materialistic that if God Himself appeared before them and gave them something on a silver platter they would say it was an hallucination. This reminds me of a psychiatrist I met years ago. One of his patients had been coming to see me for quite some time, and she was experiencing a number of quite remarkable healings. Now, I didn't give the patient any medicine. I didn't prescribe anything, treat or even touch her, or do anything medical. I talked about spiritual realities and truths that fit her specific need, and it worked, whereas a year and a half in this psychiatrist's office had not worked.

So one day he came over to see me and told me that he didn't believe in what I was doing. He thought it was terrible; aura reading was all just an hallucination, and he was going to have me arrested. Well, I let him get out all his pent-up anger, and then I began to talk to him. I showed him an excellent picture of a physical phenomenon, a materialization, taken under the most rigid conditions—not one of the Kirlian photographs, but one from a technology a little farther back than that. I said, "Doctor, how do you photograph an hallucination?" Well, he changed his mind completely after that, and he came back to see me time and again. He began meditating and practicing the things that I teach in my classes. In fact, he is now reading the aura of all his patients and saving months, if not years, of therapy time. Isn't that beautiful? So there we have another believer, who is now a far better psychiatrist, too. I'll never forget the day he called me and said, "John, I saw my first black aura. I knew immediately, intuitively, what trouble this patient was having. And as her therapy progressed the aura became lighter and lighter, and healing was at hand." That's beautiful.

In conclusion, as we ponder the mysteries of life and death let us turn again to the Bible and re-read the marvelous stories of prophecy, the appearance of angels, of apparitions, levitations, and all sorts of other marvels. Let us take hold of the true meaning of Easter and celebrate the glorious resurrection of Christ, realizing that we are thus truly liberated by the knowledge and assurance of the continuity of conscious existence. Let us welcome modern scientific research into the survival of mankind after the change called death. And let us be grateful that through the healing work of the Holy Spirit—employed by psychiatrists and psychologists, as well as physicians, priests, and ministers—we are assured that to die is not death. Thank you. *Amen.*

Christmas: A Compilation of Three Talks

Unity Temple and Heritage House
Presbyterian Chapel, San Francisco, CA
December 1981

Let us read from Saint Luke, Chapter 2, verses 25-31: *"And, behold, there was a man in Jerusalem whose name was Simon; and the same man was just and devout, waiting the consolation of Israel: and the Holy Spirit was upon him. And it was revealed unto him . . . that he should not see death before he had seen the Lord Christ. And he came by the Spirit into the temple: and when the parents brought in the child Jesus, [according to] the law . . . he took him up in his arms and blessed God, and said, 'Lord, now let . . . thy servant depart in peace, according to thy word: for mine eyes have seen thy salvation, which thou hast prepared before the face of all people.'"*

Open our eyes, dear Lord Jesus, even as the eyes of Simon were opened at the time when you were presented in the temple, that we may perceive with unfailing inner vision, and understand the presence and power of the Christ within the very temple of our being, reborn a thousand times down through the ages in consciousness, so that we may say with Simon, "Dismiss me then in peace, for I am fulfilled with the knowledge of Christ the Lord." *Amen.*

This post-Nativity story has special meaning for us all because it is a marvelous reminder of the prophetic aspects of the Christian tradition. Here was a good and devout Jewish man, Simon, who was promised by God that he would not leave this earth until his physical eyes had beheld the savior. And so it happened. How wonderful that Simon should be led, shall we say, by the Holy Spirit to walk into the temple at the precise time when Joseph and Mary were presenting Jesus, as was the custom of the day. Looking at the child, Simon knew deeply within himself that his lifelong prayer was being fulfilled at that moment. By a kind of divine intuition he knew immediately and unquestionably that he was gazing upon the Christ. He saw the light shining upon Jesus, and with a deep inner knowing Simon recognized this child as the anointed one who had come to deliver not only Israel, but all people. This gives us something to think about, for though we do not encounter the physical Jesus in these times, he is a present and living power, reborn again and again in consciousness.

Jesus is essentially a spiritual idea and a spiritual being made manifest in the flesh for the time in which he lived and taught among us. As the Christ, he is a state of being and the essence of our own nature. Jesus taught us to think in terms of Spirit, and he said that through a consciousness of the presence of God within us we would experience the light of salvation, the light of liberation.

Of all the varied and wonderful events that occur in the calendar of the Christian tradition, Christmas is the most joyous, the most simple and childlike, and the most love-filled. Indeed the birth of Christ is a marvelous symbol of the gift of life. Jesus declared that within your physical being, which is your temple, there resides eternally a spark of the Infinite. It is therefore our duty, as followers after the teacher of light, to so fan this spark of the Infinite, through deep meditation on its presence inside us, that ultimately a great conflagration takes place within that temple of our being. And so we must take hold of this consciousness, this Spirit, which is the Christ: the eternal, anointed one. To grasp that consciousness is to be reborn. Then, just as Simon was changed by a kind of divine alchemy taking place in his consciousness, so shall we be reborn and forever changed. We do this simply by observing the humility, the beauty, and the simplicity of the Christmas scene.

Today people in many different religious denominations talk about being reborn. They call themselves "born again" Christians. I think it's wonderful if you have had a rebirth experience, but we must remember that such an experience is not reserved for just a few. It is available to all of us. Every time you realize the immortal presence and the living power of the Christ, demonstrated in your being and in the most prosaic aspects of your daily life, you are reborn. Every time you conquer fear, hate, failure, and regret, or any other kind of unloveliness, the Christ child is reborn in the cradle of your heart. We want to accept the rebirth of God's presence again and again, millions of times, so that we might grow and become. When we lend ourselves to perfect faith, even as Simon did, we are permitting that consciousness of the Christ child to be reborn within us. That's what the story of Simon is all about.

Simon had yearned and prayed for a lifetime that he would not depart this world until he had seen the physical presence of the Messiah. His prayer was granted because he asked it with great longing and faith. Simon has given us a simple and direct lesson for all time. He shows us the spiritual quality of a faith that is uncomplicated, trusting, and accepting. So let us be like Simon. Let us go within and ask to become like little children, which Jesus said was the perfect way. In a certain mystical sense, Simon represents all of us. Like Simon we must ask diligently, and ask believing, that we will receive the divine qualities of humility, love, and simple trust expressed in the story of this wonderful scripture of Saint Luke.

If there was anything Christ wanted to tell us in his teaching, it was that divine spirit is forever ongoing. Those who accept the power have the power, and those who do not accept the healing power do not understand. They walk dimly, and perhaps sometimes even in darkness. You see, when an incarnation of the divine comes into the world, it is to change humanity, the world, and our consciousness. And so today we give thanks for this season of the birth of the Christ consciousness in us.

This week several Christmas services have been televised, and some were filmed in the most magnificent cathedrals and majestic places of worship in the entire world. Yet Jesus prefers to be born in the heart of every living being. That is the cradle he is looking for. It's nice to see these impressive cathedrals because they remind us of the greatness and magnificence of the Christ spirit. But the actuality of Christianity exists not in some architectural gem, but in the depths of our hearts. Let us melt the stone of ignorance that so often keeps our hearts obdurate and prevents us from accepting the glowing miracle-working presence and love that truly is the Christ spirit. That's what it's all about. That's why Jesus came into incarnation. That's why he spoke so simply and so directly to us, so that we might truly know him as an objective, as well as subjective, experience in our lives. He came so that we could know him in our everyday affairs, in the relationships we have with others, and in our own consciousness. Therefore, I urge you never to miss a day of tuning into his presence. We need the discipline of meditation in order to bring into our consciousness again and again the warmth, vitality, and joy of a presence supernal and transcendental. Jesus was trying to tell us how real divine love is: that it is the life of the soul and the real essence of our nature. He wanted us to know this divine force as totally glorious, healing, and positively beautiful. Daily renewal of the awareness of that divine love within our meditational experience is a requisite if we are going to awaken and grow. That's what we're supposed to do, and that's how we will remake the world, by remaking ourselves. We don't want to get stuck in the backwaters of spiritual stagnation, but rather move ever onward toward the inevitable realization of the Self as a true son or daughter of God, blazing with divine love for all.

Some of you may have met holy people or saints. I guess the Lord thought I needed an awful lot of help, because I have met more than a few saints in my life. I tell you, these holy people are literally consumed by the fires of divine love. And their magnetic love is a thing of such transforming power and beauty that it touches people everywhere. Those who have felt the power of this divine love—whether they are Catholic or Hindu, Baptist or Buddhist, Muslim or Mormon—all say,

"Wow, there is something really different about that person!" My dear friends, that kind of love is healing and life changing.

Now, a lot of people say, "Well, I'm no saint." Of course, we all know that. You don't have to tell us that; but you don't have to put yourself down, either. "I'm no saint . . ." Okay. But come as close as you can to being one. That doesn't mean you have to go around throwing holy water on everybody you meet. It simply means that you have to practice feeling the presence of God, receiving that divine flow of love, and sharing it with those around you.

The difference between a saint and a sinner is merely a matter of degree. A sinner is one who is still very much involved in the mundane, and a saint is one who has fanned that little spark of divinity into an all-consuming conflagration. Saints have raised a tremendous, blazing, inner fire of divine love—and they come to realize that presence as Christ, not only within themselves, but within *everyone* everywhere. Now, that doesn't mean we have to be super "goodie-two-shoes" all the time. It means that we have to develop within ourselves a state of conscious identification with this light and power, this presence and love. Didn't Jesus constantly remind us of the importance of this? And didn't he tell us that we must love, pray for, and send healing to one another?

Each one of you, in your own particular way, within the prescriptions of your individualized daily work and activities, is a minister. We are all ministers of Christ. Certainly we all have what we perceive as limitations, but we must ultimately discover that those limitations and shortcomings can be transcended. When man reaches out and touches the hem of Truth's garment, then undeniably and always a kind of inner miracle begins to take place within that consciousness, and the sinner is transformed into a saint.

Look at Saint Francis of Assisi with his great and abiding love of the Christ. Francis had a blazing love for God, and he constantly expressed his reverence for nature and all things in creation. He wrote beautiful poems in which he honored his kinship with the moon, the sun, and the stars. How wonderful that is; and what a marvelous mystic and holy man Francis was, so filled with divine radiant love for all sentient beings. But at one time, you know, he was quite a playboy. He would dress himself up in the richest apparel, made of the finest silks and satins in the land, and he would stand under the balconies of the most beautiful young signorinas in all of Italy. There he would be every night, drinking his wine, strumming his guitar, and serenading the women. Now, there was nothing really bad about that. But one day Francis was praying by himself in a little church called San Damiano, when he heard a voice calling him on the inner planes of his being. In other words, he had a mystical experience. Out of that spiritual experience came the creation of a wonderful group of men that has persisted in living the basic teachings of Francis down through seven centuries. How beautifully that spirit of divine love and brotherhood is expressed in the Franciscan friars.

When his religious order became officially accepted by the Church, Francis insisted that they simply be called the "little brothers" or "friars minor." He wouldn't allow fancy names of any kind. Francis was the first Christian to put up the Nativity scene with the manger, the shepherds, and Jesus, Mary, and Joseph. He was the one who originated that devotional act—and how beautiful it is! All through the years left to him on earth, he went about expressing Christ's love, Christ's universality of goodness. And eventually he became one of the most beloved saints in all the world, not just in the Catholic or Christian calendar. Everybody loves Saint Francis. Why? Because he took a transcendental idea from way up above and brought it down to us here on *terra firma*, and he showed us how simple and beautiful life can be when we are in harmony with all of it.

We're so apt to lose track of spiritual truths because we think they are so lofty, so high up there and out of reach, but Francis brought them down to ground level where he lived and expressed them as a constant prayer. Remember what Saint Paul wrote: *"Pray without ceasing."* (1 Thess. 5:17.) Of course, we would get nothing done if we were down on our knees all day. And we would have awful calluses too. Christ didn't mean that you should literally be on your knees all day. He meant that everything you do should be consecrated, sacred, and dedicated—from your first thought in the morning to your last prayer at night. You should consider everything you do a prayer and an act of love, offered to everyone you meet and all that comes within the orbit of your expression during the day. So even if you are a humble dishwasher, washing the dishes becomes a prayer when you so consecrate it. You don't have to wear any special garments, and you don't have to go around with your head hanging down, looking sad.

Many people have the notion that saints are sad and serious people. Saint Francis was a happy saint. That's why he attracted everybody. We love him because of the universality of his all-pervading love, his joy, and his peace. Birds came around him and wild animals sat at his feet. Why? Because they had no fear of him. Why did they have no fear of him? Because he was filled with Christ's love; and that presence was imminent, dominant, and importantly activated within his consciousness and everything he did. He expressed only love. Remember, love is just another word for God. So here is a man who certainly used the gift of life to its ultimate. Saint Francis of Assisi, born Giovanni Francesco di Bernardone, left this earth plane on October 3, 1226. That's a long time ago, yet how fresh is his memory, and how fresh are the ideals of the Franciscans.

What I want to point out today is that we must not cop out by developing within ourselves a philosophical rationale for procrastinating the divine confrontation. You know, "I'll meditate longer tomorrow. I'll be better mañana." Well, mañana never comes. Don't use your bad habits as an excuse, and don't allow your temporary shortcomings to become a reason to procrastinate the divine confrontation. Don't put off touching in to the Christ presence inside you just because you have failed in the past in some area of your life. Accept the truth of your divine nature, and understand what Saint Francis and others have taught us. Saints like Francis were happy people who understood life and joy, and who understood human love as an echo of the transcendental experience that is divine love.

Through the marvelous mystical experiences of his holy life, Francis taught everyone around him that living the Christ's teaching of love was indeed possible and practical, and that the person who steps out of his or her own limitations begins to transcend all sorrows, regrets, and mistakes. Living in the warmth and security of the ever-present spirit of the Christ, each of us can come to a new life. Every one of us can walk though life with a new confidence, a different attitude, and a posture of certainty, knowing that the universe lives inside us. The person who takes Christ at his word walks with him and Saint Francis, experiencing such joy and peace of mind and heart that there is literally nothing like it anywhere.

And so, dear friends, Christmastime is a reminder of the importance of rededicating ourselves. The Son of God came into this world and was placed in a manger of straw. Imagine the humility and poverty of that. Here was the King of Kings, the Lord of the Universe. He could have had a palace if he'd wanted one, but instead he sought to turn our minds away from things that are transitory, away from the material and passing things which are of little note. He wanted to pin our minds upon the spiritual factor of our nature, which alone can transform us from spiritual ignorance into light. So we mustn't be afraid to be a little humble, because Jesus was humble.

When we touch that light at Christmastime, we receive it as a gift of boundless love and joy. When you feel that joy and love within yourself, let it grow, and extend it outward to more and more people until it encompasses everyone everywhere. Everyone is looking for God, even the man lying in the gutter with his booze bottle. What is he doing there? He is looking for God, but he isn't finding Him in the bottle or the gutter. What should this man do? He must change his mind and be renewed by the rebirth of divine consciousness.

So try to work on that. Make a little promise to yourself that as we come into the New Year, you will never let a day go by in which you do not express some little act of kindness to someone. Now, the fact that they might not receive your kindness in the same spirit you gave it doesn't matter. If you smile at somebody on a day when their pet corn is acting up or they have a bad toothache, they might growl a little instead of saying, "Thank you." If they do that, just let it pass. It doesn't matter. If they were completely well and attentive they would respond. And remember: no good wish is ever lost. Just go about giving freely, abundantly, and joyfully. It doesn't cost you anything to smile and do little acts of kindness. And sometimes, when the occasion arises, do *big* acts of kindness. But never let the day go by without doing some act that would meet with total approval in the consciousness of the Christ.

Sometimes when a person is troubled, they are not quite able to respond when you reach out to them. Maybe they are beset with a physical illness, an emotional problem, or a financial challenge. At those times you can reach out to them silently with a quiet little prayer, a benediction, and a sense of uplift. Of course, the more you do that, the more people around you begin to recognize that there is something different about you. They see someone who has incorporated into his consciousness that marvelous sense of attunement, in which he seems to incarnate the ever-renewing qualities of love, compassion, healing, and joy, which *are* the Christ spirit.

When we read the pages of scripture, we discover that a great percentage of the message in the Four Gospels is concerned with healing, or of making whole. More marvelous than a physical healing is the total transformation of an individual. Watching someone who was rough and selfish turn into someone with a more refined spiritual quality—loving and giving, outgoing and joyful—is nothing less than miraculous. That is what Christianity is all about. That is what Christmas is all about. The decorations and beautiful flowers, the ribbons and wreaths we put up are all very nice, and we love them. But all of it is a symbol, you see, and a reminder to us that we must decorate our hearts with daily remembrance of the Christ. We must renew our contact with the all-pervading One and make our hearts His home. When we do that, changes *have to* take place within us. We can never again be the same person, because when we constantly renew the mystery of his divine presence within us, we begin to shine.

Don't be afraid to radiate that divine love, to let it out. Give abundantly of yourself spiritually, because there is an inexhaustible supply of love and compassion, of healing and bliss. You don't need to worry that maybe you're going to run out of it! The more you give, the more you get. The more you hand out through love, the more you receive.

The Christmas season is more than a time for giving gifts. It is rather sad that it has become so over-commercialized. If we are not careful, we can be swallowed up by the materialism that surrounds this wonderful event. This birth is a celebration, a spiritual event of enormous importance in our lives. We send cards, we give gifts, and that's lovely. But we must never lose sight of the fact that the primary reason for celebrating and feasting is to commemorate the birth of the Christ consciousness. We greet each other in a spirit of love and we gather together to sing joyful songs. This is all fine, and there is no reason not to be glad about all that, but it is so important to realize that the birth of the Christ is much more than a calendar event that happens only once in December. It is the birth of the Christ spirit within the temple of your being, an ongoing spiritual event. Every time we raise our consciousness above the ordinary, mundane material attachment and allow the spiritual streams of glory, light, peace, and joy to enter our minds and hearts, we are reborn by that divine and wondrous alchemy of spirit that takes place inside us. We must become more and more identified in spirit with the birth of the Christ consciousness in us. We must re-establish and rehearse, shall we say, this wondrous event in which Jesus the Christ came into the earth plane as man in order to teach, heal, deliver, and raise us up to the awareness of who we really are.

Christmas is the most joyous event of the year because it symbolizes the continual rebirth on planet earth of spiritual democracy and soul liberation. Jesus taught each and every one of us that we have a profound duty and responsibility for the development of our own spiritual nature, our own spiritual growth; and that if we neglect it we are neglecting the meaning and spirit of his physical birth upon the earth. So when you meditate and pray quietly in your room, ask that the spirit of the Christ be quickened within you so that as you go through the various events of your day you never lose sight of the fact that the birth of the child Jesus is an ongoing spiritual event within you.

You know, in many European countries people give their gifts not on December 25 but on January 6, the Feast of the Epiphany. They call that the "Little Christmas." That's when the three wise men came with gifts of gold, frankincense, and myrrh, and placed them at the feet of the holy child. My dear Irish mother was born on Christmas Day, and I was born on Little Christmas. So you can all send me a warm mental smile on the sixth of January when I'll be seventy-four years old. That will make me very happy, and it will make you feel happy too.*

So, dear friends, as we celebrate this wonderful season with good cheer and gift giving, let us pause to remember that the birth of the child of God into the earth plane is the greatest gift of all, for it is the gift of life itself. Isn't it marvelous that we are alive, and that we can think and move and create fantastic things? Isn't it a tremendous thing that we can communicate and share ideas, that we can meditate, and that we are able to comprehend to some degree what God is and what He is all about? Isn't it wonderful that His power, which *is* light and love, can become a reality to you and me as individual expressions of the divine? Isn't it marvelous, this gift of life? Suppose we had never been born? We would never have existed in all eternity, nor would we have left even a

---

* Reverend John Laurence left his body on January 12, 2003 at the age of ninety-five. Up to the final moments of his life on earth he was lovingly serving those who were at his side, asking them, "Have you had lunch? How about a cup of tea? Is there anything you need?" Finally, he turned to his beloved student-friends and asked if it was all right for him to leave. With their permission, he lifted his eyes and prepared for his ascension. With his eyes wide open and a blissful smile that graced his face, he consciously apprehended the Infinite.

blot on the page of time. But we *have* received the gift of life, and that gift is symbolized in the highest and most magnificent expression, the Nativity of the Christ.

You are selling yourself short if, when Christmas is over, you just pack up the tree trimmings and put away all the decorations in the attic until next year without pausing to think about the gift of life and what you are doing with it. Ultimately we will each be called into account for what we have done, and *not* done, with our lives. Remember that it is not just commission, but omission we are responsible for. Don't let yourself wake up one day and realize that you have wasted your life. I hear so many people bemoaning their situations, saying, "Oh, I don't know what to do with my life." When I hear people say things like that, I'd like to get a hot poker and chase them down the street, yelling, "Get up and do something! Be alive!" Sometimes you have to rouse people up from their sleep.

You know, the great teacher Paramhansa Yogananda was a true lover of Christ. He used to say that humankind suffers from spiritual ignorance, and in that ignorance he spiritually slumbers and becomes sort of catatonic. He walks through life as though he doesn't see or hear much, and he only does what he has to do. For such a person, life is terribly dull and unlovely.

Well, I haven't got time for that. I want to spend my time filled with joy and good thoughts about my fellow human beings, helping and doing good wherever I can. If my fellow human beings like me, fine. Everyone likes to be liked; but I remember one day when I was walking down Sutter Street in San Francisco, where I had a church for twenty-two years. As I started to go in the front door, a lady came along. She was a very pleasant looking woman, well dressed, and she looked directly at me. I thought perhaps she knew me from one of the services. Without a word, she walked right up to me and spat in my face. I knew right away that she didn't love me! But I wasn't going to join her in that negativity by getting mad at her. I thought, "What a pity this woman can see no good in me." At the same time, I knew she was probably teaching me a lesson in humility.

So we must be able to take the bitter with the better. Life isn't always rose petals, but neither is it always thorns. The thing is to make an effort every day, even if it is only for ten minutes, to surround yourself with the light of truth and the presence of God. Then you can meet the demands of the world. And if you have a little failure, pick up your marbles and start the game over again. Don't be discouraged, because as we return again and again to the Christ consciousness we learn that God is infinitely compassionate, always at hand, and always within us. So let us change ourselves from the spiritually blind person to the wide awake Simon: this wonderful figure in Saint Luke's gospel, who lived to see with his physical eyes the presence of the Christ. As we march into the new year, make yourself a pledge that you will never let a morning go by without having a little prayer time, a little quiet meditation, and a little inspirational reading. This way, you begin your day with a spiritual shot in the arm, shall we say; and then you will find the day more beautiful, more loving, and more joyful. As you encourage this consciousness of the presence and power of God within yourself, you begin to see—first dimly perhaps, but ultimately with great vividness—that this same presence is also in *everyone* around you. Then you will say with Simon, "Mine eyes have seen Thy salvation, which Thou hast prepared before the face of all people." Thank you. *Amen.*

John Laurence, baritone, sings before a vast NBC audience.

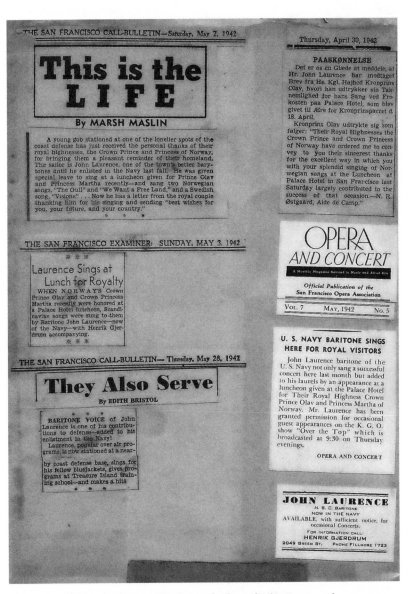

This is the LIFE

By MARSH MASLIN

A young gob stationed at one of the lonelier spots of the coast defense has just received the personal thanks of their royal highnesses, the Crown Prince and Princess of Norway, for bringing them a pleasant reminder of their homeland. The sailor is John Laurence, one of the town's better barytones until he enlisted in the Navy last fall. He was given special leave to sing at a luncheon given for Prince Olav and Princess Martha recently—and sang two Norwegian songs, "The Gull" and "We Want a Free Land," and a Swedish song, "Visions". . . Now he has a letter from the royal couple thanking him for his singing and sending "best wishes for you, your future, and your country."

* * *

※ ※ ※

Laurence Sings at Lunch for Royalty

WHEN N O R W A Y'S Crown Prince Olav and Crown Princess Martha recently were honored at a Palace Hotel luncheon, Scandinavian songs were sung to them by Baritone John Laurence—now of the Navy—with Henrik Gjerdrum accompanying.

※ ※ ※

They Also Serve

By EDITH BRISTOL

* * *

BARITONE VOICE of John Laurence is one of his contributions to defense—added to his enlistment in the Navy!

Laurence, popular over air programs, is now stationed at a near-by coast defense base, sings for his fellow bluejackets, gives programs at Treasure Island training school—and makes a hit!

* * *

PAASKØNNELSE

Det er os en Glæde at meddele, at Hr. John Laurence har modtaget Brev fra Hs. Kgl. Højhed Kronprins Olav, hvori han udtrykker sin Taknemlighed for hans Sang ved Frokosten paa Palace Hotel, som blev givet til Ære for Kronprinsparret d. 18. April.

Kronprins Olav udtrykte sig som følger: "Their Royal Highnesses the Crown Prince and Crown Princess of Norway have ordered me to convey to you their sincerest thanks for the excellent way in which you with your splendid singing of Norwegian songs at the Luncheon at Palace Hotel in San Francisco last Saturday largely contributed to the success of that occasion.—N. R. Østgaard, Aide de Camp."

OPERA AND CONCERT

A Monthly Magazine Devoted to Music and Allied Arts

Official Publication of the
San Francisco Opera Association

| VOL. 7 | MAY, 1942 | No. 5 |

U. S. NAVY BARITONE SINGS HERE FOR ROYAL VISITORS

John Laurence baritone of the U. S. Navy not only sang a successful concert here last month but added to his laurels by an appearance at a luncheon given at the Palace Hotel for Their Royal Highness Crown Prince Olav and Princess Martha of Norway. Mr. Laurence has been granted permission for occasional guest appearances on the K. G. O. show "Over the Top" which is broadcasted at 9:30 on Thursday evenings.

OPERA AND CONCERT

JOHN LAURENCE

N. B. C. BARITONE
NOW IN THE NAVY

AVAILABLE, with sufficient notice, for occasional Concerts.

FOR INFORMATION CALL:
HENRIK GJERDRUM
2049 GREEN ST.   PHONE FILLMORE 1723

These newspaper clippings are reviews of a few of John Laurence's concerts.

Elana Joan Cara was born in San Francisco, California. When she was three years old, she was placed in a Catholic home for girls called Mount Saint Joseph's. Thus began her early religious training. From a young age, she demonstrated an extraordinary musical talent and a fine singing voice. At the age of fifteen she was awarded a scholarship to the Juilliard School in New York City. Too young to enter the world of opera, she continued to develop her music skills and gained valuable performance experience as social director aboard American cruise ships. She also broadened her understanding of religion by visiting temples and holy shrines throughout the South Pacific, India, Japan, Thailand, and Bali.

In 1978 Miss Cara was introduced to Reverend John Laurence, who became her mentor, spiritual advisor, and friend. She became his secretary and driver, since he never learned to drive. For a number of years, she recorded Reverend Laurence's talks, presentations, and classes on spiritual development. She quickly became a devotee of the great Paramhansa Yogananda, and within a few years, under the direction of Kamala Silva (another disciple of Yogananda) and Reverend John Laurence, she became a devoted Kriyaban (practitioner of the Kriya Yoga meditation technique taught by Yogananda). Kamala Silva recognized Elana Joan's writing talent through the many letters they exchanged. She encouraged her to write about Reverend Laurence as an important part of her life's work. So it was with great enthusiasm and a dedicated effort that these talks have become a book titled The Light of the Christ Within.

In 1987, without ever having been on an operatic stage, mezzo-soprano Elana Joan Cara made her Metropolitan Opera and Carnegie Hall debuts, just one month apart. Her career blossomed with one success after another until she was performing with some of the world's most respected and admired singers, conductors, and directors. She has bowed before enthusiastic audiences in many major U.S. and European opera houses and symphony halls, and her list of credits is impressive.

Equally skilled in jazz, pop, oratorio, and lieder, as well as opera, Elana Joan Cara works with singers at all levels, from beginners to seasoned professionals. She currently teaches privately and conducts "Discover the Voice of Your Soul" workshops in Santa Fe, New Mexico. In addition to her work with singers, Miss Cara is devoted to her healing ministry, and to that end she offers private consultations and facilitates a twice-weekly meditation/healing circle called Mystic Heart Meditation.

~ FURTHER EXPLORATIONS ~

The original 1946 unedited edition of
Yogananda's spiritual masterpiece

AUTOBIOGRAPHY OF A YOGI
by Paramhansa Yogananda

Autobiography of a Yogi is one of the best-selling Eastern philosophy titles of all time, with millions of copies sold, named one of the best and most influential books of the twentieth century. This highly prized reprinting of the original 1946 edition is the only one available free from textual changes made after Yogananda's death. Yogananda was the first yoga master of India whose mission was to live and teach in the West.

In this updated edition are bonus materials, including a last chapter that Yogananda wrote in 1951, without posthumous changes. This new edition also includes the eulogy that Yogananda wrote for Gandhi, and a new foreword and afterword by Swami Kriyananda, one of Yogananda's close, direct disciples.

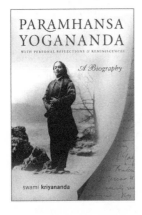

PARAMHANSA YOGANANDA
A Biography
by Swami Kriyananda

This is the moving story of Kriyananda's years with Paramhansa Yogananda, India's emissary to the West and the first yoga master to spend the greater part of his life in America. When Swami Kriyananda discovered *Autobiography of a Yogi* in 1948, he was totally new to Eastern teachings. This is a great advantage to the Western reader, since Kriyananda walks us along the yogic path as he discovers it from the moment of his initiation as a disciple of Yogananda. With winning honesty, humor, and deep insight, he shares his journey on the spiritual path through personal stories and experiences. Through more than four hundred stories of life with Yogananda, we tune in more deeply to this great master and to the teachings he brought to the West. This book is an ideal complement to *Autobiography of a Yogi*.

THE NEW PATH
My Life with Paramhansa Yogananda
by Swami Kriyananda

This is the moving story of Kriyananda's years with Paramhansa Yogananda, India's emissary to the West and the first yoga master to spend the greater part of his life in America. When Swami Kriyananda discovered *Autobiography of a Yogi* in 1948, he was totally new to Eastern teachings. This is a great advantage to the Western reader, since Kriyananda walks us along the yogic path as he discovers it from the moment of his initiation as a disciple of Yogananda. With winning honesty, humor, and deep insight, he shares his journey on the spiritual path through personal stories and experiences. Through more than four hundred stories of life with Yogananda, we tune in more deeply to this great master and to the teachings he brought to the West. This book is an ideal complement to *Autobiography of a Yogi*.

REVELATIONS OF CHRIST
Proclaimed by Paramhansa Yogananda
Presented by his disciple, Swami Kriyananda

The rising tide of alternative beliefs proves that now, more than ever, people are yearning for a clear-minded and uplifting understanding of the life and teachings of Jesus Christ. This galvanizing book, presenting the teachings of Christ from the experience and perspective of Paramhansa Yogananda, one of the greatest spiritual masters of the twentieth century, finally offers the fresh perspective on Christ's teachings for which the world has been waiting. *Revelations of Christ* presents us with an opportunity to understand and apply the scriptures in a more reliable way than any other: by studying under those saints who have communed directly, in deep ecstasy, with Christ and God.

"This is a great gift to humanity. It is a spiritual treasure to cherish and to pass on to children for generations."
—Neale Donald Walsch, author of *Conversations with God*

"Kriyananda's revelatory book gives us the enlightened, timeless wisdom of Jesus the Christ in a way that addresses the challenges of twenty-first century living."
—Michael Beckwith, Founder and Spiritual Director, Agape International Spiritual Center, author of *Inspirations of the Heart*

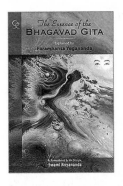

THE ESSENCE OF THE BHAGAVAD GITA
Explained by Paramhansa Yogananda
As Remembered by his disciple, Swami Kriyananda

Rarely in a lifetime does a new spiritual classic appear that has the power to change people's lives and transform future generations. This is such a book. This revelation of India's best-loved scripture approaches it from a fresh perspective, showing its deep allegorical meaning and its down-to-earth practicality. The themes presented are universal: how to achieve victory in life in union with the divine; how to prepare for life's "final exam," death, and what happens afterward; how to triumph over all pain and suffering.

"A brilliant text that will greatly enhance the spiritual life of every reader."
—Caroline Myss, author of *Anatomy of the Spirit* and *Sacred Contracts*

"It is doubtful that there has been a more important spiritual writing in the last fifty years than this soul-stirring, monumental work. What a gift! What a treasure!"
—Neale Donald Walsch, author of *Conversations with God*

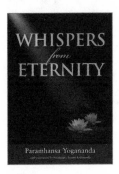

WHISPERS FROM ETERNITY
Paramhansa Yogananda
Edited by his disciple, Swami Kriyananda

Many poetic works can inspire, but few, like this one, have the power to change your life. Yogananda was not only a spiritual master, but a master poet, whose verses revealed the hidden divine presence behind even everyday things. This book has the power to rapidly accelerate your spiritual growth, and provides hundreds of delightful ways for you to begin your own conversation with God.

THE ESSENCE OF SELF-REALIZATION
The Wisdom of Paramhansa Yogananda
Recorded, Compiled, and Edited
by his disciple Swami Kriyananda

With nearly three hundred sayings rich with spiritual wisdom, this book is the fruit of a labor of love that was recorded, compiled, and edited by his disciple, Swami Kriyananda. A glance at the table of contents will convince the reader of the vast scope of this book. It offers as complete an explanation of life's true purpose, and of the way to achieve that purpose, as may be found anywhere.

~ *The* *WISDOM of YOGANANDA* *series* ~

Six volumes of Paramhansa Yogananda's timeless wisdom in an approachable, easy-to-read format. The writings of the Master are presented with minimal editing, to capture his expansive and compassionate wisdom, his sense of fun, and his practical spiritual guidance.

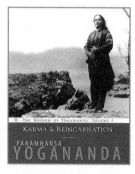
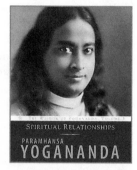

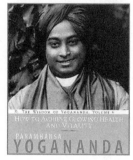

HOW TO BE HAPPY ALL THE TIME
The Wisdom of Yogananda Series, VOLUME 1

Yogananda powerfully explains virtually everything needed to lead a happier, more fulfilling life. Topics include: looking for happiness in the right places; choosing to be happy; tools and techniques for achieving happiness; sharing happiness with others; balancing success and happiness; and many more.

KARMA & REINCARNATION
The Wisdom of Yogananda Series, VOLUME 2

Yogananda reveals the truth behind karma, death, reincarnation, and the afterlife. With clarity and simplicity, he makes the mysterious understandable. Topics include: why we see a world of suffering and inequality; how to handle the challenges in our lives; what happens at death, and after death; and the purpose of reincarnation.

CRYSTAL CLARITY PUBLISHERS

Crystal Clarity Publishers offers additional resources to assist you in your spiritual journey including many other books, a wide variety of inspirational and relaxation music composed by Swami Kriyananda, and yoga and meditation videos. To see a complete listing of our products, contact us for a print catalog or see our website: www.crystalclarity.com

Crystal Clarity Publishers
14618 Tyler Foote Rd., Nevada City, CA 95959
TOLL FREE: 800.424.1055 or 530.478.7600 / FAX: 530.478.7610
EMAIL: clarity@crystalclarity.com

ANANDA WORLDWIDE

Ananda Sangha, a worldwide organization founded by Swami Kriyananda, offers spiritual support and resources based on the teachings of Paramhansa Yogananda. There are Ananda spiritual communities in Nevada City, Sacramento, and Palo Alto, California; Seattle, Washington; Portland, Oregon; as well as a retreat center and European community in Assisi, Italy, and communities near New Delhi and Pune, India. Ananda supports more than 140 meditation groups worldwide.

For more information about Ananda Sangha communities or meditation groups near you, please call 530.478.7560 or visit www.ananda.org.

THE EXPANDING LIGHT

Ananda's guest retreat, The Expanding Light, offers a varied, year-round schedule of classes and workshops on yoga, meditation, and spiritual practice. You may also come for a relaxed personal renewal, participating in ongoing activities as much or as little as you wish. The beautiful serene mountain setting, supportive staff, and delicious vegetarian food provide an ideal environment for a truly meaningful, spiritual vacation.

For more information, please call 800.346.5350
or visit www.expandinglight.org.